# 기초탄탄 GRAMMAR

# 1

Happy House

# 기초 탄탄 Grammar, 어떻게 구성했나요?

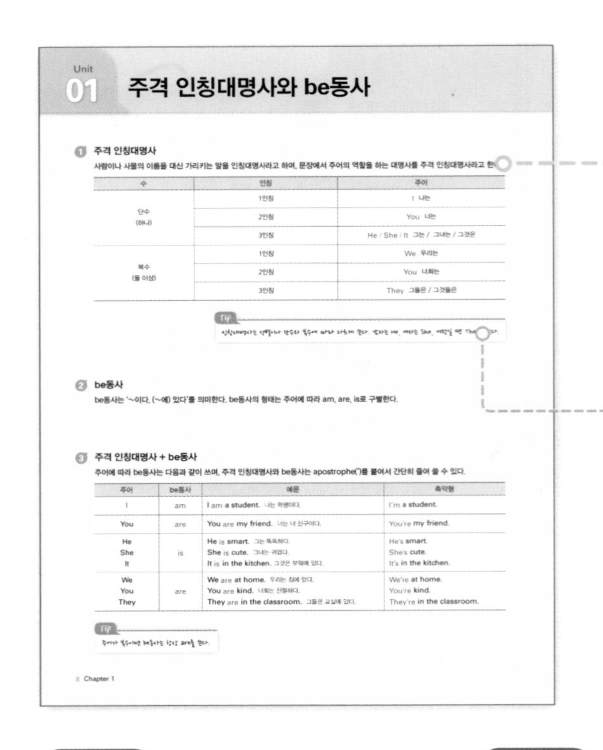

Unit 01 주격 인칭대명사와 be동사

1 주격 인칭대명사

사람이나 사물의 이름을 대신 가리키는 말을 인칭대명사라고 하며, 문장에서 주어의 역할을 하는 대명사를 주격 인칭대명사라고 한

| 수 | 인칭 | 주어 |
|---|---|---|
| 단수 (하나) | 1인칭 | I 나는 |
| | 2인칭 | You 너는 |
| | 3인칭 | He / She / It 그는 / 그녀는 / 그것은 |
| 복수 (둘 이상) | 1인칭 | We 우리는 |
| | 2인칭 | You 너희는 |
| | 3인칭 | They 그들은 / 그것들은 |

2 be동사

be동사는 '~이다, (~에) 있다'를 의미한다. be동사의 형태는 주어에 따라 am, are, is로 구별한다.

3 주격 인칭대명사 + be동사

주어에 따라 be동사는 다음과 같이 쓰며, 주격 인칭대명사와 be동사는 apostrophe(')를 붙여서 간단히 줄여 쓸 수 있다.

| 주어 | be동사 | 예문 | 축약형 |
|---|---|---|---|
| I | am | I am a student. 나는 학생이다. | I'm a student. |
| You | are | You are my friend. 너는 내 친구이다. | You're my friend. |
| He / She / It | is | He is smart. 그는 똑똑하다. She is cute. 그녀는 귀엽다. It is in the kitchen. 그것은 부엌에 있다. | He's smart. She's cute. It's in the kitchen. |
| We / You / They | are | We are at home. 우리는 집에 있다. You are kind. 너희는 친절하다. They are in the classroom. 그들은 교실에 있다. | We're at home. You're kind. They're in the classroom. |

8 Chapter 1

## 문법 개념 정리

문법의 핵심 포인트를 체계적으로 학습할 수 있도록 도표화하고 예문을 통해 쉽게 설명해 줍니다.

## Tip

놓치기 쉬운, 그러나 꼭 기억해야 할 포인트를 콕 집어 알려 줍니다.

STEP 1

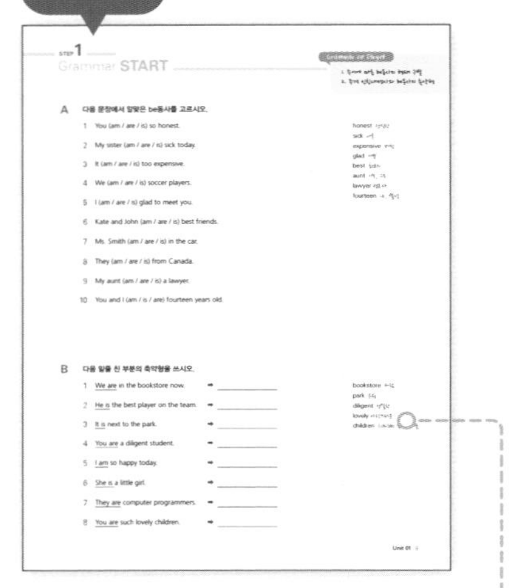

STEP 1 Grammar START

STEP 2

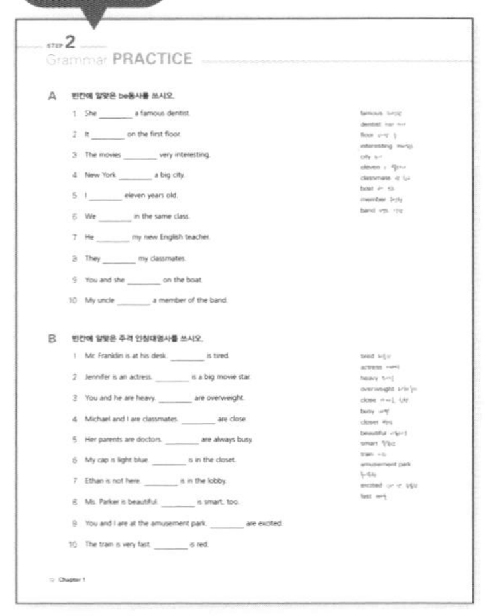

STEP 2 Grammar PRACTICE

STEP 3

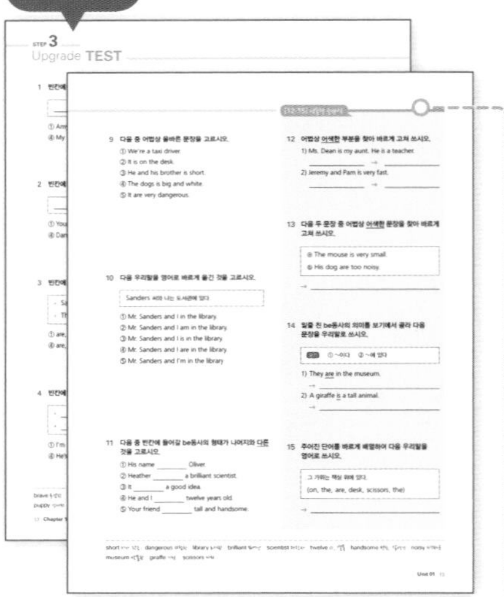

STEP 3 Upgrade TEST

## Grammar Start
### 개념 확인 문제

단원의 학습목표가 되는 문법 포인트를 콕 집어 그 원리를 확인하는 연습문제입니다.

## Grammar Practice
### 심화 학습 문제

틀린 부분 고쳐 쓰기, 문장 유형 바꿔 쓰기, 단어 배열하기, 영작하기 등 단원의 핵심 문법 포인트를 문장 속에서 파악할 수 있도록 심화된 학습을 합니다.

## Upgrade Test
### 내신 테스트형 문제

학교 내신 유형의 문제로 단원 학습 내용을 통합 응용한 테스트형 문제입니다.

## Word List

새로 나온 단어들의 우리말 뜻을 제공하여 문제풀이에 도움을 줍니다.

## 서술형 주관식

내신 서술형 주관식 문제로 실전감을 더욱 높일 수 있습니다.

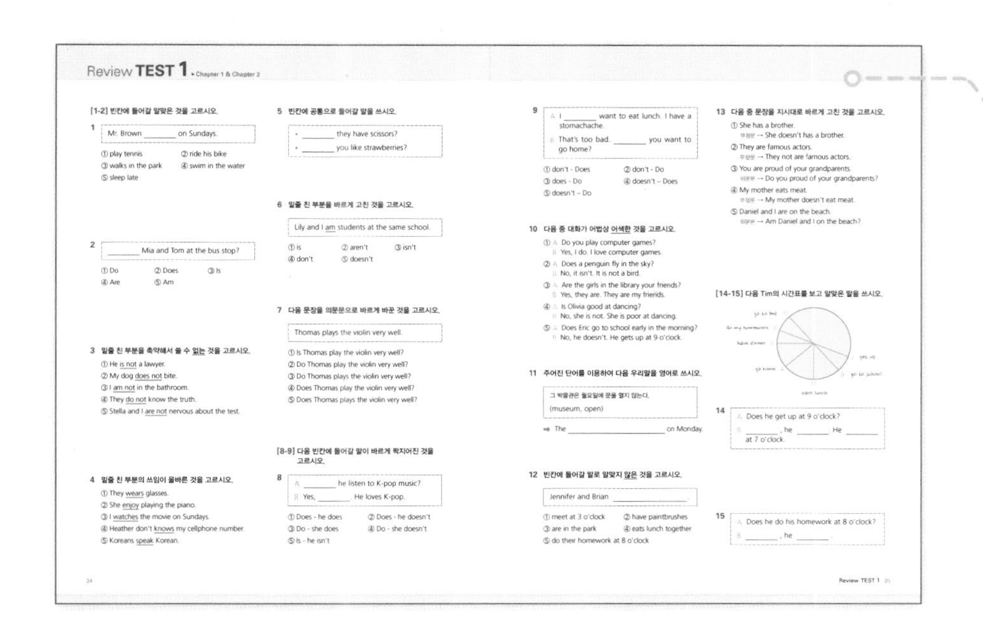

## Review Test

연계된 학습 흐름으로 구성된 두 개의 Chapter를 복습하는 문제로 다양한 유형을 다루어 줍니다.

## Workbook

각 단원의 문법 포인트를 두 페이지의 문제풀이를 통해 확인학습 할 수 있습니다.

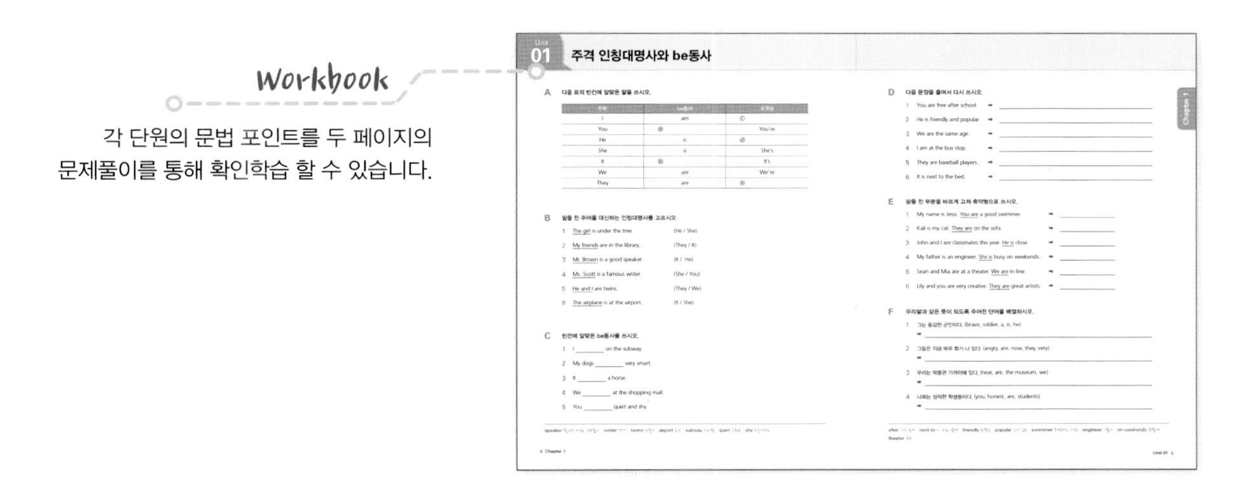

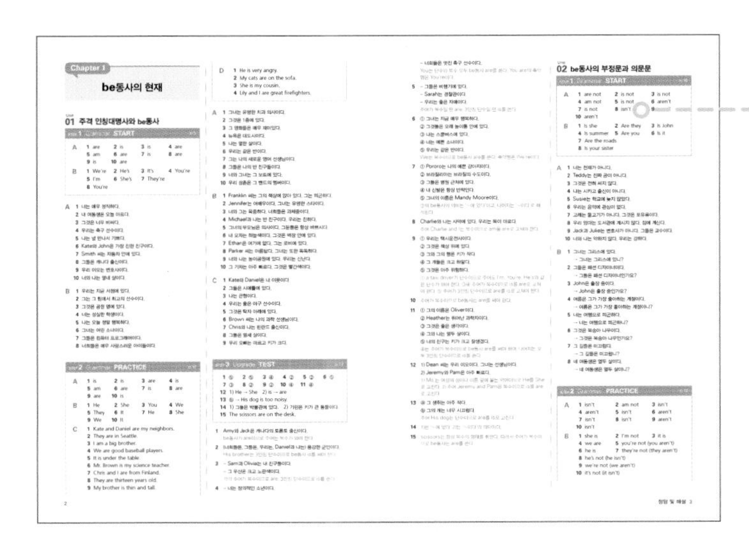

## 정답 및 해설

문장의 해석은 물론 내신형 문제의 문법 포인트를 친절하고 정확하게 해설해 줍니다.

# Contents

기초 탄탄 1
GRAMMAR

Chapter 1

# be동사의 현재

Unit 01

# 주격 인칭대명사와 be동사

## 1 주격 인칭대명사

사람이나 사물의 이름을 대신 가리키는 말을 인칭대명사라고 하며, 문장에서 주어의 역할을 하는 대명사를 주격 인칭대명사라고 한다.

| 수 | 인칭 | 주어 |
|---|---|---|
| 단수 (하나) | 1인칭 | I 나는 |
| | 2인칭 | You 너는 |
| | 3인칭 | He / She / It 그는 / 그녀는 / 그것은 |
| 복수 (둘 이상) | 1인칭 | We 우리는 |
| | 2인칭 | You 너희는 |
| | 3인칭 | They 그들은 / 그것들은 |

인칭대명사는 성별이나 단수와 복수에 따라 다르게 쓴다. 남자는 He, 여자는 She, 여럿일 땐 They를 쓴다.

## 2 be동사

be동사는 '~이다, (~에) 있다'를 의미한다. be동사의 형태는 주어에 따라 am, are, is로 구별한다.

## 3 주격 인칭대명사 + be동사

주어에 따라 be동사는 다음과 같이 쓰며, 주격 인칭대명사와 be동사는 apostrophe(')를 붙여서 간단히 줄여 쓸 수 있다.

| 주어 | be동사 | 예문 | 축약형 |
|---|---|---|---|
| I | am | I am a student. 나는 학생이다. | I'm a student. |
| You | are | You are my friend. 너는 내 친구이다. | You're my friend. |
| He<br>She<br>It | is | He is smart. 그는 똑똑하다.<br>She is cute. 그녀는 귀엽다.<br>It is in the kitchen. 그것은 부엌에 있다. | He's smart.<br>She's cute.<br>It's in the kitchen. |
| We<br>You<br>They | are | We are at home. 우리는 집에 있다.<br>You are kind. 너희는 친절하다.<br>They are in the classroom. 그들은 교실에 있다. | We're at home.<br>You're kind.<br>They're in the classroom. |

주어가 복수이면 be동사는 항상 are를 쓴다.

STEP 1

# Grammar START

Grammar on Target

1. 주어에 따른 be동사의 형태 구별
2. 주격 인칭대명사와 be동사의 축약형

## A 다음 문장에서 알맞은 be동사를 고르시오.

1 You (am / are / is) so honest.

2 My sister (am / are / is) sick today.

3 It (am / are / is) too expensive.

4 We (am / are / is) soccer players.

5 I (am / are / is) glad to meet you.

6 Kate and John (am / are / is) best friends.

7 Ms. Smith (am / are / is) in the car.

8 They (am / are / is) from Canada.

9 My aunt (am / are / is) a lawyer.

10 You and I (am / is / are) fourteen years old.

honest 정직한
sick 아픈
expensive 비싼
glad 기쁜
best 최고의
aunt 이모, 고모
lawyer 변호사
fourteen 14, 열넷

## B 다음 밑줄 친 부분의 축약형을 쓰시오.

1 We are in the bookstore now. ➡ ________________

2 He is the best player on the team. ➡ ________________

3 It is next to the park. ➡ ________________

4 You are a diligent student. ➡ ________________

5 I am so happy today. ➡ ________________

6 She is a little girl. ➡ ________________

7 They are computer programmers. ➡ ________________

8 You are such lovely children. ➡ ________________

bookstore 서점
park 공원
diligent 성실한
lovely 사랑스러운
children (child의 복수) 아이들

STEP 2

# Grammar PRACTICE

## A 빈칸에 알맞은 be동사를 쓰시오.

1 She __________ a famous dentist.

2 It __________ on the first floor.

3 The movies __________ very interesting.

4 New York __________ a big city.

5 I __________ eleven years old.

6 We __________ in the same class.

7 He __________ my new English teacher.

8 They __________ my classmates.

9 You and she __________ on the boat.

10 My uncle __________ a member of the band.

famous 유명한
dentist 치과 의사
floor 바닥, 층
interesting 재미있는
city 도시
eleven 11, 열하나
classmate 반 친구
boat 배, 보트
member 구성원
band 밴드, 악단

## B 빈칸에 알맞은 주격 인칭대명사를 쓰시오.

1 Mr. Franklin is at his desk. __________ is tired.

2 Jennifer is an actress. __________ is a big movie star.

3 You and he are heavy. __________ are overweight.

4 Michael and I are classmates. __________ are close.

5 Her parents are doctors. __________ are always busy.

6 My cap is light blue. __________ is in the closet.

7 Ethan is not here. __________ is in the lobby.

8 Ms. Parker is beautiful. __________ is smart, too.

9 You and I are at the amusement park. __________ are excited.

10 The train is very fast. __________ is red.

tired 피곤한
actress 여배우
heavy 무거운
overweight 과체중의
close 가까운, 친한
busy 바쁜
closet 벽장
beautiful 아름다운
smart 똑똑한
train 기차
amusement park 놀이공원
excited 신이 난, 흥분한
fast 빠른

## C 밑줄 친 부분을 바르게 고쳐 문장을 다시 쓰시오.

1 Kate and Daniel am my neighbors.

➡ ______________________________

2 They is in Seattle.

➡ ______________________________

3 I are a big brother.

➡ ______________________________

4 We is good baseball players.

➡ ______________________________

5 It am under the table.

➡ ______________________________

6 Mr. Brown are my science teacher.

➡ ______________________________

7 Chris and I am from Finland.

➡ ______________________________

8 They is thirteen years old.

➡ ______________________________

9 My brother are thin and tall.

➡ ______________________________

neighbor 이웃
Seattle 시애틀
baseball player 야구 선수
science 과학
Finland 핀란드
thirteen 13, 열셋
thin 마른
tall 키가 큰

## D 우리말과 같은 뜻이 되도록 주어진 단어를 바르게 배열하시오.

1 그는 화가 많이 났다. (angry, he, very, is)

➡ ______________________________

2 내 고양이들은 소파 위에 있다. (sofa, cats, are, my, the, on)

➡ ______________________________

3 그녀는 나의 사촌이다. (is, cousin, she, my)

➡ ______________________________

4 Lily와 나는 훌륭한 소방관이다. (I, firefighters, are, Lily, and, great)

➡ ______________________________

angry 화난
cousin 사촌
firefighter 소방관

STEP 3

# Upgrade TEST

**1** 빈칸에 들어갈 알맞은 것을 고르시오.

| _________ are from Toronto, Canada. |
|---|

① Amy ② Jack ③ The cat
④ My sister ⑤ Amy and Jack

**2** 빈칸에 들어갈 수 없는 것을 고르시오.

| _________ are brave soldiers. |
|---|

① You ② They ③ We
④ Daniel and I ⑤ His brother

**3** 빈칸에 들어갈 말이 바르게 짝지어진 것을 고르시오.

- Sam and Olivia _________ my friends.
- The umbrella _________ big and yellow.

① are, am ② is, are ③ is, am
④ are, is ⑤ am, is

**4** 빈칸에 공통으로 들어갈 알맞은 것을 고르시오.

- _________ a creative boy.
- _________ good soccer players.

① I'm ② You're ③ She's
④ He's ⑤ It's

**5** 빈칸에 들어갈 말을 순서대로 짝지은 것을 고르시오.

- They _________ on the airplane.
- Sarah _________ a police officer.
- We _________ good sisters.

① are - is - am ② are - is - are
③ are - are - is ④ is - is - are
⑤ is - am - are

**6** 밑줄 친 부분이 바르지 못한 것을 고르시오.

① She's so happy now.
② They're in the sandbox.
③ I'm on the school bus.
④ You're a pretty girl.
⑤ We's in the same class.

**7** 밑줄 친 부분의 의미가 나머지와 다른 것을 고르시오.

① Pororo is my pretty puppy.
② Brasilia is the capital of Brazil.
③ They are near the hospital.
④ My shoes are always very shiny.
⑤ Her name is Mandy Moore.

**8** 밑줄 친 부분 중 어법상 어색한 것을 고르시오.

① Charlie and I ② am ③ in the desert. We ④ are ⑤ thirsty.

brave 용감한 soldier 군인 umbrella 우산 creative 창의적인 airplane 비행기 police officer 경찰관 sandbox 모래 놀이통 pretty 예쁜
puppy 강아지 capital 수도 near ~ ~ 가까이에 shiny 빛나는 desert 사막 thirsty 목이 마른

9 다음 중 어법상 올바른 문장을 고르시오.

① We're a taxi driver.
② It is on the desk.
③ He and his brother is short.
④ The dogs is big and white.
⑤ It are very dangerous.

10 다음 우리말을 영어로 바르게 옮긴 것을 고르시오.

| Sanders 씨와 나는 도서관에 있다. |
|---|

① Mr. Sanders and I in the library.
② Mr. Sanders and I am in the library.
③ Mr. Sanders and I is in the library.
④ Mr. Sanders and I are in the library.
⑤ Mr. Sanders and I'm in the library

11 다음 중 빈칸에 들어갈 be동사의 형태가 나머지와 다른 것을 고르시오.

① His name _________ Oliver.
② Heather _________ a brilliant scientist.
③ It _________ a good idea.
④ He and I _________ twelve years old.
⑤ Your friend _________ tall and handsome.

## [12-15] 서술형 주관식

12 어법상 어색한 부분을 찾아 바르게 고쳐 쓰시오.

1) Ms. Dean is my aunt. He is a teacher.

_____________ → _____________

2) Jeremy and Pam is very fast.

_____________ → _____________

13 다음 두 문장 중 어법상 어색한 문장을 찾아 바르게 고쳐 쓰시오.

| ⓐ The mouse is very small.<br>ⓑ His dog are too noisy. |
|---|

→ _____________________

14 밑줄 친 be동사의 의미를 보기에서 골라 다음 문장을 우리말로 쓰시오.

| 보기 ① ~이다 ② ~에 있다 |
|---|

1) They are in the museum.

→ _____________________

2) A giraffe is a tall animal.

→ _____________________

15 주어진 단어를 바르게 배열하여 다음 우리말을 영어로 쓰시오.

| 그 가위는 책상 위에 있다.<br>(on, the, are, desk, scissors, the) |
|---|

→ _____________________

short 키가 작은 dangerous 위험한 library 도서관 brilliant 뛰어난 scientist 과학자 twelve 12, 열둘 handsome 멋진, 잘생긴 noisy 시끄러운 museum 박물관 giraffe 기린 scissors 가위

Unit 02

# be동사의 부정문과 의문문

## ❶ be동사의 부정문

be동사의 부정문은 be동사 뒤에 not을 붙이며, '~이(가) 아니다' 또는 '~에 없다'로 해석한다.
주어의 인칭과 수에 따라서 사용되는 be동사의 부정형은 다음과 같다.

| 주어 | be동사의 부정형 | 『be동사 + not』의 축약형 | 『주어 + be동사』의 축약형 |
|---|---|---|---|
| I | am not | 없음 | I'm not |
| You | are not | aren't | You're not |
| He / She / It | is not | isn't | She's not / He's not / It's not |
| We / You / They | are not | aren't | We're not / You're not / They're not |

I am a pilot. → I am not a pilot. 나는 비행기 조종사가 아니다.

He is in the library. → He is not in the library. 그는 도서관에 없다.

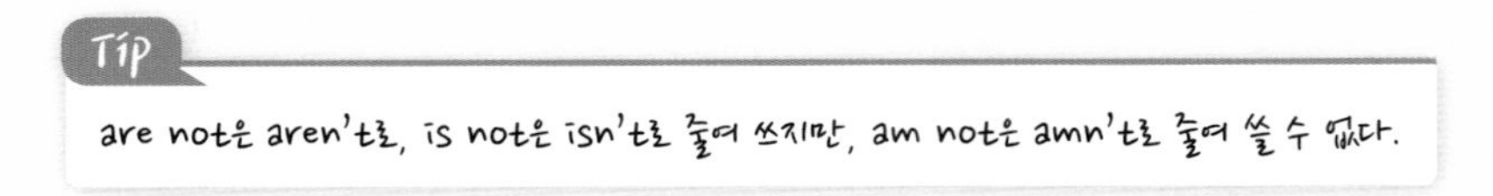


## ❷ be동사의 의문문

be동사의 의문문은 주어와 be동사의 위치를 바꾸고, 문장 끝에 물음표를 붙인다.

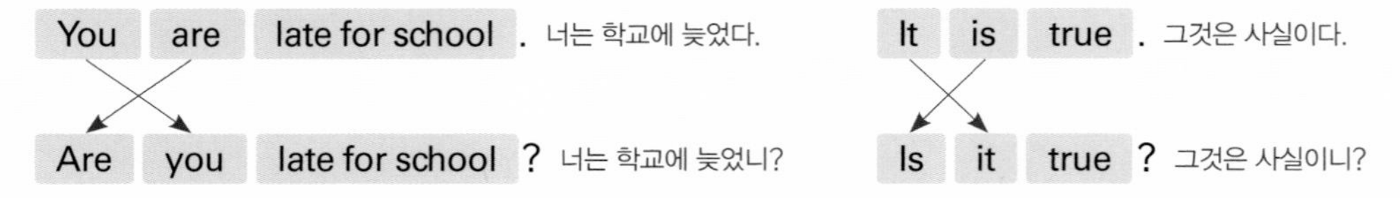


## ❸ be동사의 의문문에 대한 대답

be동사의 의문문에 대한 긍정의 대답은 『Yes, 주어 + be동사』로, 부정의 대답은 『No, 주어 + be동사 + not』의 형태이다.

| 의문문 | 긍정의 대답 | 부정의 대답 |
|---|---|---|
| Am I pretty? 내가 예쁘니? | Yes, you are. | No, you aren't. = No, you're not. |
| Are you ready? 너는 준비됐니? | Yes, I am. | No, I am not. = No, I'm not. |
| Is he busy? 그는 바쁘니?<br>Is she Korean? 그녀는 한국인이니?<br>Is it cold? 춥니? | Yes, he is.<br>Yes, she is.<br>Yes, it is. | No, he isn't. = No, he's not.<br>No, she isn't. = No, she's not.<br>No, it isn't. = No, it's not. |
| Are we late? 우리가 늦었니?<br>Are you ready? 너희는 준비됐니?<br>Are they in China? 그들은 중국에 있니? | Yes, we/you are.<br>Yes, we are.<br>Yes, they are. | No, we/you aren't. = No, we're/you're not.<br>No, we aren't. = No, we're not.<br>No, they aren't. = No, they're not. |

Tip
Yes로 대답할 경우에는 『주어 + be동사』의 축약형을 쓸 수 없다.

STEP 1
# Grammar START

Grammar on Target

1. 주어에 따른 be동사의 부정형
2. be동사의 의문문 만들기

## A 다음 문장에서 알맞은 be동사의 부정형을 고르시오.

1 You (are not / am not) a genius.

2 Teddy (is not / are not) a real bear.

3 It (are not / is not) cheap at all.

4 I (am not / is not) from Chicago.

5 Susie (is not / are not) late for school.

6 We (isn't / aren't) interested in music.

7 A whale (am not / is not) a fish. It is a mammal.

8 My mom (isn't / aren't) in the library. She is at home.

9 Jack and Julie (isn't / aren't) lawyers. They are professors.

10 You and I (am not / aren't) weak. We are strong.

genius 천재
real 진짜의
bear 곰
cheap 값싼
not ~ at all ~이 전혀 아니다
be interested in ~ ~에 관심이 있다
whale 고래
mammal 포유류
professor 교수
weak 약한
strong 강한

## B 다음 문장을 의문문으로 바꿀 때, 빈칸에 들어갈 알맞은 말을 쓰시오.

1 She is in Greece. ➡ _______ _______ in Greece?

2 They are fashion designers. ➡ _______ _______ fashion designers?

3 John is on a business trip. ➡ _______ _______ on a business trip?

4 Summer is his favorite season. ➡ _______ _______ his favorite season?

5 You are tired from the journey. ➡ _______ _______ tired from the journey?

6 It is a peach tree. ➡ _______ _______ a peach tree?

7 The roads are slippery. ➡ _______ _______ _______ slippery?

8 Your sister is twelve years old. ➡ _______ _______ _______ twelve years old?

Greece 그리스
business trip 출장
favorite 가장 좋아하는
tired 피곤한
journey 여행
peach 복숭아
slippery 미끄러운

STEP 2
# Grammar PRACTICE

## A 다음 문장을 읽고, be동사를 이용하여 문맥에 맞게 문장을 완성하시오. (축약형으로)

1 Honey is sweet. It __________ salty.

2 I am at the airport. I __________ in the movie theater.

3 She is my aunt. She __________ my mom.

4 I am older than my brother. We __________ twins.

5 The park is very quiet. It __________ noisy.

6 You and Jack are in different classes. You __________ in the same class.

7 Danny hates Amy. He __________ on good terms with her.

8 Betty has a bad voice. She __________ a good singer.

9 Hamburgers are bad for your health. They __________ healthy food.

10 The novel is interesting. It __________ boring.

sweet 달콤한
salty 짠, 짭짤한
airport 공항
aunt 이모, 고모
older 연상의
twins 쌍둥이
different 다른
on good terms with ~
~와 사이가 좋은
health 건강
healthy 건강한, 건강에 좋은
novel 소설
boring 지루한

## B 빈칸에 알맞은 말을 채워 넣어 의문문에 대한 대답을 완성하시오. (축약형으로)

1 A Is Susan an astronaut? B Yes, ____________________.

2 A Are you a pilot? B No, ____________________.

3 A Is Seoul the capital of Korea? B Yes, ____________________.

4 A Are you good swimmers? B Yes, ____________________.

5 A Am I handsome? B No, ____________________.

6 A Is he an English teacher? B Yes, ____________________.

7 A Are Ann and Jennifer of an age? B No, ____________________.

8 A Is your father a writer? B No, ____________________.

9 A Are you middle school students? B No, ____________________.

10 A Is it a ladybug? B No, ____________________.

astronaut 우주비행사
pilot 비행기조종사
capital 수도
of an age 같은 나이인
writer 작가
middle school 중학교
ladybug 무당벌레

## C 밑줄 친 부분을 바르게 고쳐 문장을 다시 쓰시오.

1 I amn't a baseball player.

➡ ____________________

2 Jennifer and I is not actresses.

➡ ____________________

3 You and he not are overweight.

➡ ____________________

4 Money aren't everything.

➡ ____________________

5 Its not that expensive.

➡ ____________________

6 Are sugar in the cupboard?

➡ ____________________

7 Is a dog and a cat under the table?

➡ ____________________

8 Am Serena good at playing the piano?

➡ ____________________

9 You ready for the baseball game?

➡ ____________________

actress 여배우
overweight 비만인, 과체중의
everything 전부, 모든 것, 중요한 것
expensive 값비싼
sugar 설탕
cupboard 찬장
be good at ~ ~을 잘하다

## D 우리말과 같은 뜻이 되도록 주어진 단어를 바르게 배열하시오.

1 나의 부모님은 백화점에 없다. (are, my parents, in the department store, not)

➡ ____________________

2 나는 그 소식에 놀라지 않는다. (not, surprised, I, at the news, am)

➡ ____________________

3 저 포도는 시지 않다. (sour, not, the grapes, are)

➡ ____________________

4 너의 컴퓨터는 고장이 났니? (your computer, is, out of order)

➡ ____________________

department store 백화점
parents 부모
be surprised at ~ ~에 놀라다
sour (맛이) 신
out of order 고장 난

STEP 3
# Upgrade TEST

**1 빈칸에 들어갈 알맞은 것을 고르시오.**

> Joe and I ________ at the snack bar.

① am ② am not ③ is not
④ is ⑤ are not

**2 밑줄 친 부분이 바르지 못한 것을 고르시오.**

① She isn't an FBI agent.
② The movie *Harry Potter* isn't boring.
③ You aren't a dentist.
④ I amn't a famous painter.
⑤ They aren't geniuses.

**3 다음 우리말을 영어로 바르게 옮긴 것을 고르시오.**

> 그들은 기술자들이 아니다.

① They isn't an engineer.
② They am not engineers.
③ They not are engineers.
④ They aren't engineers.
⑤ They're aren't engineer.

**4 빈칸에 들어갈 알맞은 것을 고르시오.**

> A Are you happy with your sneakers?
> B ________ They are too tight.

① Yes, I am. ② Yes, it is.
③ No, I am not. ④ Yes, we are.
⑤ No, they are.

**5 밑줄 친 부분이 바르지 못한 것을 고르시오.**

① I am full. I am not hungry now.
② Jane is smart. She's not a fool.
③ A Is he your brother? B No, he'snt.
④ A Are you Chinese? B No, I'm not.
⑤ A Are they from Germany? B No, they aren't.

**6 다음 짝지어진 대화 중 어색한 것을 고르시오.**

① A Are you happy with your cellphone?
B No, I'm not. It's too slow.
② A Are the birds in the cage?
B No, they aren't.
③ A Are you nervous?
B Yes, I'm nervous.
④ A Are the rich always happy?
B No, they're not always happy.
⑤ A Are you strangers here?
B No, I am not.

**7 빈칸에 들어갈 수 없는 것을 고르시오.**

> Are the boys on the ground ________?

① his brothers ② my friend
③ your classmates ④ soccer players
⑤ Michael and Brian

snack bar 분식점, 간이식당 FBI 연방수사국 agent 요원 sneakers 운동화 tight 꽉 끼는 fool 바보 Germany 독일 cellphone 휴대폰 cage 우리 nervous 초조한, 긴장한 rich 부유한 stranger 낯선 사람

8 빈칸에 들어갈 말이 바르게 짝지어진 것을 고르시오.

- They say that honesty is the best policy, but I think it ________.
- A Are you Korean?
  B ________ I'm from Seoul.

① is - No, you aren't. ② isn't - Yes, I am.
③ isn't - No, I am not. ④ isn't - Yes, you are.
⑤ aren't - No, I amn't.

9 다음 우리말을 영어로 바르게 옮긴 것을 고르시오.

Sam과 그의 남동생은 학교에 늦었니?

① Is Sam and his brother late for school?
② Do Sam and his brother late for school?
③ Am Sam and his brother late for school?
④ Sam and his brother are late for school?
⑤ Are Sam and his brother late for school?

10 다음 중 어법상 올바른 문장을 고르시오.

① Is Picasso and Braque best friends?
② Pitt and Jolie isn't from Hawaii.
③ Jesse and I am not good at dancing.
④ Are David and Joe interested in science?
⑤ James aren't embarrassed by the news.

## [11-15] 서술형 주관식

11 밑줄 친 문장에서 어법상 어색한 부분을 찾아 바르게 고쳐 쓰시오.

The cat are not behind the sofa. It is next to the chair.

→ ________________

12 주어진 단어를 바르게 배열하여 다음 우리말을 영어로 쓰시오.

Jack과 나는 실패가 두렵지 않다.
(aren't, Jack and I, failure, afraid of)

→ ________________

13 다음 문장을 인칭대명사를 이용하여 부정문과 의문문으로 바꾸시오.

Alice is proud of her parents.

1) 부정문 ________________
2) 의문문 ________________

[14-15] 다음 문장을 읽고 질문에 답하시오.

보기 Is Peter and you at the concert?

14 보기의 문장에서 틀린 부분을 고쳐 쓰시오.

________ → ________

15 보기의 질문에 부정문으로 답하시오.

→ ________________

honesty 정직 policy 정책, 방책 late 늦은, 지각한 embarrassed 당황한 behind ~ ~ 뒤에 be afraid of ~ ~을 두려워하다 failure 실패
be proud of ~ ~을 자랑스러워 하다

기초 탄탄 1
GRAMMAR

Chapter
2
일반동사의
현재
Unit 01 일반동사의 긍정문
Unit 02 일반동사의 부정문과 의문문

Unit 01

# 일반동사의 긍정문

## 1 일반동사

일반동사는 be동사와 조동사(will, can, may)를 제외한 '먹다, 가다, 좋아하다'와 같이 주어의 동작이나 상태를 나타내는 동사이다.

## 2 일반동사의 현재형

일반동사의 현재형은 일반적인 사실, 현재의 상태, 습관 및 반복적인 일상, 그리고 불변의 진리를 나타낼 때 쓰인다.

| 쓰임 | 예문 |
|---|---|
| 일반적 사실 | Koreans speak Korean. 한국인들은 한국어를 한다. |
| 현재의 상태 | She wears glasses. 그녀는 안경을 쓴다. |
| 습관 및 반복적인 일상 | I watch a movie on Saturdays. 나는 토요일마다 영화를 본다. |
| 불변의 진리 | The Earth moves around the sun. 지구는 태양 둘레를 돈다. |

Tip

속담도 늘 현재형으로 쓴다.

A rolling stone gathers no moss. 구르는 돌에는 이끼가 끼지 않는다.

## 3 일반동사의 변화 규칙

일반동사의 현재형은 주어의 인칭과 수에 따라 형태가 달라진다. 주어가 3인칭 단수일 때는 동사원형에 -(e)s를 붙이는데, 그 방법에는 다음과 같은 규칙이 있다.

| 일반동사 | 일반동사의 변화 규칙 | 주어에 따른 동사의 현재형 | |
|---|---|---|---|
| | | I, You, We, They | He, She, It, 사람 이름, 단수 명사 |
| 대부분의 동사 | -s | run, know, tell, plan | runs, knows, tells, plans |
| -o, -s, -x, -sh, -ch로 끝나는 동사 | -es | go, miss, fix, push, catch | goes, misses, fixes, pushes, catches |
| '자음 + y'로 끝나는 동사 | y → i + es | study, carry, apply, worry | studies, carries, applies, worries |
| '모음 + y'로 끝나는 동사 | -s | play, say, stay, enjoy | plays, says, stays, enjoys |
| 불규칙 동사 | 일정한 규칙 없음 | have | has |

I love music. 나는 음악을 좋아한다.
They catch the last train. 그들은 마지막 기차를 탄다.
You study hard. 너는 열심히 공부한다.
I enjoy playing soccer. 나는 축구하는 걸 즐긴다.
We have many books. 우리는 많은 책을 가지고 있다.

He loves art. 그는 미술을 좋아한다.
She catches the first train. 그녀는 첫 기차를 탄다.
Julie studies very hard. Julie는 매우 열심히 공부한다.
He enjoys playing the piano. 그는 피아노 치는 걸 즐긴다.
She has very much money. 그녀는 많은 돈을 가지고 있다.

STEP 1
# Grammar START

**Grammar on Target**

1. 주어에 따른 일반동사의 형태
2. 주어가 3인칭 단수일 때 일반동사의 변화

## A 다음 일반동사를 3인칭 단수 현재형으로 쓰시오.

1 do ➡ ________
2 have ➡ ________
3 hatch ➡ ________
4 introduce ➡ ________
5 enjoy ➡ ________
6 miss ➡ ________
7 tell ➡ ________
8 marry ➡ ________
9 relax ➡ ________
10 lay ➡ ________
11 scratch ➡ ________
12 go ➡ ________
13 worry ➡ ________
14 push ➡ ________

relax 휴식을 취하다
hatch 부화하다
introduce 소개하다
enjoy 즐기다
miss 놓치다
marry 결혼하다
lay 놓다, 두다, 알을 낳다
scratch 할퀴다, 긁다
worry 걱정하다
push 밀다

## B 다음 문장에서 알맞은 일반동사의 현재형을 고르시오.

1 Sylvia (take / takes) care of her dog.
2 I (wash / washes) the dishes every weekend.
3 They (shout / shouts) loudly.
4 My sister (make / makes) me happy.
5 Your parents (feel / feels) proud of you.
6 Mr. David (fix / fixes) his computer.
7 He (have / has) a stomachache.
8 She (carry / carries) her bag.
9 Patrick and Bella (do / does) the laundry together.
10 We (buy / buys) some vegetables.

wash the dishes 설거지를 하다
loudly 크게, 큰 소리로
feel proud of ~ ~을 자랑스러워 하다
fix 수리하다
stomachache 복통
carry 가지고 가다, 나르다
do the laundry 빨래하다
vegetable 채소

STEP 2
# Grammar PRACTICE

## A 주어진 동사를 알맞게 바꿔 현재 시제로 문장을 완성하시오.

1 Sophia __________ collecting stamps. (like)

2 He __________ his room on Mondays. (clean)

3 Charlie sometimes __________ the garden. (tend)

4 Wendy __________ her teeth after meals. (brush)

5 He __________ to solve the problem. (try)

6 Judy __________ English to poor children. (teach)

7 She __________ hard to pass the exam. (study)

8 My mom __________ flour and egg yolks to make paste. (mix)

9 They __________ TV together every evening. (watch)

10 Robin and Aaron __________ to school by bus. (go)

collect 모으다, 수집하다
stamp 우표
sometimes 때때로, 가끔
tend the garden 정원을 가꾸다
after meals 식후에
solve 풀다, 해결하다
try to ~ ~하려고 노력하다
poor 가난한
pass 합격하다
mix 섞다
flour 밀가루
yolk (계란) 노른자
paste 반죽

## B 괄호 안에서 옳은 것을 모두 고르시오.

1 (Noah and I / She / We) goes to church on Sundays.

2 (Mike / He / children) likes playing in the park.

3 (James and Nara / She / Lisa) hate to go shopping.

4 (They / Mr. Han / I) moves the table to the dining room.

5 (He / We / You) has a sore throat.

6 (She / They / Tom) helps the homeless.

7 (They / Kelley / He) wants to travel to Spain.

8 (We / They / Ms. Brown) walk the dog every morning.

9 (Mandy and George / You / She) take a vacation in England every year.

10 (She / My sister and I / Daniel) plays soccer on the weekend.

church 교회
hate 몹시 싫어하다
dining room 식당
sore throat 따가운 목구멍, 인후염
the homeless 노숙자
vacation 휴가
travel 여행하다
Spain 스페인
walk the dog 개를 산책시키다

## C 틀린 부분을 찾아 바르게 고쳐 문장을 다시 쓰시오.

1 She have a younger brother.

➡ ______________________________

2 They searches for cultural properties.

➡ ______________________________

3 He do his best to develop his company.

➡ ______________________________

4 Colin kiss his baby every morning.

➡ ______________________________

5 I hates carrots in that food.

➡ ______________________________

6 My sister and I watches a TV program.

➡ ______________________________

7 You reads an interesting novel.

➡ ______________________________

8 He go to school on time.

➡ ______________________________

9 Emma and Donald lives in Canada.

➡ ______________________________

search for ~ ~을 찾다
cultural properties 문화재
do one's best 최선을 다하다
develop 발전시키다
on time 제 때(시간)에
live 살다

## D 우리말과 같은 뜻이 되도록 주어진 단어를 바르게 배열하시오. 단, 필요에 따라 동사를 변형시켜 쓰시오.

1 Suzy는 매일 우유 한 컵을 마신다. (every day, Suzy, a cup of milk, drink)

➡ ______________________________

2 그녀는 아침마다 꽃에 물을 준다. (the flowers, water, every morning, she)

➡ ______________________________

3 그는 고장 난 텔레비전을 고친다. (the broken television, he, fix)

➡ ______________________________

4 그 쥐는 매우 빨리 움직인다. (fast, the mouse, very, move)

➡ ______________________________

a cup of milk 한 잔의 우유
water 물을 주다
broken 고장 난

STEP 3

# Upgrade TEST

**1** 빈칸에 들어갈 수 없는 것을 고르시오.

| She ________ every morning. |
|---|

① sings a song ② exercises
③ reads the newspaper ④ ride a bike
⑤ walks the dog

**2** 다음 중 짝지어진 일반동사의 3인칭 단수형이 틀린 것을 고르시오.

① do - does ② catch - catches
③ copy - copies ④ buy - buys
⑤ have - haves

**3** 밑줄 친 부분이 바르지 못한 것을 고르시오.

① She has a beautiful bracelet.
② I needs to clean my room
③ He and his dog walk along the street.
④ My cat likes playing in high places.
⑤ We eat out on Wednesdays.

**4** 빈칸에 공통으로 들어갈 알맞은 것을 고르시오.

| • ________ enjoy swimming in the pool.<br>• ________ talk about the environment. |
|---|

① It ② She ③ They
④ He ⑤ Jennifer

**5** 다음 중 어법상 올바른 문장을 고르시오.

① Stella have a driver's license.
② He and his brother play basketball.
③ A sweet mean candy in England.
④ They takes pictures of animals.
⑤ I does my homework.

**6** 빈칸에 들어갈 알맞은 것을 고르시오.

| My brother and I ________ to my mom. |
|---|

① makes breakfast
② cleans the backyard
③ give a gift
④ writes a letter
⑤ buys a flower

**7** 다음 중 틀린 문장을 올바르게 고친 것을 고르시오.

① She cross the street.
→ She crossies the street.
② I plays a computer game.
→ I plaies a computer game.
③ Emily and James participates in the contest.
→ Emily and James participate in the contest.
④ Jay speak Japanese fluently.
→ Jay speakes Japanese fluently.
⑤ My dog always bark at strangers.
→ My dog always barkes at strangers.

newspaper 신문 bracelet 팔찌 eat out 외식하다 pool 수영장 environment 환경 driver's license 운전면허증 mean 의미하다
take a picture 사진을 찍다 participate in ~ ~에 참가하다 fluently 유창하게 bark 짖다

8 밑줄 친 부분 중 어법상 어색한 것을 고르시오.

Joan ① eats breakfast every morning before she ② goes to school. She ③ leaves home at 8 o'clock and ④ meets her friend Alice. Then, they ⑤ walks to school together.

9 빈칸에 들어갈 말이 바르게 짝지어진 것을 고르시오.

- ________ waves a flag.
- ________ draw the moon.

① They - She
② We - They
③ She - He
④ She - I
⑤ I - They

10 밑줄 친 부분을 올바른 형태로 바꾸는 방식이 나머지와 다른 것을 고르시오.

① She do the laundry every Sunday.
② Kyle love her parents.
③ He play tennis on weekends.
④ Pam tell me the whole story.
⑤ My sister enjoy reading books.

11 어법상 올바른 문장의 개수를 고르시오.

- Joy studies English every day.
- I has a lot of books.
- The crocodile bird helps the crocodile.
- Dave and Lily wear the same jacket.

① 0개
② 1개
③ 2개
④ 3개
⑤ 4개

[12-15] 서술형 주관식

12 어법상 어색한 부분을 찾아 바르게 고쳐 쓰시오.

1) My father teach baseball to students.

________ → ________

2) Adams like toy soldiers very much.

________ → ________

13 주어진 단어를 바르게 배열하여 다음 우리말을 영어로 쓰시오. 단, 필요에 따라 동사를 변형시켜 쓰시오.

Sally는 그 캠프에서 자원봉사를 한다.
(Sally, at the camp, do, volunteer work)

→ ________________________

14 보기의 동사를 이용하여 현재 시제로 문장을 완성하시오.

보기 stay

1) I ________ at my grandma's house.
2) Dave ________ in bed on Sundays.
3) They ________ at home all day long.

15 주어진 단어를 이용하여 다음 우리말을 영어로 쓰시오.

그 아기는 매우 크게 운다. (cry, so loudly)

→ ________________________

leave ~ ~를 떠나다 walk to school 학교에 걸어서 가다 wave 흔들다 flag 깃발 whole 전체의, 모든 crocodile 악어 crocodile bird 악어새 camp 캠프 volunteer work 자원봉사 stay 머물다 cry 울다

Unit 02

# 일반동사의 부정문과 의문문

## 1 일반동사의 부정문

일반동사의 부정문은 동사원형 앞에 do not 또는 don't를 붙인다. 주어가 3인칭 단수일 때는 does not이나 doesn't를 붙인다.

| 주어 | 동사의 부정형 | 예문 |
|---|---|---|
| I, We, You, They | do not (don't) + 동사원형 | I like beef. I don't like pork.<br>나는 소고기를 좋아한다. 나는 돼지고기를 좋아하지 않는다. |
| He, She, It 등 3인칭 단수 | does not (doesn't) + 동사원형 | Sue drinks coffee. She doesn't drink green tea.<br>Sue는 커피를 마신다. 그녀는 녹차를 마시지 않는다. |

Tip

does not 다음에는 drinks가 아닌 동사원형 drink가 와야 한다.

## 2 일반동사의 의문문

일반동사의 의문문은 조동사 Do를 이용해서 『Do + 주어 + 동사원형 ~?』의 형태이다. 주어가 3인칭 단수일 때는 Does를 이용해서 『Does + 주어 + 동사원형 ~?』의 형태이다.

| 주어 | 동사의 의문문 | 예문 |
|---|---|---|
| I, We, You, They | Do + 주어 + 동사원형 ~? | Do you enjoy watching movies?<br>너는 영화 보는 것을 좋아하니? |
| He, She, It 등 3인칭 단수 | Does + 주어 + 동사원형 ~? | Does she speak French?<br>그녀는 프랑스어를 말하나요? |

Tip

Does 다음에는 speaks가 아닌 동사원형 speak가 와야 한다.

## 3 일반동사의 의문문에 대한 대답

일반동사의 의문문에 대한 긍정의 대답은 『Yes, 주어 + do/does』로, 부정의 대답은 『No, 주어 + don't/doesn't』의 형태이다.

| 주어 | 동사의 의문문 | 대답 |
|---|---|---|
| I, We, You, They | Do you have a cellphone? 너는 핸드폰이 있니? | Yes, I do. / No, I don't. |
| He, She, It 등 3인칭 단수 | Does she enjoy music? 그녀는 음악을 즐기니? | Yes, she does. / No, she doesn't. |

Tip

일반동사의 의문문에 대한 대답은 Yes/No로 하며, 주어를 대명사로 쓴다.

A: Does Jane join our club?

B: Yes, she does.

STEP 1

# Grammar START

Grammar on Target

1. 주어에 따른 일반동사의 부정형
2. 일반동사의 의문문 만들기

## A 다음 괄호 안에서 알맞은 것을 고르시오.

1 He (don't / doesn't) play the violin.

2 I (don't / doesn't) do chores at home.

3 Peter (don't / doesn't) like cheese.

4 We (don't / doesn't) make noise at night.

5 You and my brother (don't / doesn't) follow my advice.

6 Sally (don't / doesn't) take a nap after lunch.

7 They (don't / doesn't) eat meat.

8 You (don't / doesn't) wear jeans.

9 My cats (don't / doesn't) chase mice.

chore 허드렛일, 집안일
follow 따르다
advice 조언, 충고
take a nap 낮잠을 자다
meat 고기
jeans 청바지
chase 뒤쫓다, 추적하다
mice (mouse의 복수형) 생쥐들

## B 주어진 동사를 이용하여 일반동사의 의문문을 완성하시오.

1 ________ she ________ well? (cook)

2 ________ they ________ each other? (love)

3 ________ Steve ________ a camping car? (have)

4 ________ your brothers ________ soccer after school? (play)

5 ________ the students in this class ________ hard? (study)

6 ________ we ________ some rest for a while? (get)

7 ________ it ________ a lot in Pyeongchang? (snow)

8 ________ you ________ to bed early? (go)

9 ________ this backpack ________ to you? (belong)

cook 요리하다
after school 방과 후에
get some rest 휴식을 취하다, 쉬다
for a while 잠깐 동안
go to bed 자다
backpack 배낭, 책가방
belong to ~ ~의 것이다, ~에 속하다

STEP 2

# Grammar PRACTICE

## A 다음 문장을 부정문으로 바꿔 쓰시오. (축약형으로)

1 Jack reads comic books.

➡ Jack __________ __________ comic books.

2 They often visit London.

➡ They __________ often __________ London.

3 Sunny listens to classical music.

➡ Sunny __________ __________ to classical music.

4 Tim and I go rock climbing today.

➡ Tim and I __________ __________ rock climbing today.

5 She washes her sneakers.

➡ She __________ __________ her sneakers.

6 His dog sleeps on his bed.

➡ His dog __________ __________ on his bed.

7 You and your sister ride your bikes.

➡ You and your sister __________ __________ your bikes.

8 It matters so much in this case.

➡ It __________ __________ so much in this case.

comic book 만화책
often 종종, 자주
visit 방문하다
classical music 고전 음악, 클래식
rock climbing 암벽 등반
sneakers 운동화
ride a bike 자전거를 타다
matter 중요하다
case 경우, 사건, 사실

## B 대화를 읽고, 빈칸에 알맞은 말을 쓰시오.

1 A __________ you want some coffee?

B Yes, I __________. I __________ some coffee.

2 A __________ Joseph and you go fishing every Sunday?

B No, we __________. We play baseball.

3 A __________ your sister walk to school?

B No, she __________. She takes a bus to school.

4 A __________ Harry hurry to Hogwarts?

B Yes, he __________. He __________ to Hogwarts.

go fishing 낚시하러 가다
take a bus 버스를 타다
Hogwarts (호그와트) 해리포터에 나오는 마법학교
hurry 서두르다

## C 보기와 같이 다음 문장을 대명사를 주어로 하는 부정문과 의문문으로 바꿔 쓰시오.

> 보기 Andy watches a cartoon on TV.
> ➡ He doesn't a watch a cartoon on TV.
> ➡ Does he watch a cartoon on TV?

1 Kate has plans with her friends today.

➡ ______

➡ ______

2 Sam and his brother like potato chips very much.

➡ ______

➡ ______

3 The wind blows hard on Jeju Island.

➡ ______

➡ ______

4 My parents and I go snowboarding in winter.

➡ ______

➡ ______

have plans 약속이 있다
blow (바람이) 불다
island 섬
snowboarding 스노보드 타기

## D 우리말과 같은 뜻이 되도록 주어진 단어를 바르게 배열하시오.

1 너의 아빠는 중국에서 일하시니? (in China, your dad, work, does)

➡ ______

2 그들은 주말에 체육관에 가지 않는다. (don't, on weekends, go to the gym, they)

➡ ______

3 너와 Eric은 매일 줄넘기를 연습하니?
(practice, every day, you and Eric, jump rope, do)

➡ ______

4 그 마녀는 빗자루를 타고 날아다니니?
(the witch, on the broomstick, fly around, does)

➡ ______

gym 체육관
practice 연습하다
jump rope 줄넘기
witch 마녀
broomstick 빗자루

STEP 3
# Upgrade TEST

**1** 다음 문장을 의문문으로 바르게 바꾼 것을 고르시오.

| She likes tennis. |
|---|

① Do she likes tennis?
② Is she like tennis?
③ Has she likes tennis?
④ Does she like tennis?
⑤ Does she likes tennis?

**2** 다음 빈칸에 들어갈 Do 동사의 형태가 나머지와 다른 것을 고르시오.

① ________ your dad watch a movie?
② ________ she go out for a walk?
③ ________ it matter that much to you?
④ ________ the bus come often?
⑤ ________ you play soccer on the weekend?

**3** 다음 중 어법상 올바른 문장을 고르시오.

① I ride not a bicycle on weekdays.
② I not ride a bicycle on weekdays.
③ I am not ride a bicycle on weekdays.
④ I don't ride a bicycle on weekdays.
⑤ I doesn't ride a bicycle on weekdays.

**4** 빈칸에 들어갈 알맞은 것을 고르시오.

A Do you want to go to movies?
B ____________

① Yes, I am. ② Yes, I do. ③ Yes, I does.
④ Yes, you are. ⑤ Yes, you do.

**5** 다음 중 어법상 올바른 문장을 모두 고르시오.

① He don't exercise every day.
② Do Eric and his sister dance well?
③ Do you want to help the poor?
④ Do your father play the violin?
⑤ We doesn't go to the museum every month.

**6** 빈칸에 들어갈 말이 바르게 짝지어진 것을 고르시오.

A ________ she like cookies?
B No, she ________. She likes chocolates.

① Does - does ② Do - don't
③ Does - doesn't ④ Is - isn't
⑤ Is - doesn't

**7** 다음 중 부정문으로 바꾼 문장이 틀린 것을 고르시오.

① I have a watch.
→ I don't have a watch.
② She eats eggs.
→ She doesn't eats eggs.
③ We have a small puppy.
→ We don't have a small puppy.
④ You often play outside in winter.
→ You don't often play outside in winter.
⑤ He goes shopping.
→ He doesn't go shopping.

**8** 밑줄 친 부분 중 어법상 어색한 것을 고르시오.

① Jack doesn't have a cellphone.
② Lisa does not like fruit.
③ Children do not drink coffee.
④ My friends don't play mobile games.
⑤ Elsa and her sister doesn't eat sweets.

on weekdays 평일에 exercise 운동하다 the poor 가난한 사람들 museum 박물관 go shopping 쇼핑하러 가다 fruit 과일 sweets 사탕, 단것
have a pet 애완동물을 기르다

**9** 보기의 대답에 알맞는 질문을 고르시오.

| 보기 No, he doesn't. |
|---|

① Does your brother work in a hospital?
② Do you love movies?
③ Do we have a video camera?
④ Does your grandma have a pet?
⑤ Does your sister enter the University of Chicago this year?

**10** 다음 중 대화가 자연스럽지 않은 것을 고르시오.

① A Do they learn English at school?
B Yes, they do.
② A Do you walk to school every day?
B Yes, I do.
③ A Do you have a dishwasher?
B No, we don't.
④ A Does Jim want some cheesecake?
B No, he doesn't.
⑤ A Do you often dance with Jane?
B No, she doesn't.

**11** 다음 문장에서 틀린 부분의 개수를 고르시오.

| Mrs. Ryan is my neighbor. I meets her every morning. She greets me kindly, saying, "Good Morning, Justin." Does she works at Facebook? No, she don't. She teaches law at Yale University. |
|---|

① 0개 ② 1개 ③ 2개
④ 3개 ⑤ 4개

[12-15] 서술형 주관식

**12** 다음 대화의 빈칸에 알맞은 말을 쓰시오.

| A Do you want to go out for a walk?<br>B ____________ Wait a minute. I'll be right back with some water. |
|---|

**13** 주어진 단어를 바르게 배열하여 다음 우리말을 영어로 쓰고, 그 질문에 부정으로 답하시오.

| Cindy는 그녀의 생일파티에 대해서 아니?<br>(her birthday party, know, Cindy, about, does) |
|---|

A ____________
B ____________

**14** 주어진 단어를 이용하여 다음 우리말을 영어로 쓰시오.

| 그는 젓가락을 잘 사용하지 못한다.<br>(chopsticks, very well, use) |
|---|

→ ____________

**15** 어법상 어색한 부분을 찾아 바르게 고쳐 문장을 다시 쓰시오.

| A Do Juliet goes skiing with you?<br>B Yes, she don't. |
|---|

A ____________
B ____________

enter 들어가다, 입학하다 university 대학교 dishwasher 식기세척기 Facebook 페이스북 (미국의 유명 소셜 네트워크 서비스) chopsticks 젓가락 go skiing 스키를 타러 가다

**[1-2] 빈칸에 들어갈 알맞은 것을 고르시오.**

**1**

| Mr. Brown ________ on Sundays. |
|---|

① play tennis ② ride his bike
③ walks in the park ④ swim in the water
⑤ sleep late

**2**

| ________ Mia and Tom at the bus stop? |
|---|

① Do ② Does ③ Is
④ Are ⑤ Am

**3 밑줄 친 부분을 축약해서 쓸 수 없는 것을 고르시오.**

① He is not a lawyer.
② My dog does not bite.
③ I am not in the bathroom.
④ They do not know the truth.
⑤ Stella and I are not nervous about the test.

**4 밑줄 친 부분의 쓰임이 올바른 것을 고르시오.**

① They wears glasses.
② She enjoy playing the piano.
③ I watches the movie on Sundays.
④ Heather don't knows my cellphone number.
⑤ Koreans speak Korean.

**5 빈칸에 공통으로 들어갈 말을 쓰시오.**

- ________ they have scissors?
- ________ you like strawberries?

**6 밑줄 친 부분을 바르게 고친 것을 고르시오.**

| Lily and I am students at the same school. |
|---|

① is ② aren't ③ isn't
④ don't ⑤ doesn't

**7 다음 문장을 의문문으로 바르게 바꾼 것을 고르시오.**

| Thomas plays the violin very well. |
|---|

① Is Thomas play the violin very well?
② Do Thomas play the violin very well?
③ Do Thomas plays the violin very well?
④ Does Thomas play the violin very well?
⑤ Does Thomas plays the violin very well?

**[8-9] 다음 빈칸에 들어갈 말이 바르게 짝지어진 것을 고르시오.**

**8**

A ________ he listen to K-pop music?
B Yes, ________. He loves K-pop.

① Does - he does ② Does - he doesn't
③ Do - she does ④ Do - she doesn't
⑤ Is - he isn't

**9**

A I ________ want to eat lunch. I have a stomachache.

B That's too bad. ________ you want to go home?

① don't - Does　② don't - Do
③ does - Do　④ doesn't – Does
⑤ doesn't – Do

**10** 다음 중 대화가 어법상 <u>어색한</u> 것을 고르시오.

① A Do you play computer games?
B Yes, I do. I love computer games.

② A Does a penguin fly in the sky?
B No, it isn't. It is not a bird.

③ A Are the girls in the library your friends?
B Yes, they are. They are my friends.

④ A Is Olivia good at dancing?
B No, she is not. She is poor at dancing.

⑤ A Does Eric go to school early in the morning?
B No, he doesn't. He gets up at 9 o'clock.

**11** 주어진 단어를 이용하여 다음 우리말을 영어로 쓰시오.

그 박물관은 월요일에 문을 열지 않는다.
(museum, open)

➡ The ______________________ on Monday.

**12** 빈칸에 들어갈 말로 알맞지 <u>않은</u> 것을 고르시오.

Jennifer and Brian ________________.

① meet at 3 o'clock　② have paintbrushes
③ are in the park　④ eats lunch together
⑤ do their homework at 8 o'clock

**13** 다음 중 문장을 지시대로 바르게 고친 것을 고르시오.

① She has a brother.
부정문 → She doesn't has a brother.

② They are famous actors.
부정문 → They not are famous actors.

③ You are proud of your grandparents.
의문문 → Do you proud of your grandparents?

④ My mother eats meat.
부정문 → My mother doesn't eat meat.

⑤ Daniel and I are on the beach.
의문문 → Am Daniel and I on the beach?

**[14-15]** 다음 Tim의 시간표를 보고 알맞은 말을 쓰시오.

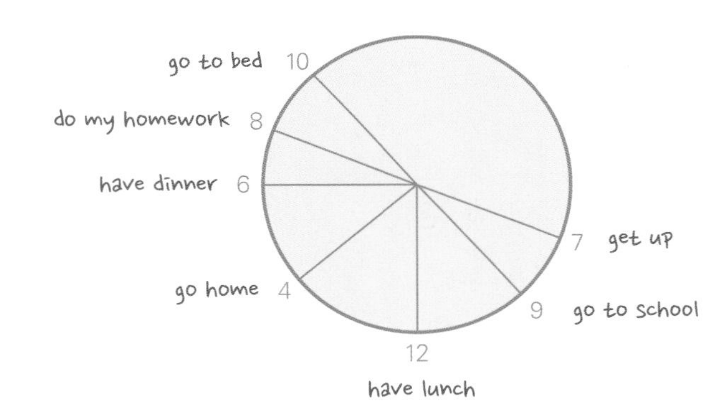


**14**

A Does he get up at 9 o'clock?

B ________, he ________. He ________ at 7 o'clock.

**15**

A Does he do his homework at 8 o'clock?

B ________, he ________.

기초 탄탄 1
GRAMMAR

Chapter 3

# 명사

Unit 01

# 셀 수 있는 명사

## 1 명사

명사는 사람, 사물, 장소 또는 추상적인 것 등의 이름을 나타내는 말이다.
명사는 bus, pencil, apple과 같이 셀 수 있는 명사와 love, hope, health와 같이 셀 수 없는 명사로 나눌 수 있다.

## 2 셀 수 있는 명사의 단수와 복수

1) 단수명사는 앞에 부정관사 a 또는 an을 붙이는데, 단수명사가 모음으로 시작할 때 an을 쓴다.

I know a boy. 나는 한 소년을 안다. He buys an orange. 그는 오렌지 하나를 산다.

2) 단수명사를 복수명사로 바꿀 때, 다음과 같은 규칙이 있다.

| 명사 | 명사의 변화 규칙 | 명사의 단수와 복수 |
|---|---|---|
| 대부분의 명사 | + -s | cat → cats, friend → friends, computer → computers, |
| '모음 + o'로 끝나는 명사 | + -s | kangaroo → kangaroos, radio → radios, zoo → zoos, bamboo → bamboos |
| '모음 + y'로 끝나는 명사 | + -s | boy → boys, toy → toys, day → days |
| '자음 + o'로 끝나는 명사 | + -es | hero → heroes, potato → potatoes, tomato → tomatoes<br>예외 photos, pianos, autos, Eskimos, kilos |
| -s, -x , -ch, -sh로 끝나는 명사 | + -es | bus → buses, box → boxes, church → churches, dish → dishes |
| '자음 + y'로 끝나는 명사 | y → i + -es | baby → babies, city → cities, lady → ladies |
| -f, -fe로 끝나는 명사 | f, fe → v + -es | half → halves, knife → knives, leaf → leaves, life → lives, thief → thieves<br>예외 roofs, chefs, chiefs, cliffs, dwarfs |
| 불규칙 | 모음이나 끝부분 변화 | man → men, woman → women, foot → feet, tooth → teeth, goose → geese, mouse → mice, child → children, ox → oxen, person → people |
| 불규칙 | 단수와 복수가 같은 형태 | deer, fish, sheep, salmon, Chinese, Japanese, Swiss |

**Tip**
셀 수 있는 명사에는 단어 자체가 복수의 의미를 갖는 집합명사가 있다.
family 가족
audience 청중
team 팀
police 경찰
cattle 가축
people 사람들

**Tip**
단수와 복수에 따라 의미가 달라지기도 한다.
arm 팔 → arms 무기
force 힘 → forces 군대
good 선 → goods 상품
wood 나무 → woods 숲
water 물 → waters 강
manner 방법 → manners 예절

## 3 항상 복수형으로 쓰는 명사

한 쌍으로 짝을 이루어서 항상 복수형으로 쓰는 명사가 있다. 이들을 셀 때는 a pair of, a couple of, a set of 등을 사용한다.

| glasses 안경, gloves 장갑, pants 바지, scissors 가위, shoes 신발, sneakers 운동화, socks 양말 |
|---|

I bought three pairs of jeans at the mall. 나는 쇼핑몰에서 세 벌의 청바지를 샀다.

**Tip**
a pair of jeans가 주어일 때는 단수동사가 와야 한다.
A pair of jeans is on the table.
청바지 한 벌이 탁자 위에 있다.

STEP 1

# Grammar START

**Grammar on Target**

1. 셀 수 있는 명사의 복수형
2. 셀 수 있는 명사의 올바른 형태

## A 다음 명사의 복수형을 쓰시오.

1 bag ➡ ____________
2 deer ➡ ____________
3 toy ➡ ____________
4 tomato ➡ ____________
5 friend ➡ ____________
6 potato ➡ ____________
7 box ➡ ____________
8 story ➡ ____________
9 wolf ➡ ____________
10 knife ➡ ____________
11 church ➡ ____________
12 photo ➡ ____________
13 chef ➡ ____________
14 city ➡ ____________
15 hero ➡ ____________
16 fish ➡ ____________
17 bamboo ➡ ____________
18 piano ➡ ____________
19 roof ➡ ____________
20 month ➡ ____________

chef 요리사
deer 사슴
hero 영웅
bamboo 대나무
roof 지붕
knife 칼, 나이프

## B 다음 문장에서 알맞은 것을 고르시오.

1 There comes (bus / a bus).

2 I buy (a orange / an orange) at the grocery store.

3 So many (man / men) come to see Jennifer Lawrence.

4 There are three (mice / mouses) in the ceiling.

5 Rachel has five (children / childs) to take care of.

6 The shepherd boy lives with 50 (sheep / sheeps) on the farm.

7 Everyone loves a gentleman with good (manner / manners).

8 She buys a pair of (jean / jeans) at the Desert Hills Outlets.

grocery store 식료품 가게
many 많은
(셀 수 있는 명사와 함께 쓰임)
ceiling 천장
take care of ~ ~를 돌보다
shepherd 양치기
solve 해결하다
everyone 모든 사람
gentleman 신사

STEP 2

# Grammar PRACTICE

## A 주어진 명사를 알맞은 형태로 바꿔 문장을 완성하시오.

1 An ant has six __________. (leg)

2 Twelve __________ are on the table. (dish)

3 __________ turn into butterflies. (caterpillar)

4 My uncle has ten __________ and six pigs. (goose)

5 Snow White meets seven __________ in the woods. (dwarf)

6 There are four __________ and two cats in the room. (puppy)

7 Two __________ speak English at the meeting. (Japanese)

8 Many __________ are pleased with the good news. (person)

9 Ms. Jones has only one __________. (child)

10 He puts both of his __________ up on the sofa. (foot)

leg 다리
caterpillar 애벌레
goose 거위
pig 돼지
dwarf 난쟁이
Japanese 일본인
pleased 기쁜
news 소식
only 유일한, 오직
both 양쪽의

## B 밑줄 친 단어를 단수는 복수로, 복수는 단수로 바꿔 문장을 다시 쓰시오.

1 Two ladies are in the red car. (a)

➡ ______________________________

2 Many boys play soccer on the playground. (a)

➡ ______________________________

3 She needs a pair of shoes for the fashion show. (five)

➡ ______________________________

4 They eat a sandwich a day. (three)

➡ ______________________________

5 A thief steals a diamond ring from the store. (two)

➡ ______________________________

lady 숙녀
thief 도둑
fashion show 패션쇼
steal 훔치다

## C 틀린 부분을 찾아 바르게 고쳐 문장을 다시 쓰시오.

1 Several dog help the blind. 몇몇 개들은 시각장애인들을 돕는다.

➡ ______________________________

2 Ann has a pairs of sneakers. Ann은 운동화 한 켤레가 있다.

➡ ______________________________

3 It makes leafs green. 그것은 나뭇잎들을 초록색으로 만든다.

➡ ______________________________

4 She needs two tomatos. 그녀는 토마토 두 개가 필요하다.

➡ ______________________________

5 Ethan needs two pair of socks. Ethan은 양말 두 켤레가 필요하다.

➡ ______________________________

6 The zoo has five kangarooes. 그 동물원에는 캥거루 다섯 마리가 있다.

➡ ______________________________

7 My dad washes the dish every morning. 우리 아빠는 매일 아침 설거지를 하신다.

➡ ______________________________

8 I brush my tooth after meals. 나는 밥을 먹은 후에 이를 닦는다.

➡ ______________________________

9 The scissor is next to the book. 가위는 책 옆에 있다.

➡ ______________________________

several 몇몇의
the blind 시각장애인들
leaf 나뭇잎
socks 양말

## D 우리말과 같은 뜻이 되도록 주어진 단어를 바르게 배열하시오.

1 네 명의 여자는 노래를 잘 부른다. (singing, women, are good at, four)

➡ ______________________________

2 그는 한 달에 청바지 한 벌을 산다. (jeans, buys, a pair of, he, each month)

➡ ______________________________

3 경찰들은 진정 영웅들이다. (are, heroes, the real, the police)

➡ ______________________________

4 Kevin은 주말마다 많은 물고기를 잡는다. (a lot of, catches, on weekends, Kevin, fish)

➡ ______________________________

month 달, 월
real 진짜의
a lot of 많은

STEP 3

# Upgrade TEST

**1** 빈칸에 들어갈 수 없는 것을 고르시오.

| There are two ________ in my room. |
|---|

① mice ② dolls ③ children
④ woman ⑤ tables

**2** 다음 중 짝지어진 단어의 관계가 나머지와 다른 것을 고르시오.

① roof - roofs
② piano - pianos
③ live - lives
④ fox - foxes
⑤ goose - geese

**3** 다음 중 셀 수 있는 명사가 아닌 것을 고르시오.

① apple ② potato
③ chief ④ coffee
⑤ watermelon

**4** 명사의 단수형과 복수형이 잘못 짝지어진 것을 고르시오.

① an ox - oxen
② a deer - deer
③ a chef - chefs
④ a tomato – tomatoes
⑤ a salmon - salmons

**5** 빈칸에 들어갈 수 없는 것을 고르시오.

| Does Noah have many ________? |
|---|

① babies ② autos ③ water
④ cattle ⑤ sheep

**6** 다음 중 어법상 어색한 문장을 고르시오.

① I exercise four day a week.
② One hundred won is not a lot of money.
③ Sheep are running on the mountain.
④ Five shirts are hanging on the clothesline.
⑤ With 100 won, you can give three bananas to a child in Rwanda.

**7** 다음 대화의 빈칸에 들어갈 수 없는 것을 고르시오.

| A May I help you?<br>B Yes, I am looking for a pair of ________.<br>A How about these?<br>B Oh, they are blue. I want red ones. |
|---|

① socks ② pants
③ gloves ④ sneakers
⑤ shirts

chief 우두머리, 지휘관 watermelon 수박 ox 황소 chef 요리사 salmon 연어 auto 자동차 look for ~ ~을 찾다

**8** 다음 중 밑줄 친 부분이 어색한 것을 고르시오.

① There are too many mistakes in report.
② There are many fallen leafs on the bench.
③ I catch plenty of fish on weekends.
④ The firefighter saved many lives from the fire.
⑤ I want to visit many beautiful cities in America.

**9** 다음 중 어법상 올바른 문장을 고르시오.

① She wears a glass.
② Look at the monkies.
③ She keeps two wolfs in her farm.
④ There are many people at Seoul Station.
⑤ We need ten boxs for toys.

**[10-11]** 다음 중 어법상 어색한 문장을 고르시오.

**10** ① There are two photos on my desk.
② A onion has a strong taste.
③ There are seven days in a week.
④ They sell various goods in the store.
⑤ We catch many fish in the sea every weekend.

**11** ① Do you have woods in this town?
② I raise many lilies.
③ She has two oranges for lunch.
④ Are these your boxes?
⑤ I drink three milks every day.

## [12-15] 서술형 주관식

**12** 어법상 어색한 부분을 찾아 바르게 고쳐 쓰시오.

| The scissor cut well. |
|---|

__________ → __________

**13** 보기에서 알맞은 명사를 골라 단수형 또는 복수형으로 바꿔 문장을 완성하시오.

| 보기 tooth shoes hero |
|---|

1) They are __________ of the Olympics.
2) I brush my __________ three times a day.
3) She wants to buy two pairs of __________.

**14** 어법상 어색한 부분을 찾아 바르게 고쳐 문장을 다시 쓰시오.

| The waitress puts five fork and five knife on the table. |
|---|

→ ______________________________

______________________________

**15** 주어진 단어를 바르게 배열하여 다음 우리말을 영어로 쓰시오.

| 우리는 아프리카의 아이들에게 50켤레의 운동화를 보낸다.<br>(send, sneakers, in Africa, fifty pairs of, to children, we) |
|---|

→ ______________________________

______________________________

mistake 실수, 오류 fallen leaf 낙엽 bench 긴 의자 life 생명 fire 불 a(the) fire 화재 various 다양한 goods 물품, 상품 waitress 여종업원 send 보내다

Unit 02

# 셀 수 없는 명사

## 1 셀 수 없는 명사의 종류

셀 수 없는 명사에는 고유명사, 추상명사, 물질명사가 있다. 셀 수 없으므로 a/an을 붙일 수 없고, 복수형으로도 쓸 수 없다.

| 셀 수 없는 명사 | | 예문 |
|---|---|---|
| 고유명사 | 세상에 하나밖에 없는 사람, 사물, 장소 | the Sahara, the Eiffel Tower, Mount Everest, London, Korea, Tom, December 등<br>He lives in Seoul. 그는 서울에 산다. |
| 추상명사 | 눈에 보이지 않는 추상적인 개념이나 감정 | love, peace, hope, success, wisdom, beauty, advice, experience, honesty, information, knowledge 등<br>I have a lot of homework to do. 나는 해야 할 숙제가 많다. |
| 물질명사 | 일정한 형태가 없거나 형태가 있더라도 세기 힘든 물질 | water, air, salt, sugar, rice, cheese, coffee, milk, sand, dust, fire, glass, gold, hair, light, paper, pizza 등<br>I want to drink a cup of coffee. 나는 한 잔의 커피를 마시고 싶다. |

**Tip**
고유명사의 첫 글자는 항상 대문자이다.

**Tip**
furniture, money, homework과 같이 사물의 집합체를 나타내는 명사도 셀 수 없다.

## 2 셀 수 없는 명사의 수량 표현

물질명사는 다음과 같이 모양이나 물질을 담는 용기, 계량 단위를 셈으로써 수를 표현할 수 있다.

| 단위 명사 | | 명사 | 예문 |
|---|---|---|---|
| 모양에 따른 측정 단위 | a piece of 한 조각 | cake, bread, paper, furniture | I have two pieces of cake for dessert. 나는 디저트로 케이크 두 조각을 먹는다.<br>A bar of soap is in the bathroom. 욕실에 비누 한 개가 있다. |
| | a sheet of 한 장 | paper | |
| | a slice of 한 쪽 | cheese, bread, bacon, pizza | |
| | a loaf of 한 덩어리 | bread | |
| | a bar of 한 개 | soap, chocolate | |
| 용기에 따른 측정 단위 | a cup of 한 컵 | coffee, tea, water | I want to drink a cup of green tea. 나는 녹차 한 잔을 마시고 싶다.<br>Bring me a glass of orange juice. 나에게 오렌지 주스 한 잔 갖다 줘. |
| | a glass of 한 잔 | milk, juice, water | |
| | a bottle of 한 병 | wine, beer, milk, water, juice | |
| | a bag of 한 자루(부대) | sugar, rice, flour | |
| | a box of 한 상자 | fruit | |
| 무게에 따른 측정 단위 | a pound of 1파운드 | beef | They eat a pound of beef a day. 그들은 하루에 쇠고기 1파운드를 먹는다. |
| | a kilo of 1킬로 | sugar | |
| 많고 적음의 정도 표시 | much, a lot of, lots of 많은 / a little 조금 있는 / little 거의 없는 / some 약간의 / no 전혀 없는 | | I have some money with me. 나는 약간의 돈을 가지고 있다 |

**Tip**
advice나 information과 같은 추상명사도 a piece of로 수량을 표시할 수 있다.
She gave me a piece of advice. 그녀가 나에게 한마디의 조언을 해주었다.

STEP 1

# Grammar START

**Grammar on Target**

1. 셀 수 있는 명사와 셀 수 없는 명사
2. 셀 수 없는 명사의 수량 표현

## A 다음 문장에서 알맞은 것을 고르시오.

1 (Ryan / A Ryan) is my beloved son.

2 I have some (moneys / money) with me.

3 She has some (experience / experiences) in the field.

4 Heather drinks two cups of (coffee / coffees) a day.

5 A closet is a piece of (a furniture / furniture).

6 I need some (information / informations) about New York.

7 There is little (sugar / sugars) in the pot.

8 Barcelona is the capital of (a Spain / Spain).

9 The museum is open daily except on (Monday / a Monday).

10 (Knowledge / A knowledge) and wisdom are the real power.

beloved 사랑하는
experience 경험
field 들판, 분야
drink 마시다
closet 옷장
piece 한 조각(부분, 점, 장)
furniture 가구
little 아주 적은, 거의 없는
pot 항아리, 단지
daily 매일의, 나날의
except ~ ~을 제외하고
knowledge 지식
wisdom 지혜

## B 다음 문장에서 알맞은 수량 표현을 고르시오.

1 Eric puts (a sheet of / a glass of) paper on my desk.

2 The chef needs (a box of / a bottle of) fruit every day.

3 There is (a slice of / a glass of) milk on the table.

4 I like to drink (a pound of / a cup of) coffee in the morning.

5 Here is (a bar of / a kilo of) soap for you.

6 (A bottle of / A loaf of) bread is only two dollars.

7 Mom brings me (a piece of / a bar of) cake after dinner.

8 The mouse eats (a bottle of / a slice of) cheese in the kitchen.

sheet 시트, 한 장, 한 판
fruit 과일
slice (얇게 썬) 조각
glass 유리 잔
bring 가져오다, 데려오다
soap 비누
dinner 저녁식사

STEP 2

# Grammar PRACTICE

## A 주어진 우리말을 이용하여 빈칸에 알맞은 말을 쓰시오.

1 나는 저녁 식사 후 그에게 녹차 한 잔을 가져다 준다.

➡ I bring him __________ __________ of green tea after dinner.

2 찬장 안에 와인 아홉 병이 있다.

➡ There are nine __________ of __________ in the cupboard.

3 그녀는 그 가게에서 과일 두 상자를 산다.

➡ She buys __________ __________ of fruit at the store.

4 할머니는 나에게 매일 조언 한 가지를 해 주신다.

➡ Grandma gives me __________ __________ of advice every day.

5 그는 보통 샌드위치에 치즈 세 장을 넣는다.

➡ He usually puts three __________ of __________ on his sandwich.

6 Jessica는 매일 아침 오렌지 주스를 한 잔 마신다.

➡ Jessica drinks __________ __________ of orange juice every morning.

furniture 가구
bottle 병
wine 와인
cupboard 찬장
advice 조언, 충고
cheese 치즈
juice 주스

## B 괄호 안에서 알맞은 것을 모두 고르시오.

1 There is (a lot of / much / many) dust around.

2 I have a fried egg with (a / two / a glass of) milk for breakfast.

3 Charlie needs (a sheet of / a piece of / a loaf of) paper.

4 She wants to buy (some / three / a bottle of) furniture for her new house.

5 (A cup of / A glass of / A slice of) water is on the table.

6 There is (a / a lot of / a little) snow on the roof.

7 Emma toasts (a loaf of / two loaves of / a cup of) bread every morning.

8 He has a slice of (cheese / bread / pizza) with his salad.

a lot of 많은
dust 먼지
fried 기름에 튀긴
some 약간의
roof 지붕
toast 굽다
salad 샐러드

## C 틀린 부분을 찾아 바르게 고쳐 문장을 다시 쓰시오.

1 My country has many snow in winter.

➡ ________________________________

2 I have some bread with a butter for breakfast.

➡ ________________________________

3 An Eiffel Tower is a symbol of Paris.

➡ ________________________________

4 They have a lot of homeworks.

➡ ________________________________

5 My family has four pound of beef a week.

➡ ________________________________

6 He needs a lot of moneys to enjoy the sport.

➡ ________________________________

7 She wants to visit toronto this winter vacation.

➡ ________________________________

8 We can see beautiful flowers in an April.

➡ ________________________________

9 I usually drink three cup of coffees a day.

➡ ________________________________

butter 버터
symbol 상징
Paris 파리
beef 쇠고기
vacation 방학
April 4월

## D 우리말과 같은 뜻이 되도록 주어진 단어를 바르게 배열하시오.

1 그건 식은 죽 먹기다. (is, cake, a piece of, it)

➡ ________________________________

2 그는 일을 마친 후에 물 한 병을 마신다. (a bottle of, after work, drinks, he, water)

➡ ________________________________

3 식탁 위에 주스 두 잔이 있다. (juice, on the table, are, two glasses of, there)

➡ ________________________________

4 나는 방과 후에 해야 할 일이 많다. (work, have, after school, a lot of, I, to do)

➡ ________________________________

STEP 3
# Upgrade TEST

**[1-2] 다음 중 어법상 틀린 것을 고르시오.**

**1** ① a cup of coffee ② a sheet of paper
③ a glass of juice ④ a box of fruit
⑤ a slice of sugar

**2** ① two bottles of water
② three cups of green tea
③ two slices of bacon
④ three piece of pizzas
⑤ four boxes of fruit

**3 다음 중 어법상 올바른 문장을 고르시오.**

① Sam gives me an advice.
② Sam gives me a piece of advice.
③ Sam gives me two piece of advices.
④ Sam gives me a piece of an advice.
⑤ Sam gives me two pieces of advices.

**4 다음 빈칸에 가장 적절한 말을 고르시오.**

| I want to drink ________ milk. |
|---|

① a bar of ② a piece of
③ a glass of ④ a loaf of
⑤ a slice of

**5 빈칸에 들어갈 수 없는 것을 고르시오.**

| Jane has two pieces of ________. |
|---|

① beer ② cake
③ furniture ④ paper
⑤ advice

**6 다음 밑줄 친 부분이 올바른 것을 고르시오.**

① You wear a pair of glass.
② I have four cups of teas in every morning.
③ Sally buys a pound of beef.
④ He eats three piece of chocolate cakes.
⑤ Tom pours a bucket of waters on his garden.

**7 빈칸에 들어갈 말이 바르게 짝지어진 것을 고르시오.**

| John has ________ money, so he can buy ________ cars. |
|---|

① a lot of - little
② few - little
③ many - much
④ a lot of - a lot of
⑤ a little - lots of

bacon 베이컨 beer 맥주 bucket 양동이

**8** 빈칸에 들어갈 말로 가장 알맞은 것을 고르시오.

| Jessica doesn't have ________ in her apartment. |
|---|

① many furnitures ② much furniture
③ a lot of furnitures ④ a few furnitures
⑤ a number of furniture

**[9-10] 다음 중 어법상 올바른 문장을 고르시오.**

**9** ① Horse is a useful animal.
② Some child are playing in the park.
③ I saw two ox on my way home.
④ I have lots of homework to do.
⑤ He has many informations on the issue.

**10** ① The health is very important.
② Seoul is the capital of a Korea.
③ The spoons are made of silvers.
④ Please give me some advice.
⑤ I have a few money with me.

**11** 밑줄 친 부분이 바르지 못한 것을 고르시오.
① Light travels faster than sound.
② She steps on the sands at the beach.
③ There is a lot of butter on the table.
④ There are three Toms in our class.
⑤ I have a piece of paper.

## [12-15] 서술형 주관식

**12** 어법상 어색한 부분을 찾아 바르게 고쳐 쓰시오.

| No news are good news. |
|---|

________ → ________

**13** 어법상 어색한 부분을 두 군데 찾아 바르게 고쳐 쓰시오.

| Frog lives in a fresh water. |
|---|

1) ________ → ________
2) ________ → ________

**14** 다음 우리말을 영어로 옮길 때 빈칸에 알맞은 말을 쓰시오.

| 아빠는 매일 아침에 커피 한 잔을 드신다. 엄마는 아침으로 1) 빵 두 조각을 드시고 나는 2) 우유 한 잔을 마신다. 우리는 아침마다 바쁘다. |
|---|

↓

| Dad drinks a cup of coffee in every morning. Mom has 1) ________, and I drink 2) ________ for breakfast. We are busy every morning. |
|---|

1) ________
2) ________

**15** 주어진 단어를 이용하여 다음 우리말을 영어로 쓰시오.

| 나는 물 두 병을 마시고 싶다.<br>(drink, a bottle of) |
|---|

→ ________

apartment 아파트 useful 유용한 issue 주제, 문제 frog 개구리 fresh water 민물 light 빛 travel 이동하다, 여행하다 sound 소리 beach 해변

기초 탄탄 1
GRAMMAR

Chapter 4

# 대명사

Unit 01 인칭대명사와 재귀대명사

Unit 02 지시대명사와 부정대명사

Unit 01
# 인칭대명사와 재귀대명사

| 수 | 인칭 | 인칭대명사 | | | 소유대명사 (~의 것) | 재귀대명사 (~ 자신) |
|---|---|---|---|---|---|---|
| | | 주격 (~은/는/이/가) | 소유격 (~의) | 목적격 (~을/를) | | |
| 단수 | 1 | I | my | me | mine | myself |
| | 2 | You | your | you | yours | yourself |
| | 3 | He<br>She<br>It | his<br>her<br>its | him<br>her<br>it | his<br>hers<br>- | himself<br>herself<br>itself |
| 복수 | 1 | We | our | us | ours | ourselves |
| | 2 | You | your | you | yours | yourselves |
| | 3 | They | their | them | theirs | themselves |

## 1 인칭대명사

사람이나 사물의 이름을 대신 가리키는 말을 인칭대명사라고 하며, 문장 안에서 역할에 따라 주격, 소유격, 목적격으로 구분한다. 주격은 주어, 목적격은 목적어의 역할을 하며, 소유격은 '~의'로 해석되며 항상 명사 앞에 나온다.

| 주격 (~은/는/이/가) | 소유격 (~의) | 목적격 (~을/를) |
|---|---|---|
| She is my best friend.<br>그녀는 나의 가장 좋은 친구야. | He is our math teacher.<br>그는 우리의 수학선생님이야. | I am glad to meet you.<br>나는 너를 만나서 기뻐. |

**Tip**
대명사의 소유격 앞에는 a, an, the와 같은 관사가 올 수 없다.

## 2 소유대명사

소유대명사는 '소유격 + 명사'를 대신하는 대명사로서 문장에서 주어, 목적어, 보어 역할을 한다.

| 소유격 (~의) | 소유대명사 (~의 것) |
|---|---|
| This is my book. 이것은 나의 책이다.<br>That is your shirt. 저것은 너의 셔츠이다.<br>It is our dog. 그것은 우리의 개이다. | This book is mine. 이 책은 나의 것이다.<br>That shirt is yours. 저 셔츠는 너의 것이다.<br>The dog is ours. 그 개는 우리의 것이다 |

**Tip**
대명사 외에 '~의 (것)'을 나타낼 때는 명사 뒤에 's를 붙인다.
Harry's glasses are on the desk. Harry의 안경은 책상 위에 있다.
The glasses are Harry's. 그 안경은 Harry의 것이다.

## 3 재귀대명사

재귀대명사는 인칭대명사의 소유격이나 목적격에 -self나 -selves를 붙인 형태로, 반복해서 주어 자신을 지칭할 때 사용한다.

| 재귀 용법 (~ 자신) | 강조 용법 (직접) |
|---|---|
| He blames himself for the mistake.<br>그는 그 실수에 대해서 자신을 비난한다.<br>→ 목적어로 쓰여 생략할 수 없음 | He himself cleans his room.<br>그는 그의 방을 직접 청소한다.<br>→ 주어를 강조하는 데 쓰여 생략 가능 |

**Tip**
재귀대명사의 관용표현
by oneself 홀로
by itself 자동으로
for oneself 스스로
introduce oneself 자기소개를 하다
between ourselves 우리끼리만
talk to oneself 혼잣말하다
enjoy oneself 즐거운 시간을 보내다
Help oneself. 마음껏 드세요.

STEP 1

# Grammar START

Grammar on Target

1. 인칭대명사의 구분과 쓰임
2. 소유대명사와 재귀대명사의 역할과 쓰임

## A 다음 문장에서 알맞은 인칭대명사를 고르시오.

1 Angela is my cousin. (It / She / You) lives in London.

2 My favorite actor is Tom Cruise. I like (his / her / their) smile.

3 Mom and Dad are in the living room. (We / They / She) look happy.

4 Paul has a dog. He takes (its / it) to the park every day.

5 I have a brother. (He / Him / His) name is David.

6 Jack and I play soccer every Saturday. (You / They / We) are good players.

7 Big Bang has five members. I want to meet (you / them / us) for real.

8 Your little sister has curly hair. I like (your / her / our) hair.

9 The people are next to the red car. It is (they / them / their) car.

10 My dog loves me so much. It follows (me / mine / myself) everywhere.

cousin 사촌
favorite 좋아하는
look ~해 보이다
member 구성원
for real 실제로, 진짜로
curly 곱슬곱슬한
everywhere 어디나

## B 다음 문장에서 알맞은 대명사를 고르시오.

1 The new bike is (mine / myself).

2 My mom fixes her car (hers / herself).

3 Jason looks at (his / himself) in the mirror.

4 This is yours, and that is (theirs / themselves).

5 Your father's eyes are blue, but (yours / yourself) are brown.

6 Their way of life is different from (ours / ourselves).

7 You prepare breakfast (yours / yourself) for your family.

8 The lake is famous for (it / its) beautiful scenery.

fix 고치다
brown 갈색의
be different from ~
~와 다르다
prepare 준비하다
is famous for ~
~로 유명하다
beautiful 아름다운
scenery 경치, 풍경

STEP 2
# Grammar PRACTICE

## A 주어진 대명사를 빈칸에 알맞은 형태로 바꿔 쓰시오.

1 ________ team has a lot of fans. (we)

2 I often talk to ________. (I)

3 Juliet loves ________ so much. (he)

4 Sophia ________ solves the problem. (she)

5 He borrows her pencil, and she borrows ________ ruler. (he)

6 My dog wags ________ tail back and forth. (it)

7 Computers help ________ study alone. (we)

8 Our house is white, and ________ is brown. (they)

solve 해결하다
borrow 빌리다
ruler 자
tail 꼬리
wag (꼬리나 머리를) 흔들다
back 앞으로
forth 뒤로
alone 혼자

## B 밑줄 친 부분을 알맞은 대명사로 바꿔 쓰시오.

1 I like Peter, but Peter likes Monica.
➡ I like ________, but ________ likes her.

2 My mom watches the drama on Sundays.
➡ ________ watches ________ on Sundays.

3 That is your cellphone, and this is my cellphone.
➡ That is ________, and this is ________.

4 Noel doesn't live with his parents.
➡ ________ doesn't live with ________.

5 The dog is not Tiffany's, but it is Brian's.
➡ The dog is not ________, but it is ________.

6 My family and I visit my aunt's house in Paris every summer.
➡ ________ visit ________ house in Paris every summer.

7 Vivian's grandfather gives Vivian a red tomato.
➡ ________ gives ________ a red tomato.

aunt 이모, 고모
watch 보다
cellphone 휴대폰

## C 틀린 부분을 찾아 바르게 고쳐 문장을 다시 쓰시오.

1 They puppies are small and cute.

➡ ______________________________

2 John has new jacket. I like him jacket.

➡ ______________________________

3 The umbrella is not mine, but it is yourself.

➡ ______________________________

4 He meets hers at eight o'clock every morning.

➡ ______________________________

5 She invites our to the Christmas party every year.

➡ ______________________________

6 He is very talented. Their parents are proud of him.

➡ ______________________________

7 She does homework her at seven every day.

➡ ______________________________

8 It isn't my wallet. My is long and black.

➡ ______________________________

9 Her children eat themself without her help.

➡ ______________________________

talented 재능이 있는
long 긴
wallet 지갑
help 도움

## D 우리말과 같은 뜻이 되도록 주어진 단어를 바르게 배열하시오.

1 나의 고양이가 그의 개 옆에 있다. (next to, my, his, is, cat, dog)

➡ ______________________________

2 돌고래는 어미로부터 많은 것을 배운다.
(learns, its, a dolphin, from, mother, many things)

➡ ______________________________

3 Olivia의 집은 우리집 맞은 편에 있다. (across from, house, Olivia's, ours, is)

➡ ______________________________

4 그녀는 스스로를 자랑스러워 한다. (herself, of, is, she, proud)

➡ ______________________________

next to ~ ~의 옆에
dolphin 돌고래
learn 배우다
thing (유형, 무형의) 것
across from ~ ~의 바로 맞은편에

# Upgrade TEST

**1** 다음 중 짝지어진 단어의 관계가 나머지와 다른 것을 고르시오.

① I - my ② He - his
③ It - it's ④ She - her
⑤ They - their

**2** 다음 중 밑줄 친 부분이 어색한 것을 고르시오.

① She's sick now.
② I know them well.
③ They really like us.
④ He plays the piano.
⑤ Its very expensive.

**3** 빈칸에 들어갈 말로 알맞은 것을 고르시오.

> This is her cellphone.
> = This cellphone is ________.

① she ② her
③ her's ④ hers
⑤ she's

**4** 다음 밑줄 친 재귀대명사 중 생략할 수 있는 것을 고르시오.

① I met President Obama himself.
② Susan often says to herself.
③ The criminal killed himself.
④ The door opens of itself.
⑤ Between ourselves, I like her.

**5** 밑줄 친 부분 중 어법상 틀린 것을 고르시오.

> A Is this ① his bag?
> B No, ② it isn't ③ his. It's ④ her, but these bags are ⑤ ours.

**6** 밑줄 친 부분의 쓰임이 나머지와 다른 것을 고르시오.

① This is our car.
② Are you Susie's sister?
③ Parents should take care of their babies.
④ My name is Jason.
⑤ Daniel is a friend of his.

**7** 빈칸에 들어갈 알맞은 것을 고르시오.

> It's too hot today. Please give ________ a bottle of water.

① mine ② he ③ her
④ our ⑤ theirs

this 이것 these 이것들 met (meet 만나다)의 과거 president 대통령 criminal 범인 kill 죽다 should ~ ~해야 한다
have(has) to ~ ~해야 한다

**8** 밑줄 친 부분이 바르지 못한 것을 고르시오.

① She loves herself very much.
② I enjoy myself at the party.
③ He has to take care of himself from now on.
④ You have to go there by yourself.
⑤ They built the bridge for theirselves.

**9** 다음 밑줄 친 재귀대명사 중 생략할 수 없는 것을 고르시오.

① She hurt herself cutting potatoes.
② I want to solve this problem myself.
③ The news itself is very shocking.
④ He cleans his room himself.
⑤ The witch is evil itself.

**10** 빈칸에 들어갈 말이 바르게 짝지어진 것을 고르시오.

- Sam's opinion is different from ________.
- They can't agree with ________.

① them - his
② their - him
③ they - himself
④ theirs - him
⑤ themselves - he

**11** 빈칸에 들어갈 알맞은 것을 고르시오.

He is too busy to help you with your homework. You have to do it ________.

① beside yourself
② to yourself
③ for yourself
④ of yourself
⑤ on yourself

## [12-15] 서술형 주관식

**12** 어법상 어색한 부분을 찾아 바르게 고쳐 쓰시오.

Her hair is the same color as your.

________ → ________

**[13-14]** 다음 우리말을 영작할 때 빈칸에 들어갈 알맞은 말을 쓰시오.

**13**

내 소개를 할게. 내 이름은 Jane이야.
Let me introduce ________. My name is Jane.

→ ________

**14**

Harry, 와줘서 고마워. 마음껏 먹어.
Harry, thank you for coming. ________ ________.

→ ________

**15** 주어진 단어를 바르게 배열하여 다음 우리말을 영어로 쓰시오.

그 칫솔은 나의 것이다. 너의 것은 하얀색이다.
(white, is, yours, the toothbrush, is, mine)

→ ________

hurt 다치게 하다　shocking 충격적인　witch 마녀　evil 악, 사악함　opinion 의견　be different from ~ ~와 다르다　agree with ~ ~에 동의하다
as ~ ~처럼, ~같은

Unit 02

# 지시대명사와 부정대명사

## 1 지시대명사

셀 수 없는 명사에는 고유명사, 추상명사, 물질명사가 있다. 셀 수 없으므로 a/an을 붙일 수 없고, 복수형으로도 쓸 수 없다.

| | 가까이 있는 대상 | | 멀리 있는 대상 | |
|---|---|---|---|---|
| 단수 | this<br>이것, 이 사람 | This is my bag.<br>이것은 내 가방이다 | that<br>저것, 저 사람 | That is your bag.<br>저것은 너의 가방이다. |
| 복수 | these<br>이것들, 이 사람들 | These are my sons.<br>이들은 내 아들들이다. | those<br>저것들, 저 사람들 | Those are soldiers.<br>저들은 군인들이다. |

Tip
That is는 줄여서 That's로 쓸 수 있지만, This is, These are, Those are는 줄여 쓸 수 없다.

지시대명사가 사람인 경우에는 다시 언급할 때 he, she, they로, 사물인 경우에는 it, they로 쓴다.

| 사람 | 사물 |
|---|---|
| This is my cousin Susan. She is a dentist.<br>이 사람은 내 사촌 Susan이다. 그녀는 치과의사이다. | This is my new jacket. I bought it in the U.S.<br>이것은 내 새 재킷이다. 나는 그것을 미국에서 샀다. |

this, that, these, those는 뒤에 오는 명사를 꾸며주는 지시형용사로 쓰일 수 있다.
This ride is very exciting. 이 탈것은 매우 신난다.

## 2 부정대명사

부정대명사란 정해지지 않은 사람이나 사물을 가리킬 때 사용하는 대명사이다.

1) one 하나, 한 사람

앞에서 언급된 특정한 사람이나 사물을 가리킬 땐 it, they를, 막연한 사람이나 사물을 가리킬 땐 one(단수), ones(복수)를 쓴다.

| 지시대명사 it, they | 부정대명사 one, ones |
|---|---|
| I have a pen. You can use it.<br>나는 펜이 있어. 네가 그 펜을 써도 돼. | I need an umbrella. Please lend me one.<br>나는 우산이 필요해. 하나 빌려줘. |

Tip
일반적인 사람을 나타낼 때에도 one을 쓰는데, 이 경우에 복수형은 쓰지 않는다.
One should respect one's parents. 사람은 자신의 부모님을 존경해야 한다.

2) one, other, another 하나, 나머지 하나, 다른 하나

| 표현 | 의미 | 예문 |
|---|---|---|
| one ~ the other ... | (둘 중) 하나 ~ 나머지 하나 ··· | One is a daughter, and the other is a son.<br>한 명은 딸이고, 나머지 한 명은 아들이다. |
| one ~ the others ... | (여럿 중) 하나 ~ 나머지 전부 ··· | One is white, and the others are black.<br>하나는 하얀색이고, 나머지는 전부 검정색이다. |
| one ~ another ~ the other ... | (셋 중) 하나 ~ 다른 하나 ~ 나머지 하나 ··· | One is red, another is blue, and the other is pink.<br>하나는 빨간색, 다른 하나는 파란색, 나머지 하나는 분홍색이다. |
| some ~ others ... | (전체 중) 일부 ~ 다른 일부 ··· | Some like Angelina, and others like Jessica.<br>어떤 이들은 Angelina를 좋아하고, 다른 이들은 Jessica를 좋아한다. |

Tip
전체의 수가 명확할 때에는 'some ~ the others ... (일부 ~ 나머지 전부 ···)'를 쓴다.

STEP 1

# Grammar START

Grammar on Target

1. 지시대명사의 구분과 쓰임
2. 부정대명사의 역할과 쓰임

## A 다음 괄호 안에서 알맞은 것을 고르시오.

1 (This / These) are my friends Tom and Peter.

2 Is (this / these) a comfortable chair?

3 (That / Those) are my grandparents.

4 Are (that / those) real flowers?

5 (This / These) baby does not cry.

6 (This / These) is my brother. (He / It) is a teacher.

7 Are (that / those) your shoes? (It / They) are so beautiful.

8 (This / These) windows are clean, but (that / those) curtains are dirty.

9 (That's / Thoes's) my favorite tree. (It / They) is an apple tree.

10 (This / These) rabbits are white, and (that / those) rabbits are black.

comfortable 편안한
chair 의자
real 진짜의, 현실의
window 창문
curtain 커튼
dirty 더러운

## B 다음 문장에서 알맞은 말을 보기에서 골라 쓰시오.

| 보기 | one | ones | the other | another | the others | some |
|---|---|---|---|---|---|---|

1 These shoes are too tight. I need bigger ________.

2 I don't have a bicycle. I want to buy ________.

3 This spoon is dirty. Please give me ________ one.

4 One is Korean, and ________ ________ are Japanese.

5 I have three shirts. One is green, ________ is pink, and the other is purple.

6 ________ like winter, and others like summer.

7 Jack has two sons. ________ is a lawyer, and ________ ________ is a firefighter.

tight 단단한, 꽉 조이는
son 아들
Japanese 일본인

STEP 2
# Grammar PRACTICE

## A 주어진 우리말을 이용하여 빈칸에 알맞은 말을 쓰시오.

1 A 저 노란 코트는 그녀의 것이니? B 응, 맞아.

➡ A Is __________ yellow coat hers? B Yes, it is.

2 A 이 상자들은 너의 것이니? B 아니, 그렇지 않아.

➡ A Are __________ boxes yours? B No, __________ aren't.

3 이건 널 위한 선물이야. 네 마음에 들었으면 좋겠어.

➡ __________ is a present for you. I hope you like __________.

4 어떤 사람들은 야구를 좋아하고, 또 다른 사람들은 축구를 좋아한다.

➡ __________ like baseball, and __________ like soccer.

5 난 빨간 양말을 좋아하지 않아요. 파란 게 있나요?

➡ I don't like red socks. Do you have blue __________?

6 나는 개 두 마리가 있다. 한 마리는 크고, 다른 한 마리는 아주 작다.

➡ I have two dogs. __________ is big, and the __________ is very small.

7 이 네 명의 소녀들은 자매이다. 한 명은 키가 작고, 나머지는 모두 키가 크다.

➡ __________ four girls are sisters. One is short, and the __________ are tall.

8 저 카메라들은 비싸지만, 나도 하나 사고 싶다.

➡ __________ cameras are expensive, but I want to buy __________.

9 사람은 어려운 때를 대비해서 저축해야 한다.

➡ __________ should save for a rainy day.

10 나는 항상 하얀색 운동화를 사고, Kate는 항상 분홍색 운동화를 산다.

➡ I always buy white sneakers, and Kate buys pink __________.

11 그녀는 풍선 열 개를 가지고 있다. 하나는 파란색이고, 나머지는 모두 노란색이다.

➡ She has ten balloons. __________ is blue, and the __________ are yellow.

12 나는 접시 세 개가 있다. 하나는 동그라미, 다른 하나는 네모, 나머지 하나는 직사각형이다.

➡ I have three dishes. __________ is a circle, __________ is a square, and the __________ is a rectangle.

present 선물
camera 카메라
expensive 비싼
save 저축하다
balloon 풍선
square 정사각형
rectangle 직사각형

## B 밑줄 친 부분을 바르게 고쳐 문장을 다시 쓰시오.

1 These is my brother Harry.

➡ ______________________________

2 A Do you need this book? B Yes, I need one.

➡ ______________________________

3 Can I borrow that white chairs?

➡ ______________________________

4 You can see those man in front of the door.

➡ ______________________________

5 Look at the ring. One looks great.

➡ ______________________________

6 I have two sweaters. It is yellow, and the other is blue.

➡ ______________________________

7 There are three pigs. One is fat, the other is chubby, and another is skinny.

➡ ______________________________

8 Some children likes cucumbers, and another don't like them.

➡ ______________________________

in front of ~ ~의 앞에
sweater 스웨터
ring 반지
pig 돼지
fat 뚱뚱한
skinny 마른
cucumber 오이

## C 우리말과 같은 뜻이 되도록 주어진 단어를 바르게 배열하시오.

1 저 아이들은 너의 사촌들이니? (children, are, those, cousins, your)

➡ ______________________________

2 그는 또 다른 책을 읽고 싶어한다. (another, read, he, wants, book, to)

➡ ______________________________

3 어떤 학생들은 수학을 좋아하고, 다른 학생들은 영어를 좋아한다.
(like, others, English, students, some, and, math)

➡ ______________________________

4 가방이 두 개 있다. 하나는 너의 것이고, 다른 하나는 나의 것이다.
(the other, is, mine, and, yours, is, one)

➡ There are two bags. ______________________________

STEP 3
# Upgrade TEST

**1 다음 중 어법상 올바른 문장을 고르시오.**

① These're cookies.
② A this flower is beautiful.
③ That is a police station.
④ This's my father.
⑤ Those man is Mr. White.

**2 밑줄 친 that의 쓰임이 나머지와 다른 것을 고르시오.**

① That is yours.
② That bike over there is mine.
③ I don't like this, but I like that.
④ What do you think about that?
⑤ That's all right.

**3 빈칸에 들어갈 말이 바르게 짝지어진 것을 고르시오.**

> I have two pants. ________ is blue, and ________ is black.

① One - two
② One - another
③ One - the other
④ One - other
⑤ The first – the second

**4 빈칸에 들어갈 알맞은 것을 고르시오.**

> The ears of a rabbit are larger than ________ of a cat.

① it
② this
③ that
④ these
⑤ those

**5 빈칸에 들어갈 알맞은 것을 고르시오.**

> A How about this hat?
> B I don't like it. Show me ________.

① one
② other
③ the other
④ another
⑤ some

**6 빈칸에 알맞은 것을 고르시오.**

> I bought a book and gave ________ to John.

① one
② it
③ this
④ the one
⑤ ones

**7 다음 중 어법상 어색한 문장을 고르시오.**

① One should respect one's parents.
② I prefer white wine to red one.
③ She needs a chair. Please lend her one.
④ Look at the gloves. I like them very much.
⑤ I have an extra box. You can use it.

police station 경찰서 lager (large의 비교급) 더 큰 than ~ ~보다 How(What) about ~? ~는 어때? bought (buy의 과거형) 샀다
gave (give의 과거형) 주었다 respect 존경하다 prefer ~ to ... ...보다 ~를 더 좋아하다 wine 포도주 extra 여분의, 추가의

**8** 밑줄 친 부분이 바르지 못한 것을 고르시오.

① One is red, and the other is blue.
② One is a dog, and the others are cats.
③ Some like water, and others like juice.
④ Would you like another cup of coffee?
⑤ My cellphone is too old. I want new ones.

**9** 다음 중 어법상 올바른 문장을 고르시오.

① Some are green, and other are red.
② The climate here is hotter than it in Seoul.
③ Some like apples, and anothers like oranges.
④ I don't like white shoes. Do you have black ones?
⑤ One is a rose, other is a lily, and the other is a tulip.

**10** 밑줄 친 부분이 어법상 틀린 것을 고르시오.

① Can you show me another shirt?
② Do you have an umbrella? I need it.
③ One is a spoon, and the other is a fork.
④ As for sugar, too much of it is bad for your health.
⑤ Health is more important than wealth. This is useless without that.

**11** 빈칸에 들어갈 알맞은 말을 고르시오.

There are a hundred children in this kindergarten. Some prefer foreign teachers, and ________ prefer Korean teachers.

① other ② others ③ the other
④ anothers ⑤ the others

## [12-15] 서술형 주관식

**12** 다음 우리말을 영어로 옮길 때 빈칸에 들어갈 알맞은 말을 쓰시오.

일본의 인구수가 한국의 인구수보다 많다.

↓

The population of Japan is larger than ________ of Korea.

→ ____________________

**[13-14]** 어법상 어색한 부분을 찾아 바르게 고쳐 쓰시오.

**13**

Jack has three sons. One is a lawyer, the other is a teacher, and the other is a singer.

____________ → ____________

**14**

There are two pairs of socks. The yellow one is yours.

____________ → ____________

**15** 주어진 우리말과 단어를 이용하여 두 번째 문장을 영어로 쓰시오.

There are five baby white tigers. 한 마리는 수컷이고, 나머지 전부는 암컷이다. (male, female)

→ ____________________

climate 기후 hotter (hot의 비교급) 더 더운 lily 백합 tulip 튤립 as for ~ ~에 관해서 wealth 재산 useless 쓸모 없는 kindergarten 유치원 foreign 외국의 population 인구 white tiger 흰 호랑이 male 남성, 수컷 female 여성, 암컷

**1** 다음 중 짝지어진 명사의 단수형과 복수형이 <u>틀린</u> 것을 고르시오.

① helmet - helmets ② leaf - leaves
③ potato - potatoes ④ zoo - zoos
⑤ box - boxs

**2** 빈칸에 들어갈 수 <u>없는</u> 것을 고르시오.

| ________ is good for our health. |
|---|

① Yoga ② Fresh fruit
③ Deep sleep ④ Books
⑤ Exercise

**3** 명사의 복수형이 <u>잘못</u> 사용된 문장을 고르시오.

① Let's drink some water.
② I lost my membership cards.
③ Kangaroos have a long tail.
④ They want to buy three knifes.
⑤ She has ten pairs of shoes.

**4** 빈칸에 들어갈 말이 바르게 짝지어진 것을 고르시오.

| 신사 숙녀 여러분, 와 주셔서 감사합니다.<br>________ and ________, thanks for coming. |
|---|

① Lady - gentleman
② Ladys - gentleman
③ Ladies - gentlemen
④ Ladys – gentlemen
⑤ Ladies – gentlemens

**5** 다음 중 <u>틀린</u> 문장을 고르시오.

① Schools need to teach students manners.
→ 학교에서 학생들에게 예절을 가르쳐야 한다.
② I like to swim in the waters.
→ 나는 물속에서 수영하는 것을 좋아한다.
③ She looks at goods on display.
→ 그녀는 진열된 물건을 바라보고 있다.
④ Many wild animals live in the woods.
→ 숲 속에는 많은 야생 동물들이 살고 있다.
⑤ He talks about North Korea's arms program.
→ 그는 북한의 무기 프로그램에 대해 이야기한다.

**[6-7]** 밑줄 친 부분이 바르지 <u>못한</u> 것을 고르시오.

**6** ① <u>Oxen</u> are important to farmers.
② A pair of <u>gloves</u> is in the washing machine.
③ Your <u>geese</u> are running away.
④ Snow White lives with <u>dwarfs</u>.
⑤ I spend all my times studying for <u>testes</u>.

**7** ① He drinks <u>a cup of coffee</u>.
② She buys <u>two loaf of bread</u>.
③ There are <u>three glasses of milk</u>.
④ We need <u>two bags of rice</u>.
⑤ Mia wants <u>a slice of pizza</u> for lunch.

**8** 주어진 단어를 이용하여 다음 우리말을 영어로 쓰시오.

| 나는 운동화 두 켤레가 필요하다. (sneakers) |
|---|

➡ ______________________________

**[9-10] 다음 빈칸에 들어갈 말이 바르게 짝지어진 것을 고르시오.**

**9**

나는 너무 배가 고프다. 내 것을 다 먹고 나서 그녀의 것도 먹고 싶다.

➡ I am so hungry. I want to eat ________ after finishing ________.

① her – my
② her – mine
③ hers - mine
④ hers – my
⑤ hers – myself

**10**

• I often talk to ________.
• He practices the piano all by ________.

① me - him
② mine - his
③ myself – himself
④ me - himself
⑤ myself – his

**11** 밑줄 친 부분을 생략할 수 없는 것을 고르시오.

① I myself made this cake.
② They blamed themselves.
③ He himself is the father of two daughters.
④ She herself is only eleven years old.
⑤ I teach him himself to drive.

**12** 다음 중 재귀대명사가 잘못 쓰인 문장을 고르시오.

① You yourself are responsible.
② We meet Justin Bieber ourself.
③ They themselves take care of the dog.
④ History repeats itself.
⑤ The doctors study cancer themselves.

**13** 빈칸에 들어갈 말이 바르게 짝지어진 것을 고르시오.

• I like two sports. ________ is baseball, and ________ is tennis.
• I don't like the color. Show me ________.

① It - another - others
② One - another - the other
③ One - the others - one
④ One - the other - ones
⑤ One - the other - another

**[14-15] 다음 빈칸에 알맞은 말을 쓰시오.**

**14**

어떤 이들은 개를 좋아하고, 다른 이들은 고양이를 좋아한다.

➡ ________ like dogs, and ________ like cats.

**15**

오늘은 음료가 무료입니다. 마음껏 드시기 바랍니다.

➡ Drinks are free today. ________ ________ to anything.

기초 탄탄 1
GRAMMAR

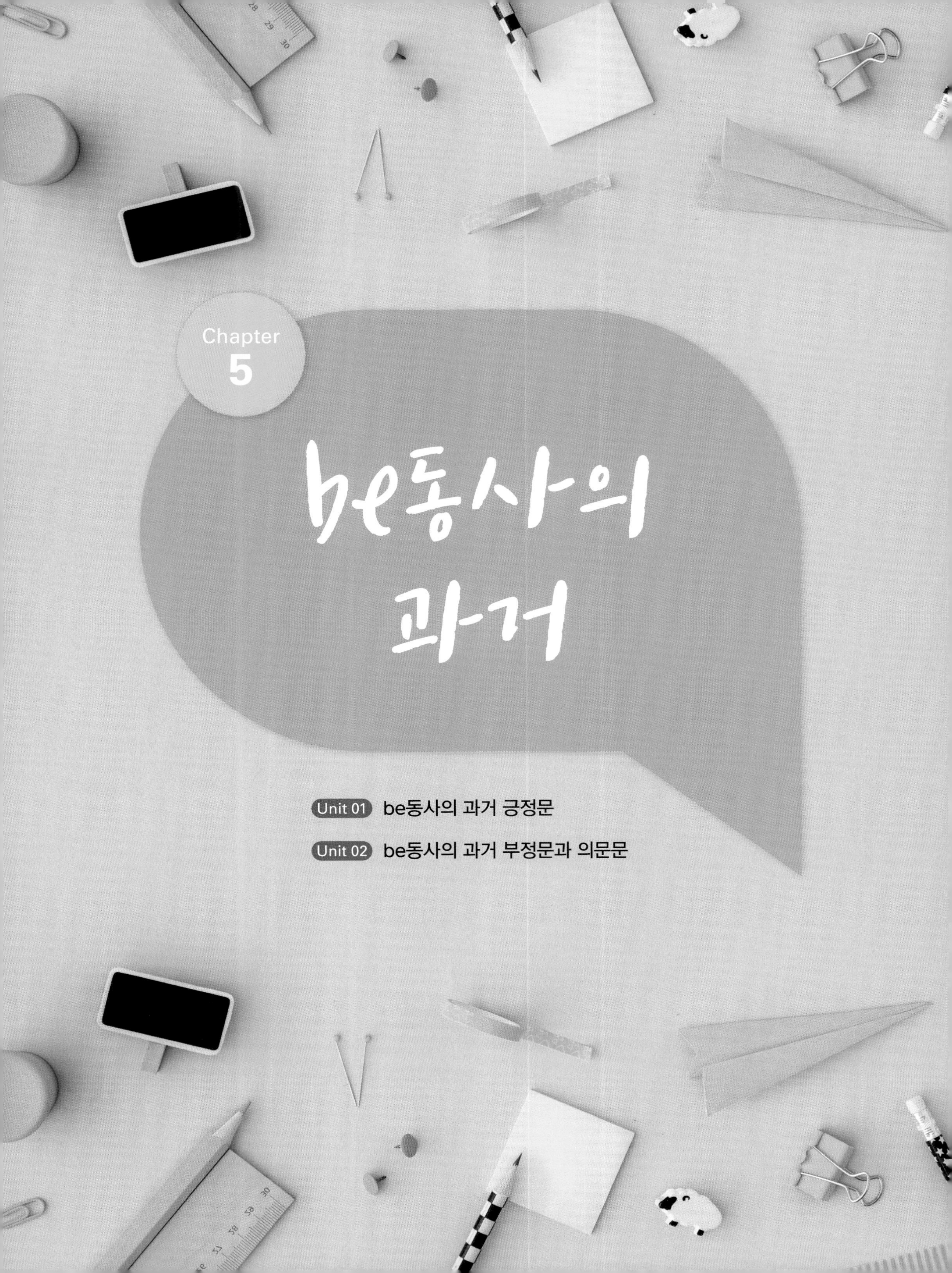

Chapter 5

# be동사의 과거

Unit 01 be동사의 과거 긍정문

Unit 02 be동사의 과거 부정문과 의문문

Unit 01

# be동사의 과거 긍정문

## 1 be동사의 과거형

주어의 과거 상태를 나타낼 때 be동사의 과거형 was, were를 사용한다. 주어의 인칭과 수에 따라 다음과 같이 구별하여 사용하며 '~이었다, ~에 있었다'로 해석한다.

| 수 | 인칭 | 주어 | 현재형 | 과거형 |
|---|---|---|---|---|
| 단수 | 1인칭 | I | am | was |
| | 2인칭 | You | are | were |
| | 3인칭 | He<br>She<br>It | is | was |
| 복수 | 1인칭 | We | are | were |
| | 2인칭 | You | | |
| | 3인칭 | They | | |

## 2 be동사의 과거형 문장

주어의 과거 기분, 직업, 신분 등을 나타내는 be동사의 과거형 문장은 주로 부사 'yesterday, last, ago' 등을 함께 사용한다.

| 주어 | be동사의 과거형 | 예문 |
|---|---|---|
| I | was | I was busy yesterday. 나는 어제 바빴다. |
| You | were | You were sick last night. 너는 지난 밤에 아팠다. |
| He<br>She<br>It | was | He was late for school this morning. 그는 오늘 아침 지각했다.<br>She was short two years ago. 그녀는 2년 전에 키가 작았다.<br>It was my mistake. 그것은 내 실수였다. |
| We<br>You<br>They | were | We were in Paris last Sunday. 우리는 지난 일요일에 파리에 있었다.<br>You were twelve years old last year. 너희들은 작년에 열두 살이었다.<br>They were at a movie theater an hour ago. 그들은 한 시간 전에 극장에 있었다. |

Tip

주어가 단수일 땐 was, 복수일 땐 were를 쓴다. 단, 주어가 You일 때는 언제나 were를 쓴다.

The victory was yours yesterday, but it's mine now.
승리는 어제 너의 것이었지만, 오늘은 나의 것이다.
People were very angry with her.
사람들은 그녀에게 매우 분노했다.

STEP 1
# Grammar START

Grammar on Target

1. 주어에 따른 be동사의 과거형 구별
2. be동사의 현재형과 과거형

## A 다음 문장에서 알맞은 be동사를 고르시오.

1 You (was / were) a great police officer.

2 She (was / were) pleased with the news.

3 I (was / were) sure of my success in the project.

4 We (was / were) in Mexico two weeks ago.

5 They (are / was / were) at the museum yesterday afternoon.

6 It (is / was / were) in my bag two hours ago.

7 James and I (are / was / were) in Barcelona a year ago.

8 Last year, Michael (was / were) a student. Now, he (is / was / were) a teacher.

9 It (is / was / were) rainy ten minutes ago. Now, it (is / was / were) sunny.

10 They (are / was / were) sad last night, but they (was / were) happy tonight.

be pleased with ~ ~에 기뻐하다
be sure of ~ ~에 확신을 가지다, ~을 믿다
success 성공
ago ~ 전에
last 지난, 바로 앞의
now 지금, 이제
tonight 오늘밤

## B 빈칸에 알맞은 be동사를 쓰시오.

1 Last week, I __________ at my grandma's house.

2 You __________ absent from school last Monday.

3 Last year, my cat __________ fat. Now, it __________ skinny.

4 Mia and Harry __________ in the same class last year.

5 It __________ too hot last summer, and it __________ too cold last winter.

6 I __________ eleven years old last year. This year, I __________ twelve years old.

7 We __________ full now. Thirty minutes ago, we __________ very hungry.

8 He __________ at the amusement park two hours ago. Now, he __________ at home.

absent 결석한
last year 작년
this year 올해
full 배부른, 가득한
amusement park 놀이공원

# STEP 2 Grammar PRACTICE

## A 밑줄 친 부분을 바르게 고쳐 쓰시오.

1. She were lazy. ➡ ____________
2. You are excited about it yesterday. ➡ ____________
3. I were in the library two hours ago. ➡ ____________
4. They was in New York last year. ➡ ____________
5. It is windy last weekend. ➡ ____________
6. His car is black last year. ➡ ____________
7. We was very tired last week. ➡ ____________
8. My parents are in China 2 years ago. ➡ ____________
9. That pretty girl were my best friend. ➡ ____________

lazy 게으른
windy 바람이 많이 부는
tired 피곤한

## B 주어진 우리말을 이용하여 빈칸에 알맞은 말을 쓰시오.

1. 우리는 2010년에 보스톤에 있었다. 그때 나는 행복했었다.
   ➡ We ________ in Boston in 2010. I ________ happy at that time.
2. Amy의 생일은 지난 주 수요일이었다. 오늘은 Michelle의 생일이다.
   ➡ Amy's birthday ________ last Wednesday. Today ________ Michelle's birthday.
3. 작년에, 엄마와 나는 플로리다에 있었고, 아빠는 인도에 있었다.
   ➡ Last year, Mom and I ________ in Florida, and Dad ________ in India.
4. 그날은 크리스마스였고, 그녀는 크리스마스 파티에 있었다.
   ➡ It ________ Christmas, and she ________ at the Christmas party.
5. 작년에 그것은 저렴했다. 그러나 올해 그것은 비싸다.
   ➡ Last year, it ________ cheap. But it ________ expensive this year.
6. 내 여동생과 나는 지난 달에 아팠지만, 지금 우리는 건강하다.
   ➡ My sister and I ________ sick last month, but now we ________ healthy.

at that time 그때
cheap (값이) 싼
Christmas 크리스마스, 성탄절
healthy 건강한
expensive 비싼

## C 다음 문장을 과거 시제로 바꿔 쓰시오.

1 I am a brave firefighter.

➡ ____________________

2 Sally and Emma are neighbors.

➡ ____________________

3 He is a famous singer.

➡ ____________________

4 You are in the hospital.

➡ ____________________

5 One of my gloves is under the sofa.

➡ ____________________

6 We are bored with the class.

➡ ____________________

7 Mr. Brown is an honest lawyer.

➡ ____________________

8 Chris and I are good at English.

➡ ____________________

neighbor 이웃
hospital 병원
honest 정직한

## D 우리말과 같은 뜻이 되도록 주어진 단어를 바르게 배열하시오.

1 그는 10년 전에 유명한 야구선수였다.
(a famous baseball player, was, he, ten years ago)

➡ ____________________

2 그 아이들은 공포영화 때문에 겁에 질렸다.
(were, the children, the horror movie, terrified by)

➡ ____________________

3 나는 어젯밤에 너무 피곤하고 졸렸다. (was, I, sleepy, and, so, last night, tired)

➡ ____________________

4 그녀의 부모님은 5분 전에 나와 함께 있었다.
(with me, five minutes ago, were, her parents)

➡ ____________________

terrified 무서워하는, 겁이 난
horror 공포
sleepy 졸린

STEP 3

# Upgrade TEST

**1 빈칸에 들어갈 수 없는 것을 고르시오.**

| I was busy ________. |
|---|

① then ② two days ago
③ last Sunday ④ now
⑤ yesterday

**2 빈칸에 들어갈 알맞은 것을 고르시오.**

| We ________ in London last year. |
|---|

① are ② is ③ were
④ was ⑤ have been

**3 다음 우리말을 영어로 바르게 옮긴 것을 고르시오.**

| 그녀는 어제 숙제 하느라 바빴다. |
|---|

① She is busy doing her homework yesterday.
② She was busy doing her homework yesterday.
③ She were busy doing her homework yesterday.
④ She has been busy doing her homework yesterday.
⑤ She had been busy doing her homework yesterday.

**4 다음 중 빈칸에 들어갈 말이 나머지와 다른 것을 고르시오.**

① I _______ ill in bed yesterday.
② Sam _______ busy last weekend.
③ She _______ in London two weeks ago.
④ The soccer game _______ very exciting last night.
⑤ There _______ many people here in 1997.

**5 밑줄 친 be동사의 형태가 옳지 않은 것을 고르시오.**

① Your book was on the desk.
② She was beside herself with envy.
③ The task was beyond his ability.
④ They were at a loss with the results.
⑤ A lot of questions was unanswered until recently.

**6 다음 중 어법상 옳지 않은 문장을 고르시오.**

① Shakespeare was born in 1564.
② He is in the basement yesterday.
③ In the box was a pretty doll an hour ago.
④ He is in good health now.
⑤ In the old days, people believed that the Earth was flat.

**7 밑줄 친 부분 중 어법상 어색한 것을 고르시오.**

Hi. My name ① is Henry. ② I'm from Canada. I ③ have a twin brother. His name ④ is Mike. We ⑤ was in Toronto last week.

beside oneself 제정신이 아닌 envy 질투 beyond one's ability 능력 밖인 a number of 다수의 unanswered 대답이 안 된, 해결 되지 못한 recently 최근에 be at a loss 당황하다 believe 믿다 flat 평평한

**8** 빈칸에 들어갈 말이 바르게 짝지어진 것을 고르시오.

> When it ________ so cold last year,
> Tom and I ________ on the frozen river.

① is - are ② was - was
③ were - was ④ were - were
⑤ was - were

**9** 다음 중 어법상 올바른 문장을 고르시오.

① His birthday were last Friday.
② She was angry now.
③ Galileo said that the Earth was round.
④ I will take care of your baby while you were away.
⑤ Many people were against the government on the day in 1960.

**[10-11]** 다음 중 어법상 어색한 것을 고르시오.

**10** ① In the past, there was an old church here.
② Sarah and we was in Paris last year.
③ There were so many salmon in the river.
④ Sujin was in Seoul for ten years until then.
⑤ Water is composed of hydrogen and oxygen.

**11** ① She was an actress ten years ago.
② I was very interested in science then.
③ In the refrigerator, the old food was rotten.
④ Dinosaurs were everywhere on the Earth in the Jurassic Period.
⑤ Tony and I was at the National Children's Science Center yesterday.

## [12-15] 서술형 주관식

**[12-13]** 어법상 어색한 부분을 찾아 바르게 고쳐 쓰시오.

**12**

> They was unhappy with the announcement by the government.

________ → ________

**13**

> The news were so shocking then.

________ → ________

**14** 주어진 단어를 이용하여 다음 우리말을 영어로 쓰시오.

> 그녀는 그때 물리학을 매우 좋아했다.
> (be fond of, physics, then)

→ ________________

**15** 주어진 단어를 바르게 배열하여 다음 우리말을 영어로 쓰시오.

> 그들은 월요일마다 매우 바빴다.
> (busy, on Mondays, were, very, they)

→ ________________
________________

angry 화난 take care of ~ ~를 돌보다 be against ~ ~에 반대하다 government 정부 be composed of ~ ~로 구성되어 있다 hydrogen 수소 oxygen 산소 actress 여자배우 rotten 썩은, 부패한 dinosaur 공룡 Jurassic Period 쥐라기 national 국가의, 국립의 announcement 발표, 소식 shocking 충격적인 be fond of ~ ~을 좋아하다 physics 물리학

# Unit 02 be동사의 과거 부정문과 의문문

## 1 be동사의 과거 부정문

be동사의 과거 부정문은 be동사의 과거형 뒤에 not을 붙이며, '~이 아니었다' 또는 '~에 없었다'로 해석한다.
주어의 인칭과 수에 따라서 사용되는 be동사의 과거 부정형은 다음과 같다.

| 주어 | be동사의 과거 부정형 | 축약형 | 예문 |
|---|---|---|---|
| I | was not | wasn't | I wasn't a genius. 나는 천재가 아니었다. |
| You | were not | weren't | You weren't at the bus stop. 너는 버스 정류장에 있지 않았다. |
| He<br>She<br>It | was not | wasn't | He wasn't at home yesterday. 그는 어제 집에 없었다.<br>She wasn't a great doctor. 그녀는 훌륭한 의사가 아니었다.<br>It wasn't her mistake. 그것은 그녀의 실수가 아니었다. |
| We<br>You<br>They | were not | weren't | We weren't in Paris. 우리는 파리에 있지 않았다.<br>You weren't honest. 너희들은 정직하지 않았다.<br>They weren't cowards. 그들은 겁쟁이가 아니었다. |

**Tip**
주어가 단수일 땐 was not 또는 줄여서 wasn't, 복수일 땐 were not 또는 weren't를 쓴다.
단, 주어가 You일 때는 언제나 were not 또는 weren't를 쓴다.

## 2 be동사의 과거 의문문

be동사의 과거 의문문은 주어와 be동사의 위치를 바꾸고, 문장 끝에 물음표를 붙인다.
주어가 단수이면 『Was + 주어 + ~?』의 형태이고, 주어가 복수이면 『Were + 주어 + ~?』의 형태이다.

| be동사의 과거형 | 주어 | 예문 | 대답 | |
|---|---|---|---|---|
| | | | 긍정의 대답 | 부정의 대답 |
| Was | I | Was I in the classroom?<br>내가 그 교실에 있었니? | Yes, you were. | No, you weren't. |
| Were | you | Were you angry with me?<br>너 나한테 화났었니? | Yes, I was. | No, I wasn't. |
| Was | he<br>she<br>it | Was he interested in sports?<br>그는 운동에 관심이 있었니?<br>Was she in Rome?<br>그녀는 로마에 있었니?<br>Was it cold outside?<br>바깥은 추웠니? | Yes, he was.<br>Yes, she was.<br>Yes, it was. | No, he wasn't.<br>No, she wasn't.<br>No, it wasn't. |
| Were | we<br>you<br>they | Were we on the right bus?<br>우리가 맞는 버스를 탔었니?<br>Were you there with him?<br>너희도 그와 함께 거기 있었니?<br>Were they excited yesterday.<br>그들은 어제 재미있어 했니? | Yes, we/you were.<br>Yes, we were.<br>Yes, they were. | No, we/you weren't.<br>No, we weren't.<br>No, they weren't. |

**Tip**
부정으로 물을 때에는 『Wasn't + 주어 ~?』 또는 『Weren't + 주어 ~?』의 형태이다.
부정으로 물었더라도, 맞으면 무조건 Yes로, 틀리면 No로 대답한다.

STEP 1

# Grammar START

Grammar on Target

1. 주어에 따른 be동사의 과거 부정형
2. be동사의 과거 의문문 만들기

## A 다음 문장에서 알맞은 것을 고르시오.

1 I (was not / were not) brave enough to tell the truth.

2 You (was not / were not) satisfied with the test results.

3 This (was not / were not) his first time in San Francisco.

4 New clothes (was not / were not) important to her.

5 The backpack (was not / were not) mine. It was Ryan's.

6 Your sister (wasn't / weren't) here two hours ago.

7 The sun was very hot, but I (wasn't / weren't) thirsty.

8 My parents (wasn't / weren't) in the department store yesterday.

9 Helen and Lynn (wasn't / weren't) sisters. They were friends.

10 Olivia's birthday (wasn't / weren't) last Tuesday. It was Wednesday.

enough 충분한
truth 진실, 사실
be satisfied with ~ ~에 만족하다
result 결과
important 중요한
first time 처음
department store 백화점

## B 다음 문장을 의문문으로 바꿀 때, 빈칸에 들어갈 알맞은 말을 쓰시오.

1 We were very sleepy. ➡ ________ ________ very sleepy?

2 Lily was hungry last night. ➡ ________ ________ hungry last night?

3 You were busy yesterday. ➡ ________ ________ busy yesterday?

4 He was short only a year ago. ➡ ________ ________ short only a year ago?

5 They were at the park. ➡ ________ ________ at the park?

6 It was a national holiday. ➡ ________ ________ a national holiday?

7 She was very sick last month. ➡ ________ ________ very sick last month?

8 His socks were full of holes. ➡ ________ ________ ________ full of holes?

national holiday 국경일
full of ~ ~로 가득찬
hole 구멍, 구덩이

STEP 2

# Grammar PRACTICE

## A 다음 문장을 읽고, be동사를 이용하여 문맥에 맞게 문장을 완성하시오. (축약형으로)

1 She __________ sleepy last night, but now she is very sleepy.

2 Your shoes __________ here yesterday. They were on the shelf.

3 Charlie __________ interested in music. But now he is a musician.

4 The shop __________ open this morning. It was closed today.

5 They __________ good players last year, but this year they are good.

6 He __________ in Jakarta, Indonesia, 2 years ago. He was in Russia.

7 The cat __________ on the wall. It was in front of the door.

8 We __________ at Disneyland last weekend. We were at Universal Studios.

9 It __________ noisy outside last night. It was so quiet.

10 Mr. Baker __________ my math teacher. He was my science teacher.

closed 닫힌, 문을 닫은
shelf 선반
be interested in ~ ~에 관심이 있다
musician 음악가
Indonesia 인도네시아
Jakarta 자카르타 (인도네시아의 수도)
wall 담, 벽

## B 빈칸에 알맞은 말을 채워 넣어 의문문에 대한 대답을 완성하시오. (축약형으로)

1 A Was he a tour guide? B Yes, __________________.

2 A Were you at home yesterday? B No, __________________.

3 A Was the party fun last night? B Yes, __________________.

4 A Were they proud of their son? B Yes, __________________.

5 A Was she really beautiful? B No, __________________.

6 A Was Tony late for school today? B Yes, __________________.

7 A Were we there last Monday? B No, __________________.

8 A Was she your teacher last year? B No, __________________.

9 A Was the English test easy? B No, __________________.

10 A Was it your brother's? B Yes, __________________.

tour guide 여행 가이드
fun 재미있는, 즐거운
easy 쉬운

## C 밑줄 친 부분을 바르게 고쳐 문장을 다시 쓰시오.

1 You not were a teacher.

➡ ______________________________

2 Olivia and Ethan wasn't in Seoul last year.

➡ ______________________________

3 Are you a member of Boy Scouts 5 years ago?

➡ ______________________________

4 Last night, he weren't afraid of the dark.

➡ ______________________________

5 Is your uncle a police officer at that time?

➡ ______________________________

6 Was the mice under the sink?

➡ ______________________________

7 Harry and I aren't absent from school last Wednesday.

➡ ______________________________

8 At that time, the girl were both pretty and smart.

➡ ______________________________

be afraid of ~ ~을 두려워하다
dark 어둠
sink 싱크대, 개수대
both A and B A와 B 둘 다

## D 우리말과 같은 뜻이 되도록 주어진 단어를 바르게 배열하시오.

1 Ethan이 10분 전에 여기 있었니? (ago, Ethan, ten, minutes, was, here)

➡ ______________________________

2 나의 부모님은 작년에 런던에 계시지 않았다.
(in London, not, my parents, were, last year)

➡ ______________________________

3 한 달 전에, 저 딸기들은 달지 않았다.
(a month ago, sweet, those strawberries, weren't)

➡ ______________________________

4 어젯밤에 그 샐러드는 맛이 있었니? (delicious, was, last night, the salad)

➡ ______________________________

delicious 아주 맛있는

STEP 3
# Upgrade TEST

**[1-2] 빈칸에 들어갈 알맞은 것을 고르시오.**

**1**

A ________ you busy last week?
B No, I wasn't.

① Is ② Are
③ Was ④ Were
⑤ Has been

**2**

A Was she late for school this morning?
B No, ________.

① she was ② she isn't
③ she wasn't ④ she hasn't
⑤ she didn't

**3 빈칸에 wasn't가 들어갈 수 없는 것을 고르시오.**

① He ________ late for school yesterday.
② Susan ________ happy at that time.
③ They ________ at the meeting last Friday.
④ Joshua ________ at his father's birthday party.
⑤ There ________ a shopping mall here 2 years ago.

**4 밑줄 친 부분 중 어색한 것을 고르시오.**

A ① Were you and Jessie at home last night?
B ② Yes, we were.
A Can you tell me where you ③ were then?
B Of course. We ④ were at the movie theater.
A ⑤ Was the movie interesting?
B Yes, it was.

**5 다음 우리말을 영어로 바르게 옮긴 것을 고르시오.**

Mary와 Jane은 작년에 뉴욕에 있었니?

① Was Mary and Jane in New York last year?
② Were Mary and Jane in New York last year?
③ Was Mary and Jane be in New York last year?
④ Did Mary and Jane be in New York last year?
⑤ Did Mary and Jane were in New York last year?

**6 빈칸에 알맞은 것을 고르시오.**

A Were Jin and you interested in the story?
B Yes, ________.

① she was ② they are
③ they were ④ we were
⑤ I was

**7 다음 중 어법상 어색한 문장을 고르시오**

① Jim wasn't sick yesterday.
② Was Sunny a singer then?
③ George wasn't satisfied with the test results.
④ Eric and his brother was here three hours ago.
⑤ They weren't detectives but criminals.

be interested in ~ ~에 관심이 있다 be satisfied with ~ ~에 만족하다 test result 시험결과 detective 형사, 탐정 criminal 범인

**8** 빈칸에 들어갈 말이 바르게 짝지어진 것을 고르시오.

| |
|---|
| A ________ Lucy married to him last year?<br>B No, she ________. She married him two years ago. |

① Were - was
② Was - were
③ Wasn't - was
④ Were - weren't
⑤ Was - wasn't

**9** 다음 중 어법상 올바른 문장을 고르시오.

① Qin Shi Huang is the first king to unite China.
② I wasn't hardly aware of the fact until recently.
③ The first Disneyland is founded in 1955.
④ The exhibitions weren't that fun at that time.
⑤ Was you a policeman ten years ago?

**10** 다음 중 어법상 어색한 문장을 고르시오.

① You was back home at nine.
② There weren't any books.
③ Light is faster than sound.
④ In the past, there were no cars.
⑤ Was John scared while watching the horror movie?

**11** 다음 대답에 대한 질문으로 알맞은 것을 고르시오.

| |
|---|
| No, she wasn't. She was interested in music. |

① Did Sally be interested in art?
② Is Sally interesting in art now?
③ Was Sally interested in art when she was young?
④ Wasn't Sally interesting in art recently?
⑤ Didn't Sally be interested in art then?

## [12-15] 서술형 주관식

**[12-13]** 어법상 어색한 부분을 찾아 바르게 고쳐 쓰시오.

**12**

| |
|---|
| Emily and her sister wasn't at the café last night. She was at the concert hall. |

1) ____________ → ____________
2) ____________ → ____________

**13**

| |
|---|
| A Was Noah and his brother in the library?<br>B No, he wasn't. They were in the playground. |

1) ____________ → ____________
2) ____________ → ____________

**14** 주어진 단어를 바르게 배열하여 다음 우리말을 영어로 쓰고, 긍정으로 대답하시오.

| |
|---|
| 그녀는 젊었을 때 미인이었나요?<br>(a beauty, when she was young, she, was) |

1) ________________________
2) ________________________

**15** 주어진 단어를 이용하여 다음 우리말을 영어로 쓰시오.

| |
|---|
| 대부분의 아이들이 그날 학교에 있지 않았다.<br>(at school, most of, on that day) |

→ ________________________
________________________

Qin Shi Huang 진시황제 unite 통일하다 whole 전체의, 모든 hardly 거의 ~ 않다 be aware of ~ ~을 알고 있다 recently 최근에 found 설립하다 exhibition 전시회 fun 재미있는 scared 무서워하는 horror 공포, 전율

기초 탄탄 1
GRAMMAR

Chapter 6

# 일반동사의 과거

Unit 01 일반동사의 과거 긍정문

Unit 02 일반동사의 과거 부정문과 의문문

Unit 01

# 일반동사의 과거 긍정문

## 1 일반동사의 과거 시제의 용법

일반동사의 과거형은 과거에 발생한 동작이나 상태, 또는 역사적 사실을 말할 때 사용한다.

| 과거 시제의 쓰임 | 예문 |
| --- | --- |
| 과거의 동작, 습관 | He fixed his car yesterday. 그는 어제 그의 차를 고쳤다. |
| 과거의 상태 | A church stood here in the past. 과거에는 여기에 교회가 서있었다. |
| 역사적 사실 | Columbus discovered America in 1492. 콜럼버스는 1492년에 미대륙을 발견했다. |

be동사의 과거형 문장과 마찬가지로 과거 시점을 나타내는 'yesterday, last, ago' 등과 함께 사용된다.

## 2 일반동사의 과거형 변화 규칙

일반동사의 과거형은 주어의 인칭과 수에 상관없이 동사원형에 -ed를 붙이며 불규칙하게 변하는 경우가 있다.

| 일반동사 | | 변화 규칙 | 일반동사의 과거형 |
| --- | --- | --- | --- |
| 규칙 변화 | 대부분의 동사 | + -ed | want → wanted, help → helped, talk → talked, watch → watched, enjoy → enjoyed, play → played |
| | '모음 + -y'로 끝나는 동사 | | |
| | '자음 + y'로 끝나는 동사 | y → i + -ed | study → studied, try → tried, worry → worried, cry → cried |
| | e로 끝나는 동사 | + -d | like → liked, live → lived, die → died |
| | '단모음 + 단자음'으로 끝나는 동사 | 자음을 한 번 더 쓰고 + -ed | drop → dropped, hug → hugged, plan → planned, stop → stopped, fit → fitted |
| 불규칙 변화 | 형태가 같은 동사 | | cut, put, read, hit, cost, set, let, shut, hurt |
| | 불규칙하게 변하는 동사 | | come → came, buy → bought, say → said, go → went, drink → drank, tell → told, know → knew, fly → flew, catch → caught, build → built, sleep → slept, pay → paid, win → won, meet → met, blow → blew, break → broke, feel → felt, drive → drove, begin → began, leave → left, ride → rode, stand → stood, throw → threw, run → ran, teach → taught, sit → sat, eat → ate |

Tip

pp.126-128 불규칙 동사표 참조

STEP 1

# Grammar START

Grammar on Target

1. 일반동사의 과거형 규칙 변화
2. 일반동사의 과거형 불규칙 변화

## A 다음 일반동사의 과거형을 쓰시오.

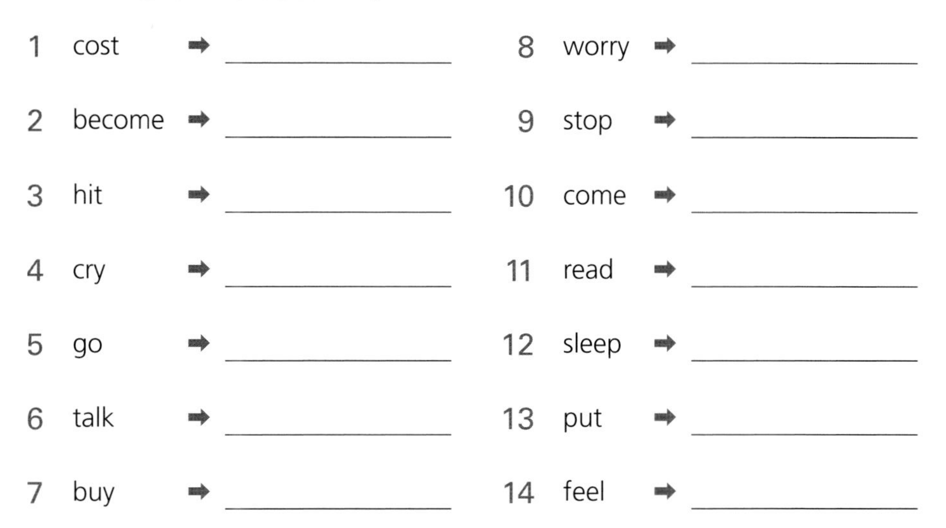

1 cost ➡ ____________

2 become ➡ ____________

3 hit ➡ ____________

4 cry ➡ ____________

5 go ➡ ____________

6 talk ➡ ____________

7 buy ➡ ____________

8 worry ➡ ____________

9 stop ➡ ____________

10 come ➡ ____________

11 read ➡ ____________

12 sleep ➡ ____________

13 put ➡ ____________

14 feel ➡ ____________

cost 비용이 들다
become 되다
hit 치다
worry 걱정하다
come 오다
put 놓다
feel 느끼다

## B 다음 문장에서 알맞은 일반동사의 과거형을 고르시오.

1 Susan (liveed / lived) here before.

2 I (enjoyed / enjoied) watching the movie very much.

3 They (wantd / wanted) to stay at home on rainy days.

4 Ryan (dropped / droped) several books on the floor.

5 World War II (broke / breaked) out in 1939.

6 He (studyed / studied) very hard to pass the exam.

7 I (used / usied) to take a walk after dinner.

8 We (cut / cuted) the papers with the scissors.

9 Noel (helpped / helped) the old woman up.

10 She (liked / likied) the big pond in front of her house.

stay 머무르다
go out 외출하다
break out (전쟁, 질병이) 발발하다, 발생하다
used to ~ (과거의 습관, 상태) ~하곤 했다

STEP 2
# Grammar PRACTICE

## A 주어진 동사를 알맞게 바꿔 과거 시제로 문장을 완성하시오.

1 I __________ for eight hours a day. (sleep)

2 He __________ the box on the shelf yesterday. (put)

3 Eskimos __________ their homes with ice. (build)

4 My brother __________ for his English test. (study)

5 You __________ to bed at nine o'clock last night. (go)

6 We __________ him a lot of questions in class. (ask)

7 They __________ their violins for the concert. (play)

8 At last, the Korean team __________ the final game. (win)

9 Jordan __________ working as a fashion model two years ago. (begin)

10 Kate __________ to my house and __________ me with science. (come, help)

put 놓다, 두다, 넣다
Eskimo 에스키모인
build 짓다, 세우다
ask 질문하다, 요청하다
in class 수업 중에
at last 마침내, 드디어
final 마지막의
win 이기다
begin 시작하다

## B 다음 문장을 과거 시제로 바꿔 쓰시오.

1 I meet her at the airport today.

➡ ________________________________________ yesterday.

2 He catches a lot of fish every weekend.

➡ ________________________________________ last weekend.

3 Serena drinks a glass of milk now.

➡ ________________________________________ an hour ago.

4 We pay a lot of money for the house.

➡ ________________________________________ a year ago.

5 Noah stops his work and eats lunch at twelve every day.

➡ ________________________________________ two hours ago.

catch 잡다
pay 지불하다
stop 멈추다

## C 틀린 부분을 찾아 바르게 고쳐 문장을 다시 쓰시오.

1 The train leave for London an hour ago.

➡ ______________________________

2 He runs one hundred meters in eleven seconds yesterday.

➡ ______________________________

3 In 1997, Jason and Olivia live in Paris.

➡ ______________________________

4 She really wants to went her home two hours ago.

➡ ______________________________

5 My dad buyed a new TV a month ago.

➡ ______________________________

6 She reads to her child last night.

➡ ______________________________

7 They arrive at the station ten minutes ago.

➡ ______________________________

8 I was very sad and cry all day long.

➡ ______________________________

9 She sliped on the ice and break her leg last week.

➡ ______________________________

leave for ~ ~을 향해 떠나다
run 달리다
arrive 도착하다
cry 울다
slip 미끄러지다
break 깨뜨리다, 부러지다

## D 우리말과 같은 뜻이 되도록 주어진 단어를 바르게 배열하시오. 단, 필요에 따라 동사를 변형시켜 쓰시오.

1 그녀는 작년에 보스톤에 살았다. (last year, live, in Boston, she)

➡ ______________________________

2 그는 해안 고속도로를 따라 운전했다. (drive, he, the coastal highway, along)

➡ ______________________________

3 그 아이는 그의 강아지를 껴안고 뽀뽀했다. (kiss, his puppy, hug, the child, and)

➡ ______________________________

4 나는 작년에 자전거를 타고 학교에 다녔다. (ride, I, to school, last year, my bike)

➡ ______________________________

drive 운전하다
coastal 해안의
highway 고속도로
hug 껴안다
kiss 키스하다
ride 타다

STEP 3
# Upgrade TEST

**[1-2] 빈칸에 들어갈 수 없는 것을 고르시오.**

**1**

I went to the Museum of Modern Art ________.

① this morning
② yesterday
③ a week ago
④ last Friday
⑤ since 1998

**2**

They ________ last night.

① went to the movies.
② stayed at home
③ rode their bikes
④ did their homework
⑤ walk their dog in the park

**3 다음 중 짝지어진 동사의 과거형이 틀린 것을 고르시오.**

① slide - slided
② copy - copied
③ spread - spread
④ hold - held
⑤ find - found

**4 다음 중 어법상 올바른 문장을 고르시오.**

① We are so active at that time.
② He uses to take a walk after dinner.
③ She reads the book yesterday.
④ There came many people at the concert.
⑤ Jennifer has a great time at the party last Saturday.

**[5-7] 다음 중 어법상 어색한 문장을 고르시오.**

**5**
① I get up at 6 a.m. every day.
② World War II break out in 1939.
③ Rome was not built in a day.
④ Sam told me that honesty is the best policy.
⑤ She bought a book yesterday.

**6**
① Steve has a master's degree.
② They go to church every Sunday.
③ Many people died in the accident.
④ Water boils at 100℃.
⑤ I live in Europe then.

**7**
① Shawn went to Yale University in 2018.
② You were absent from school yesterday.
③ In the past, people believed that the Earth is flat.
④ Light moves faster than sound.
⑤ Thomas Edison invented the electric light bulb.

spread 펼치다, 퍼뜨리다 slide 미끄러지다 active 활동적인 absent 결석한

**8** 다음 우리말을 영어로 바르게 옮긴 것을 고르시오.

| 그녀는 그 순간 거짓말을 했다. |
|---|

① She tells a lie at that moment.
② She told a lie at that moment.
③ She tolds a lie at that moment.
④ She did told a lie at that moment.
⑤ She has told a lie at that moment.

**[9-10]** 다음 중 과거 시제가 바르게 쓰인 문장을 고르시오.

**9** ① She crossied the street.
② The water fell to the ground.
③ Emily taken part in the contest.
④ James speaked French at the meeting.
⑤ I plaied a computer game yesterday.

**10** ① He stoped smoking yesterday.
② Carson copyed the article.
③ She holded me by the hand.
④ They left the building early this morning.
⑤ We losed all our money during the journey.

**11** 다음 중 어법상 올바른 문장을 고르시오.
① She did visited her parents' farm.
② We cryed out when we heard the news.
③ Julie cames to see me yesterday.
④ They spreaded the rumor on purpose.
⑤ Wisely, you paid attention to my advice.

## [12-15] 서술형 주관식

**12** 어법상 어색한 부분을 찾아 바르게 고쳐 쓰시오.

| Columbus discovers America in 1492. |
|---|

________ → ________

**13** 주어진 단어를 바르게 배열하여 다음 우리말을 영어로 쓰시오.

우리 집 앞에는 연못이 있었다.
(used, a pond, to, in front of, be)

→ There ____________ my house.

**14** 어법상 어색한 부분을 세 군데 찾아 바르게 고쳐 쓰시오.

Yesterday, my dad and I went to Burger King. We orderred two shrimp burgers, large French fries, and a mango jellyade. All of them costed us 15,000 won. He handed the cashier 20,000 won. The cashier gived him his change.

1) ________ → ________
2) ________ → ________
3) ________ → ________

**15** 주어진 단어를 이용하여 다음 우리말을 영어로 쓰시오.

Brian은 아침을 먹은 후에 수학을 공부했고, 그런 다음에 축구를 했다.
(after breakfast, and then, play soccer, study math)

→ ____________________
____________________

cross 건너다 contest 대회 meeting 회의 smoking 흡연 copy 복사하다 article (신문, 잡지 등의) 기사 journey 여행 rumor 소문 on purpose 의도적으로 wisely 현명하게 pay attention to ~ ~에 주의하다 order 주문하다 cost (비용이) 들다 hand 건네주다, 넘겨주다 cashier 계산원 change 거스름돈

Unit 02

# 일반동사의 과거 부정문과 의문문

## 1 일반동사의 과거 부정문

일반동사의 과거 부정문은 주어의 인칭과 수에 상관없이 동사원형 앞에 did not이나 didn't를 붙인다.

| 주어 | 동사의 부정형 | 예문 |
|---|---|---|
| I<br>You<br>He / She / It<br>We / You / They | did not (didn't) + 동사원형 | I didn't go there last night. 나는 어젯밤에 그곳에 가지 않았다.<br>You didn't play soccer yesterday. 너는 어제 축구를 하지 않았다.<br>She didn't cheat on the test. 그녀는 시험에서 부정행위를 하지 않았다.<br>They didn't have lunch today. 그들은 오늘 점심을 먹지 않았다. |

**Tip**
didn't 다음에는 반드시 동사원형이 온다.
→ She didn't cheats on the test. (×)

## 2 일반동사의 과거 의문문

일반동사의 과거 의문문은 주어의 인칭과 수에 상관없이 주어 앞에 Did를 쓰며 『Did + 주어 + 동사원형 ~?』의 형태이다.

| 주어 | 동사의 의문문 | 예문 |
|---|---|---|
| I<br>You<br>He / She / It<br>We / You / They | Did + 주어 + 동사원형 ~? | Did I tell you about my family? 내가 우리 가족에 대해 말했던가?<br>Did you enjoy watching the movie? 그 영화 재미있었니?<br>Did she call you last night? 그녀가 어젯밤에 너한테 전화했니?<br>Did they enter the room? 그들은 방에 들어갔니? |

**Tip**
Did 다음에는 반드시 동사원형이 온다.
→ Did she calls you last night? (×)

## 3 일반동사의 과거 의문문에 대한 대답

긍정의 대답은 『Yes, 주어 did.』로, 부정의 대답은 『No, 주어 didn't.』의 형태이다.

| 긍정의 대답 | | | 부정의 대답 | | |
|---|---|---|---|---|---|
| Yes, | I<br>you<br>he / she / it<br>we / you / they | did. | No, | I<br>you<br>he / she / it<br>we / you / they | didn't. |

A Did you meet Lily yesterday? 너 어제 Lily 만났니? B Yes, I did. 응, 만났어.
A Did he tell a lie to his mom? 그가 엄마한테 거짓말했니? B No, he didn't. 아니, 안 했어.

STEP 1

# Grammar START

Grammar on Target

1. 일반동사의 과거 부정문 만들기
2. 일반동사의 과거 의문문 만들기

## A 다음 괄호 안에서 알맞은 것을 고르시오.

1 He (don't / doesn't / didn't) go to school on Saturdays.

2 I (don't / doesn't / didn't) lose my wallet yesterday.

3 It didn't (rain / rains / rained) last weekend.

4 We (don't / doesn't / didn't) read the manual at that time.

5 Andy and you didn't (build / builds / built) a snowman that day.

6 You (don't / doesn't / didn't) invite him to your birthday party last year.

7 She didn't (write / writes / wrote) her name down on her test paper.

8 They didn't (eat / eated / ate) fast food for their health.

9 Leo (don't / doesn't / didn't) have the courage to fight for justice at that time.

wallet 지갑
manual 설명서
courage 용기
fight 싸우다
build(make) a snowman 눈사람을 만들다
invite 초대하다
test paper 시험지
justice 정의, 공평

## B 주어진 동사를 이용하여 일반동사의 과거 의문문을 완성하시오.

1 __________ she __________ her ring? (find)

2 __________ they __________ the tickets already? (buy)

3 __________ Daniel __________ his holiday? (enjoy)

4 __________ you __________ for me after school? (wait)

5 __________ the children __________ to their teacher? (talk)

6 __________ we __________ the bathroom window? (lock)

7 __________ Heather __________ her homework an hour ago? (finish)

8 __________ you __________ sugar in my coffee? (put)

9 __________ he __________ the soccer game last night? (watch)

already 이미, 벌써
wait 기다리다
talk 말하다
lock 잠그다
bathroom 욕실
finish 끝내다, 마치다

STEP 2
# Grammar PRACTICE

## A 다음 문장을 부정문으로 바꿔 쓰시오. (축약형으로)

1 I saw many kinds of kangaroos in Australia.
➡ I __________ __________ many kinds of kangaroos in Australia.

2 She came to my house with her cat.
➡ She __________ __________ to my house with her cat.

3 The hen laid a golden egg every day.
➡ The hen __________ __________ a golden egg every day.

4 My dad sold his old car to my uncle.
➡ My dad __________ __________ his old car to my uncle.

5 It happened very often.
➡ It __________ __________ very often.

6 Andera looked like a supermodel.
➡ Andera __________ __________ like a supermodel.

7 They bought new bats and gloves.
➡ They __________ __________ new bats and gloves.

8 He drank three cups of coffee today.
➡ He __________ __________ three cups of coffee today.

kind 종류, 유형
hen 암탉
lay 놓다, 낳다
golden 황금빛의
sell 팔다
happen 일어나다, 발생하다
look like ~ ~인 것처럼 보이다, ~할 것 같다
bat 방망이, 배트

## B 대화를 읽고, 빈칸에 알맞은 말을 쓰시오.

1 A __________ you have breakfast?
B Yes, I __________. I __________ some bread two hours ago.

2 A __________ Leonardo paint Mona Lisa's eyebrows?
B No, he __________. It was a fashion to shave them at that time.

3 A __________ your sisters sing songs on the stage?
B No, they __________. They played the piano and the violin.

4 A __________ she care for hurt and sick soldiers?
B Yes, she __________. She also established hospitals.

have 가지다, 먹다
eyebrow 눈썹
fashion 유행, 인기
shave 깎다, 면도하다
stage 무대, 단계
hurt 다친
soldier 군인
establish 설립하다, 개설하다

## C 다음 문장을 부정문과 의문문으로 바꿔 쓰시오.

1 He wrote many fairy tales for children.

➡ ______________________________

➡ ______________________________

2 She delivered food to poor people.

➡ ______________________________

➡ ______________________________

3 They loved to invent things.

➡ ______________________________

➡ ______________________________

4 Mr. Brown taught her about the solar system.

➡ ______________________________

➡ ______________________________

5 Helen tried to communicate with other people.

➡ ______________________________

➡ ______________________________

fairy tale 동화
deliver 배달하다, 전하다
poor 가난한
invent 발명하다
teach 가르치다
solar system 태양계
try 노력하다, 애쓰다
communicate 의사소통을 하다

## D 우리말과 같은 뜻이 되도록 주어진 단어를 바르게 배열하시오.

1 너의 캐나다 친구는 너에게 이메일을 보냈니?
(Canadian friend, you, did, an email, your, send)

➡ ______________________________

2 그는 역사상 가장 유명한 야구선수가 되었니?
(the most famous baseball player, he, in history, become, did)

➡ ______________________________

3 그녀는 그 문제를 우연히 발견하지 않았다.
(discover, she, by accident, the problem, didn't)

➡ ______________________________

4 그들은 신발을 신지 않고 조용히 걸었다.
(didn't, shoes, walked, and, softly, wear, they)

➡ ______________________________

fairy tale 동화
deliver 배달하다, 전하다
poor 가난한
invent 발명하다
teach 가르치다
solar system 태양계
try 노력하다, 애쓰다
communicate 의사소통을 하다

STEP 3
# Upgrade TEST

**1** 빈칸에 들어갈 말이 바르게 짝지어진 것을 고르시오.

| We ______ ______ to the speech yesterday. |
|---|

① wasn't, listen
② weren't, listen
③ don't, listened
④ didn't, listen
⑤ didn't, listened

**2** 다음 문장을 의문문으로 바르게 바꾼 것을 고르시오.

| She had a great time at the party. |
|---|

① Do she had a great time at the party?
② Does she had a great time at the party?
③ Did she has a great time at the party?
④ Had she a great time at the party?
⑤ Did she have a great time at the party?

**[3-4]** 다음 중 어법상 어색한 문장을 고르시오.

**3** ① Did Sarah give you the book?
② Did you went to the concert?
③ Tom took a walk after dinner last night.
④ Did you watch a movie yesterday?
⑤ They didn't want to do their chores.

**4** ① I did my math homework.
② I went to the movies with my friends.
③ I watch a movie *Ice Age 2* yesterday.
④ I read an interesting book.
⑤ I took care of my younger brother.

**[5-6]** 다음 대화의 빈칸에 들어갈 알맞은 것을 고르시오.

**5**

A ______________________
B No, he didn't. He played mobile games.

① What did Jim do yesterday?
② Did she play mobile games?
③ Was he playing mobile games then?
④ Did Brian do his homework last night?
⑤ Didn't Jason went to the movies last night?

**6**

A Did you go to the aquarium last Sunday?
B ______________

① Yes, I wasn't.
② No, I was.
③ Yes, I didn't.
④ Yes, I did.
⑤ No, I did.

**7** 다음 문장을 부정문으로 바르게 바꾼 것을 고르시오.

| She attended the reading club meeting yesterday. |
|---|

① She not attended the reading club meeting yesterday.
② She wasn't attended the reading club meeting yesterday.
③ She didn't attend the reading club meeting yesterday.
④ She didn't attended the reading club meeting yesterday.
⑤ She didn't attends the reading club meeting yesterday.

speech 연설 chore 허드렛일, 집안의 자질구레한 일 aquarium 수족관

**8** 다음 중 대화가 자연스러운 것을 고르시오.

① A Did you eat lunch?
   B Yes, I eat spaghetti for lunch.
② A Did you go there?
   B No, I don't. I will go there at ten o'clock.
③ A Did you go to Tokyo Disneyland yesterday?
   B Yes, I did. I went there with my parents.
④ A Did Serena bring an orange last night?
   B No, she brings a really big watermelon.
⑤ A Did you have a great time there?
   B Yes, I do.

**9** 다음 대답에 대한 질문으로 알맞은 것을 고르시오.

| No, he didn't. |
|---|

① Did your brother worked at a bank then?
② Wasn't Jane tired last night?
③ Did Timothy wants to join the club?
④ Did Sam open this document in the afternoon?
⑤ Does your son go to church?

**10** 빈칸에 들어갈 알맞은 것을 고르시오.

A Did you finish your homework?
B _____ I was busy taking care of my sister.

① Yes, I didn't. ② No, I wasn't.
③ Yes, I did. ④ No, I didn't.
⑤ No, I don't.

**11** 다음 중 어법상 어색한 문장을 고르시오.

A ① Did you go to the movie yesterday?
B ② Yes, I was.
A ③ How was the movie?
B ④ It was very fun and thrilling.
⑤ Everyone liked the movie *Avengers*.

## [12-15] 서술형 주관식

**[12-13]** 주어진 단어를 이용하여 다음 우리말을 영어로 쓰시오.

**12**

그들은 어제 모형 비행기를 완성하지 못했다.
(complete, model airplane)

→ ______________________

**13**

그들은 벽돌로 그 집을 지었나요?
(build, house, with bricks)

→ ______________________

**14** 다음 문장을 의문문으로 바꿔 쓰시오.

| She had a stomachache yesterday. |
|---|

→ ______________________

**15** 어법상 어색한 부분을 찾아 바르게 고쳐 문장을 다시 쓰시오.

A Does Jimin went fishing last Saturday?
B Yes, she doesn't.

A ______________________
B ______________________

watermelon 수박 document 서류, 문서 complete 완료하다 model airplane 모형 비행기 brick 벽돌 stomachache 복통, 위통

**1** 빈칸에 공통으로 들어갈 말을 쓰시오.

- I ________ a teacher.
- The police afficer ________ nice to me.

① am ② is
③ was ④ were
⑤ have

**2** 다음 중 어법상 올바른 문장을 고르시오.

① I were not rich.
② You and John was not sick.
③ You weren't fat.
④ Cathy weren't clever.
⑤ We wasn't tall.

**[3-4]** 다음 의문문 중 잘못된 문장을 고르시오.

**3** ① Was Jessica afraid of the mouse?
② Were your dad a teacher?
③ Were your friends on your side?
④ Was Johnny in the hospital?
⑤ Were our classrooms empty?

**4** ① Wasn't our teacher Tom?
② Weren't you there?
③ Weren't the doctors busy?
④ Wasn't we on one team?
⑤ Wasn't Irene her name?

**5** 빈칸에 들어갈 알맞은 것을 고르시오.

Mia and Tom ________ in Busan last year.
Mia와 Tom은 작년에 부산에 있지 않았다.

① isn't ② aren't ③ wasn't
④ weren't ⑤ didn't

**6** 주어진 단어를 이용하여 다음 우리말을 영어로 쓰시오.

너는 어젯밤에 피곤했니?
(tired)

➡ ________________________________

**7** 밑줄 친 일반동사의 과거형이 잘못된 것을 고르시오.

① They ate lunch.
② My wife put our baby in the bed.
③ She sats on the chair.
④ Your girlfriend took my book.
⑤ He looked the same as his brother.

**8** 다음 중 어법상 올바른 문장을 고르시오.

① We didn't felt cold.
② They didn't heared music.
③ He didn't visits my grandmother.
④ I didn't see the police.
⑤ She didn't got a good score on the test.

**9** 빈칸에 들어갈 말이 바르게 짝지어진 것을 고르시오.

A ________ he take care of his dog?
B Yes, he did. He ________ a lot of time with his dog.

① Is - spent ② Was - spent
③ Did - spend ④ Did - spends
⑤ Did - spent

**10** 다음 중 어법상 어색한 문장을 고르시오.

① Did you told her the truth?
② Did he ask you to bring my suit?
③ Did I explain this question?
④ Did she go on a shopping trip?
⑤ Did we learn this grammar?

**11** 주어진 단어를 각 빈칸에 알맞은 형태로 쓰시오.

A You didn't ________ your room. (clean)
B I'm sorry. I ________ sick all day yesterday. (be)

**12** 다음 대화에서 어색한 것을 모두 고르시오.

A ① Did you see the news last night?
B ② Yes, I do. ③ Are you talking about air pollution?
A ④ Yes, I am. I had a sore throat. So I drank a lot of water. Now I ⑤ felt okay.
B I am glad to hear that.

**13** 지시대로 고친 문장이 틀린 것을 고르시오.

① I am a singer.
과거 부정문 → I wasn't a singer.
② Rachel speaks to her teacher.
과거 의문문 → Did Rachel speak to her teacher?
③ Harry goes on a trip.
과거 의문문 → Did Harry goes on a trip?
④ Nicky is jealous of you.
과거 의문문 → Was Nicky jealous of you?
⑤ They are ready to leave.
과거 의문문 → Were they ready to leave?

**[14-15]** 주어진 단어를 이용하여 우리말을 영어로 쓰시오.

**14**

A 나 어제 10km 달렸어. (run, 10 km)
B 정말? 다리는 괜찮았어? (your legs, okay)

⬇

A ________________________
B Really? ________________________

**15**

A 내가 핸드폰 잃어버렸다고 얘기했니? (tell)
B 아니. 난 몰랐어. (know)

⬇

A ________________ that I lost my phone?
B No, you didn't. ________________ that.

기초 탄탄 1
GRAMMAR

Chapter 7

# 진행 시제

Unit 01

# 현재진행형

## 1 현재진행형의 긍정문

현재진행형은 현재 진행중인 동작을 나타내며 '~하고 있다' 또는 '~하는 중이다'로 해석한다.
주어의 인칭에 따라 『주어 + be동사 + 동사원형 -ing』의 형태이며, 동사원형에 -ing를 붙이는 방법은 다음과 같다.

| 동사 | 동사의 변화 규칙 | 동사의 진행형 |
|---|---|---|
| 대부분의 동사 | 동사원형 + -ing | crying, drinking, eating, flying, going, jumping, learning, listening, looking, sleeping, talking, walking, watching |
| -e로 끝나는 동사 | e를 빼고 + -ing | come → coming, dance → dancing, give → giving, have → having, take → taking, write → writing |
| -ie로 끝나는 동사 | -ie → -y + -ing | die → dying, lie → lying, tie → tying |
| 단모음 + 단자음으로 끝나는 동사 | 끝 자음을 한 번 더 쓰고 + -ing | cut → cutting, get → getting, hit → hitting, plan → planning, put → putting, run → running, sit → sitting |

현재 She waits for the elevator.
그녀는 엘리베이터를 기다린다.

현재진행 She is waiting for the elevator.
그녀는 엘리베이터를 기다리고 있다.

**Tip**

소유나 상태를 나타내는 have, like, need, want, believe, know, taste 등은 진행형으로 쓸 수 없다.
She is having a car. (x) ⟶ She has a car. (o)
The food is tasting good. (x) ⟶ The food tastes good. (o)

그러나, have가 '시간을 보내다' 또는 '먹다'의 의미일 경우에는 진행형이 가능하다.
I am having a great time. (o) 난 멋진 시간을 보내고 있다.
She is having lunch. (o) 그녀는 점심을 먹고 있다.

## 2 현재진행형의 부정문

현재진행형의 부정문은 be동사 뒤에 not을 붙이고, '~하고 있지 않다'로 해석한다.

| 주어 | 현재진행형의 부정형 | 예문 |
|---|---|---|
| I | am + not + -ing | I am not singing a song. 나는 노래를 부르고 있지 않다. |
| He / She / It | is + not + -ing | He is not playing a computer game now. 그는 지금 컴퓨터 게임을 하고 있지 않다. |
| We / You / They | are + not + -ing | We are not planning to visit Africa. 우리는 아프리카를 방문할 계획을 하고 있지 않다. |

## 3 현재진행형의 의문문

주어의 인칭에 따라 『be동사 + 주어 + -ing ~?』의 형태이다. 대답은 Yes / No로 한다.

| 주어 | 현재진행형의 의문문 | 예문 |
|---|---|---|
| I | Am + 주어 + -ing? | Am I watching TV? 내가 TV를 보고 있니?<br>Yes, you are. / No, you aren't. |
| he / she / it | Is + 주어 + -ing? | Is she sleeping now? 그녀는 지금 자고 있니?<br>Yes, she is. / No, she isn't. |
| we / you / they | Are + 주어 + -ing? | Are they moving tables downstairs? 그들은 테이블을 아래층으로 옮기고 있니?<br>Yes, they are. / No, they aren't. |

STEP 1

# Grammar START

**Grammar on Target**

1. 현재진행형 만들기
2. 현재진행형의 부정문과 의문문

## A 다음 괄호 안에서 알맞은 것을 고르시오.

1 You (walk / are walking) in the park now.

2 I (am reading / is reading) comic books.

3 He is (listen / listening) to music in his room.

4 My cats are (sleeping / sleepping) on my bed.

5 It is (snows / snowing) outside now.

6 The children are (dancing / danceing) in the flowerbed.

7 Bella (has / is having) a slice of bread for breakfast now.

8 We are (go / going) to a seafood restaurant on the beach.

9 A boy and his dog are (lieing / lying) on the grass.

outside 바깥쪽, 밖
snow 눈이 내리다
flowerbed 꽃밭, 화단
seafood 해산물
restaurant 식당
beach 해변
grass 풀, 잔디

## B 주어진 말을 이용하여 현재진행형의 부정문과 의문문을 완성하시오.

1 They __________ __________ __________ in the pool. (not, swim)

2 __________ you __________ enough water? (drink)

3 __________ he __________ the tomatoes into thin slices. (cut)

4 You __________ __________ __________ a truck now. (not, drive)

5 __________ Noah and Lua __________ in the sand with a shovel? (dig)

6 __________ the wind __________ a lot now? (blow)

7 My dad __________ __________ __________ to my graduation. (not, come)

8 __________ the policeman __________ after the murderer? (run)

9 She __________ __________ __________ the piano at the Arts Center. (not, play)

pool 수영장
thin 얇은, 가는
slice 조각, 부분
drive 운전하다
truck 트럭
graduation 졸업, 졸업식
policeman 경찰관
murderer 살인범
run after ~
~을 따라가다, 뒤쫓다

STEP 2

# Grammar PRACTICE

## A 밑줄 친 부분을 바르게 고쳐 쓰시오.

1 I am not sit next to him. ➡ ____________

2 Does he looking for his cap? ➡ ____________

3 Is Olivia clean her room now? ➡ ____________

4 The students not are learning about politics. ➡ ____________

5 The mouse is move a slice of cheese. ➡ ____________

6 You don't giving me advice. ➡ ____________

7 Are she sending a text message to her mom? ➡ ____________

8 He is having a new computer. ➡ ____________

sit 앉다
look for ~ ~을 찾다
politics 정치
text message 문자 메시지

## B 주어진 단어와 우리말을 이용하여 빈칸에 알맞은 말을 쓰시오.

1 뉴욕에서 즐거운 시간을 보내고 있니? (have)

➡ ________ you ________ a great time in New York?

2 한 아기는 자고 있고, 다른 아기는 울고 있다. (sleep, cry)

➡ One baby is ________, and the other baby is ________.

3 그는 자전거를 타고 학교에 다닌다. 지금은 걸어서 학교에 가고 있다. (walk)

➡ He ________ to school by bicycle. Now, he ________ ________ to school.

4 A 그들은 손을 씻고 있니? B 응, 씻고 있어. (wash)

➡ A ________ they ________ their hands? B Yes, they ________.

5 Charlie는 침대에 누워 있다. 그는 아파 보인다. (lie, look)

➡ Charlie ________ ________ in his bed. He ________ sick.

6 그녀는 지금 이를 닦고 있지 않다. 그녀는 숙제를 하고 있다. (brush, do)

➡ She ________ ________ her teeth now. She is ________ her homework.

at that time 그때
cheap (값이) 싼
expensive 비싼

## C 보기와 같이 다음 문장을 부정문과 의문문으로 바꿔 쓰시오.

보기 She is riding a roller coaster.
➡ She isn't riding a roller coaster.
➡ Is she riding a rollor coaster?

1 The boy is kicking a ball.
➡ ______
➡ ______

2 They are working hard.
➡ ______
➡ ______

3 He is enjoying his trip to New Orleans.
➡ ______
➡ ______

4 Bees are flying around the flowers.
➡ ______
➡ ______

roller coaster 롤러코스터
kick (발로) 차다
work 일하다
hard 열심히
bee 벌

## D 우리말과 같은 뜻이 되도록 주어진 단어를 바르게 배열하시오. 단, 필요에 따라 동사를 변형시켜 쓰시오.

1 나는 공항에 갈 준비를 하고 있다. (am, the airport, leave for, I, to, prepare)
➡ ______

2 그녀는 자기 아이들을 돌보고 있다. (her, she, children, take care of, is)
➡ ______

3 Kevin은 지금 사회 공부를 하고 있지 않다. (not, Kevin, social studies, is, study)
➡ ______

4 너 지금 그에게 네 비밀을 말하고 있는 거야? (secret, him, are, tell, you, now, your)
➡ ______

leave for ~ ~로 떠나다
prepare 준비하다
take care of ~ ~을 돌보다
social studies 사회 (과목)
tell 말하다, 이야기하다
secret 비밀

STEP 3

# Upgrade TEST

**1** 짝지어진 동사의 진행형이 틀린 것을 고르시오.

① set - setting ② eat - eatting
③ stop - stopping ④ close - closing
⑤ lie - lying

**2** 빈칸에 들어갈 알맞은 것을 고르시오.

> A What are you doing now?
> B I ________ a picture.

① take ② am taking
③ took ④ taking
⑤ am going to take

**3** 다음 밑줄 친 부분의 쓰임이 나머지 넷과 다른 것을 고르시오.

① The baby is sleeping.
② My mom is cooking now.
③ This book is very interesting.
④ A dog is running down the street.
⑤ They are playing soccer on the playground.

**4** 다음 우리말을 영어로 바르게 옮긴 것을 고르시오.

> Tom과 나는 컴퓨터 게임을 하고 있는 중이다.

① Tom and I play computer games.
② Tom and I plays computer games.
③ Tom and I is playing computer games.
④ Tom and I am playing computer games.
⑤ Tom and I are playing computer games.

**[5-6]** 다음 질문에 대한 답으로 알맞은 것을 고르시오.

**5**

> What is she doing?

① She goes to school.
② She is being a student.
③ She went shopping yesterday.
④ She is cleaning her room now.
⑤ She is going to visit her parents in Paris.

**6**

> Is it raining in Seoul now?

① No, it is. ② Yes, it isn't.
③ No, it isn't. ④ Yes, it does.
⑤ No, it doesn't.

**7** 다음 중 어법상 올바른 문장을 고르시오.

① The blue shirt is becoming you.
② Jessica is resembling her mother now.
③ This building is belonging to my dad.
④ The committee is consisting of eleven members.
⑤ We are having a great time here in New York.

**8** 다음 우리말을 영어로 바르게 옮긴 것을 고르시오.

> 너와 Jack은 카드놀이를 하고 있니?

① Is you and Jack playing cards?
② Are you and Jack playing cards?
③ Do you and Jack is playing cards?
④ Do you and Jack be playing cards?
⑤ Does you and Jack playing cards?

resemble 닮다 committee 위원회 consist of ~ ~으로 구성되다 belong to ~ ~의 것이다(속하다)

**[12-15] 서술형 주관식**

**9** 빈칸에 들어갈 말이 바르게 짝지어진 것을 고르시오.

- George ________ the mountain every Sunday.
- Helen ________ the piano now.

① is climbing, plays
② is climbing, is playing
③ climbed, is playing
④ climbed, played
⑤ climbs, is playing

**10** 다음 질문에 대한 대답으로 올 수 없는 것을 고르시오.

Daniel, what are you doing now?

① I'm having a book.
② I'm swimming in the pool.
③ I'm taking a picture.
④ I'm watching an action movie.
⑤ I'm drawing several cartoon scenes.

**11** 다음 중 어법상 올바른 문장을 고르시오.

① It is sounding great.
② I am walking my dog every day.
③ Sandra was reading a book now.
④ They are wanting to meet you.
⑤ I am having lunch now.

**12** 어법상 어색한 부분을 찾아 바르게 고쳐 쓰시오.

He is appearing very sad.

________ → ________

**13** 어법상 어색한 부분을 모두 찾아 바르게 고쳐 쓰시오.

The moles is diging a hole now.

1) ________ → ________
2) ________ → ________

**14** 주어진 단어를 이용하여 다음 우리말을 영어로 쓰시오.

그는 지금 침대에 누워있습니까?
(lie, on the bed)

→ ________________

**15** 주어진 단어를 이용하여 다음 우리말을 영어로 쓰고, 그 질문에 부정으로 답하시오.

그들은 아프리카를 방문할 계획을 하고 있습니까?
(plan, to visit, Africa)

1) ________________
2) ________________

appear ~인 것 같다, ~처럼 보이다 mole 두더지 dig (땅을) 파다 plan 계획을 세우다

Unit 02

# 과거진행형

## 1 과거진행형의 긍정문

과거진행형은 과거 어느 시점에 진행중이었던 동작을 나타내며 '~하고 있었다' 또는 '~하는 중이었다'로 해석한다.
주어의 인칭에 따라 『주어 + be동사의 과거 (was / were) + 동사원형 -ing』의 형태이다.

| 주어 | 과거진행형 | 예문 |
|---|---|---|
| I / He / She / It | was + -ing | I was doing my math homework.<br>나는 수학 숙제를 하는 중이었다. |
| We / You / They | were + -ing | They were eating bananas then.<br>그들은 그때 바나나를 먹고 있었다. |

현재진행 It is raining. 비가 오고 있다.
과거진행 It was raining. 비가 오고 있었다.

Tip
주로 과거 시점을 나타내는 then, at that time, at the moment, when 등과 함께 쓰인다.

## 2 과거진행형의 부정문

과거진행형의 부정문은 be동사의 과거 뒤에 not을 붙이고, '~하고 있지 않았다'로 해석한다.

| 주어 | 과거진행형 | 예문 |
|---|---|---|
| I / He / She / It | was + not + -ing<br>= wasn't + -ing | She wasn't sleeping at that time.<br>그때 그녀는 자고 있지 않았다. |
| We / You / They | were + not + -ing<br>= weren't + -ing | They weren't paying attention to me at the moment.<br>그들은 그 순간에 나에게 주의를 기울이고 있지 않았다. |

## 3 과거진행형의 의문문

주어의 인칭에 따라 『be동사의 과거 (Was / Were) + 주어 + -ing ~?』 의 형태이다. 대답은 Yes / No로 한다.

| 주어 | 과거진행형 | 예문 |
|---|---|---|
| I / He / She / It | Was + 주어 + -ing ~? | Was she practicing playing the violin last night?<br>그녀는 어젯밤에 바이올린 연주를 연습하고 있었니?<br>Yes, she was. / No, she, wasn't. |
| We / You / They | Were + 주어 + -ing ~? | Were you planning to move to Chicago then?<br>당신들은 그때 시카고로 이사 갈 계획을 세우고 있었나요?<br>Yes, we were. / No, we weren't. |

STEP 1

# Grammar START

Grammar on Target

1. 과거진행형 만들기
2. 과거진행형의 부정문과 의문문

## A 다음 괄호 안에서 알맞은 것을 고르시오.

1 I (am / was) drawing a picture of my dog then.

2 You (are / were) running across the street now.

3 She (is / was) stirring soup at 7 this morning.

4 They (is climbing / were climbing) a mountain at that time.

5 A man (is standing / was standing) in front of the door last night.

6 Clouds (was floating / were floating) in the sky that afternoon.

7 A girl was crying for her mother (at that time / now).

8 We were (not making / making not) a Christmas tree then.

9 Tim and Max (was having / were having) lunch together.

draw 그리다
across 건너서, 가로질러
stir 휘젓다
climb 오르다
float 떠다니다, 뜨다

## B 주어진 말을 이용하여 과거진행형의 부정문과 의문문을 완성하시오.

1 He ________ ________ ________ his homework last night. (not, do)

2 ________ my grandparents ________ at us? (smile)

3 Serena ________ ________ ________ in the library yesterday. (not, study)

4 ________ Heather and Lily ________ Spanish? (practice)

5 The man ________ ________ ________ a seatbelt at that time. (not, wear)

6 She ________ ________ ________ the house then. (not, clean)

7 ________ the witness ________ at the moment? (lie)

8 ________ they ________ down a mountain? (ski)

9 I ________ ________ ________ in a loud voice then. (not, complain)

practice 연습하다, 실행하다
seatbelt 안전벨트
wear a seatbelt 안전벨트를 매다
witness 목격자, 증인
complain 불평하다
loud 시끄러운
ski 스키를 타다

STEP 2
# Grammar PRACTICE

## A 밑줄 친 부분을 바르게 고쳐 쓰시오.

1 He was ride a bicycle. ➡ __________

2 Were Emma speaking to Noah? ➡ __________

3 The beast didn't looking in the mirror then. ➡ __________

4 Was Bella play tennis around 5 o'clock? ➡ __________

5 They not were getting on a bus then. ➡ __________

6 Were the elephants use their trunks? ➡ __________

7 She is having a great time then. ➡ __________

8 Did you watching TV at that time? ➡ __________

beast 짐승, 야수
get on ~ ~에 타다
trunk
(코끼리의) 코, 나무의 몸통

## B 주어진 단어와 우리말을 이용하여 빈칸에 알맞은 말을 쓰시오.

1 마녀가 백설공주에게 사과를 주고 있었다. (give)
➡ The witch ________ ________ an apple to Snow White.

2 우리는 어젯밤 공포 영화를 보고 있지 않았다. (watch)
➡ We ________ ________ a horror movie last night.

3 저녁식사 후에, 나는 평소와 다름없이 책을 읽고 있었다. (read)
➡ After dinner, I ________ ________ a book as usual.

4 얼룩말이 연못 근처에서 물을 마시고 있었니? (drink)
➡ ________ a zebra ________ water near a pond?

5 Mia는 거리에서 춤을 추고 있지 않았다. 그녀는 바이올린을 연주하고 있었다. (dance, play)
➡ Mia ________ ________ on the street. She ________ ________ the violin.

6 A 그때, 그들은 동시에 일어나고 있었니? (stand)
B 아니, 그렇지 않아.
➡ A At that time, ________ they ________ up at the same time?
B No, they ________.

witch 마녀
as usual 평소와 다름없이
near ~에 가까이에
pond 연못

## C 보기와 같이 다음 문장을 부정문과 의문문으로 바꿔 쓰시오.

| 보기 | Peter Pan and Wendy were flying in the sky. |
|---|---|
| | ➡ Peter Pan and Wendy weren't flying in the sky. |
| | ➡ Were Peter Pan and Wendy flying in the sky? |

1 He was going straight to his home.

➡ ______________________

➡ ______________________

2 Mom and Dad were cooking together in the kitchen.

➡ ______________________

➡ ______________________

3 I was taking a shower at that time.

➡ ______________________

➡ ______________________

4 Daniel was fighting with John at that time.

➡ ______________________

➡ ______________________

straight 똑바로, 일직선의, 곧장
go straight 직진하다, 직행하다
take a shower 샤워를 하다
fight 싸우다

## D 우리말과 같은 뜻이 되도록 주어진 단어를 바르게 배열하시오. 단, 필요에 따라 동사를 변형시켜 쓰시오.

1 나는 그때 설거지를 하고 있었다. (the dishes, I, wash, then, was)

➡ ______________________

2 소녀들은 친구들에게 손을 흔들고 있었니? (to their friends, were, the girls, wave)

➡ ______________________

3 우리는 그때 강에서 수영하고 있지 않았다.
(swim, at that time, we, in the river, weren't)

➡ ______________________

4 큰 개가 아이들을 향해서 짖고 있었니? (at the children, the big dog, bark, was)

➡ ______________________

wash the dishes 설거지를 하다
wave 흔들다
river 강
bark 짖다

STEP 3

# Upgrade TEST

**1 다음 중 어법상 어색한 문장을 고르시오.**

① Is Jack doing the dishes now?
② What were you doing at that time?
③ Shawn was playing the guitar at that time.
④ He wasn't cleaning his room before sunset.
⑤ Julie and her husband was decorating their house then.

**2 빈칸에 들어갈 알맞은 것을 고르시오.**

A What were you doing then?
B I ________ my homework.

① do ② did
③ am doing ④ was doing
⑤ were doing

**3 다음 질문의 대답으로 알맞은 것을 고르시오.**

Were they paying attention to my speech?

① Yes, they didn't. ② No, they did.
③ Yes, they were. ④ Yes, they weren't
⑤ No, they were.

**4 다음 대답에 대한 질문으로 알맞은 것을 고르시오.**

Yes, she was.

① Does she read books now?
② Did Sarah go to school yesterday?
③ Is Katie playing the violin now?
④ Was Nicole cooking at around 7?
⑤ Were you and Betty having a great time there?

**[5-6] 다음 우리말을 영어로 바르게 옮긴 것을 고르시오.**

**5**

한 달 전에 너희들은 캐나다의 해안가를 여행하고 있었니?

① Did you travel along the Canadian coast a month ago?
② Are you traveling along the Canadian coast a month ago?
③ Was you traveling along the Canadian coast a month ago?
④ Were you traveling along the Canadian coast a month ago?
⑤ Have you been traveling along the Canadian coast?

**6**

우리가 그 건물을 떠났을 때 비가 오고 있었다.

① It was raining when we left the building.
② It rained when we were leaving the building.
③ We left the building when it rained.
④ It had been raining after we left the building
⑤ It has been raining when we left the building.

**7 다음 중 어법상 올바른 문장을 고르시오.**

① We are swimming in the pool then.
② She were making the sculpture at that time.
③ Brad was going to visit us in London tomorrow.
④ Susan and her sister was traveling around the world.
⑤ Cindy and I were wondering if you could help us.

sunset 일몰, 해넘이 decorate 장식하다 travel 여행하다 coast 해안 when ~ ~할 때 sculpture 조각 wonder 궁금해하다

**8** 다음 문장의 주어를 대명사로 바꾸고 부정문으로 알맞게 바꾼 것을 고르시오.

| Megan and I were sleeping then. |
|---|

① She wasn't sleeping then.
② I wasn't sleeping then.
③ They weren't sleeping then.
④ We weren't sleeping then.
⑤ She and I wasn't sleeping then.

**9** 다음 우리말을 영어로 바르게 옮긴 것을 고르시오.

| Garry는 공항에서 혼잣말을 하고 있었다. |
|---|

① Garry talks to himself at the airport.
② Garry talked to himself at the airport.
③ Garry is talking to himself at the airport.
④ Garry was talking to himself at the airport.
⑤ Garry were talking to himself at the airport.

**10** 다음 대답의 질문으로 알맞은 것을 고르시오.

| No, she wasn't. She was drawing a picture. |
|---|

① Was Sophie a singer at that time?
② Did Brian read a magazine?
③ Is John doing the dishes?
④ Does Jane clean her room?
⑤ Was Katherine watching a movie?

**11** 다음 중 어법상 어색한 문장을 고르시오.

① We were practicing playing the piano then.
② I was doing my chores at home at that time.
③ It was snowing when we went out last night.
④ They were having a sports car two years ago.
⑤ Mary was listening to a lecture this morning.

## [12-15] 서술형 주관식

**12** 어법상 어색한 부분을 찾아 바르게 고쳐 쓰시오.

| I am doing my homework two hour ago. |
|---|

_______________ → _______________

**[13-14]** 주어진 단어를 이용하여 다음 우리말을 영어로 쓰시오.

**13**

| 그녀는 한동안 감기로 시달리고 있었다.<br>(suffer from, a cold, for a while) |
|---|

→ _______________________________

**14**

| 그는 어젯밤에 빨간 양말을 찾고 있었니?<br>(look for, red socks, last night) |
|---|

→ _______________________________

**15** 다음 문장을 과거진행형의 부정문으로 바꾸시오.

| You didn't plan to move to Chicago then. |
|---|

→ _______________________________

talk to oneself 혼잣말하다 lecture 강의 chore 허드렛일, 잡일 practice 연습하다 suffer from ~ ~으로 고통 받다 cold 감기 look for ~ ~를 찾다

기초 탄탄 1
GRAMMAR

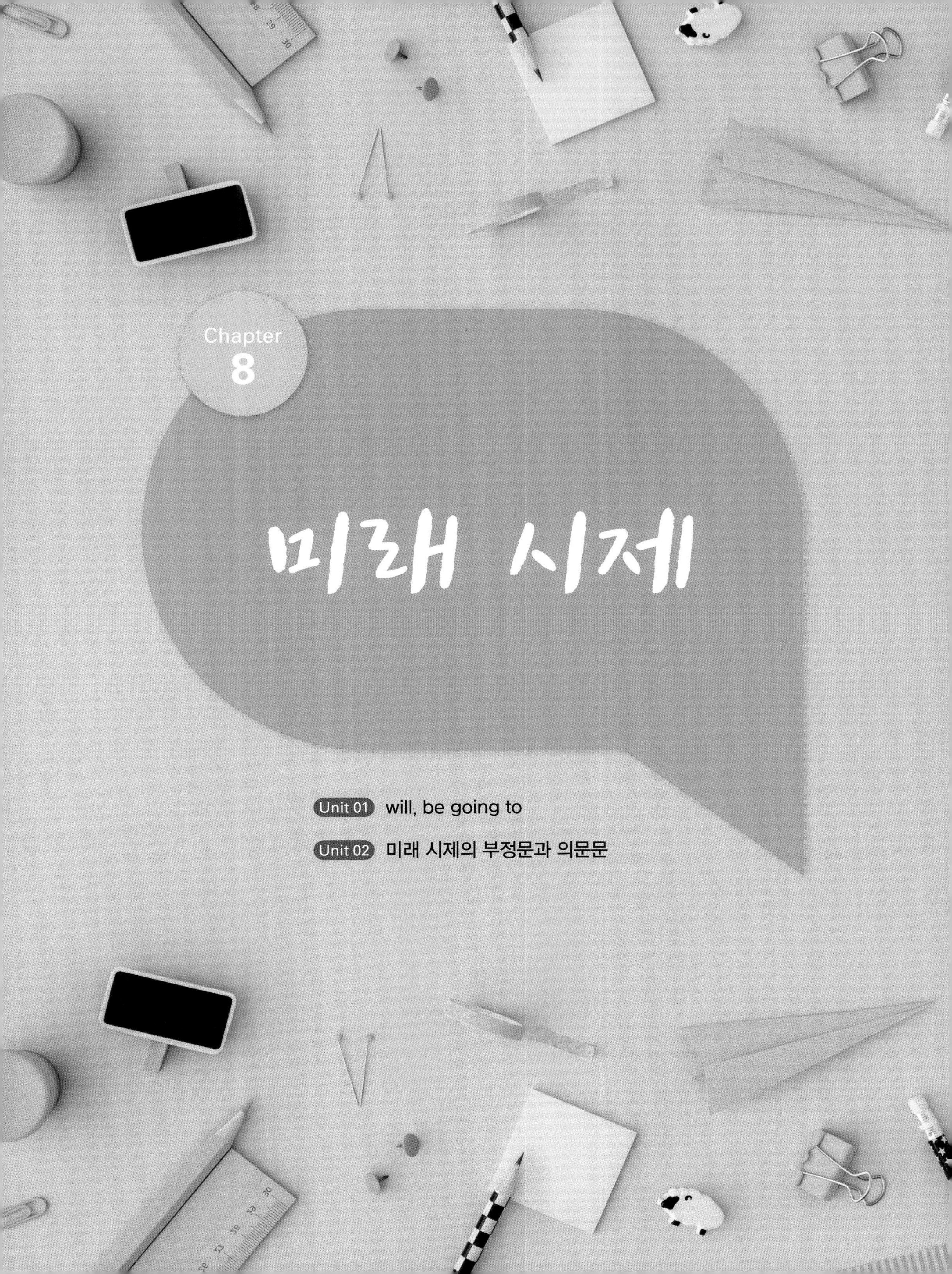

Chapter 8

# 미래 시제

Unit 01

# will, be going to

## 1 will

단순한 미래에 대한 추측, 순간적인 화자의 결정이나 의지를 나타낼 때 『will + 동사원형』을 사용하며 '~일 것이다' 또는 '~할 것이다'로 해석한다. 주로 미래를 나타내는 tomorrow, soon, next time, later 등과 함께 쓰인다.

| | 상태 | 동작 |
|---|---|---|
| 과거 | It was sunny yesterday. 어제는 날씨가 맑았다. | I ate lunch then. 나는 그때 점심을 먹었다. |
| 현재 | It is sunny today. 오늘은 날씨가 맑다. | I eat lunch now. 나는 지금 점심을 먹는다. |
| 미래 | It will be sunny tomorrow. 내일은 날씨가 맑을 것이다. | I will eat lunch soon. 나는 곧 점심을 먹을 것이다. |

**Tip**

대명사가 주어인 경우 『대명사 + will』을 I'll, You'll, He'll, She'll, It'll, We'll, They'll과 같이 줄여서 쓸 수 있다.
He'll be a great scientist. 그는 훌륭한 과학자가 될 것이다.

## 2 be going to

be going to도 미래에 대한 추측을 나타낼 때 사용되지만, 말하는 순간에 화자의 결정이나 의지를 나타내는 will과 달리, be going to는 미리 계획된 미래의 일정을 나타낼 때 사용된다. 주어의 인칭에 따라 『be동사 + going to + 동사원형』의 형태이며 '~할 예정이다' 또는 '~할 것이다'로 해석한다.

| | 상태 | 동작 |
|---|---|---|
| 의미 | 미래에 대한 추측<br>(화자의 의지에 의해 순간적으로 결정된 일을)<br>~할 것이다 | 미래에 대한 추측<br>(이미 계획된 대로 혹은 예정된 대로)<br>~할 것이다 |
| 형태 | will + 동사원형 | be동사 + going to + 동사원형 |
| 예문 | I will show you my new cellphone.<br>내 새 휴대폰을 보여줄게. | I am going to move to New York.<br>나는 뉴욕으로 이사를 갈 거야. |

**Tip**

주어와 be동사는 I'm, You're, He's, She's, It's, We're, They're과 같이 줄여서 쓸 수 있다.
She's going to travel to Africa. 그녀는 아프리카로 여행을 갈 것이다.

STEP 1

# Grammar START

Grammar on Target

1. 미래 시제의 두 가지 형태
2. 과거, 현재, 미래 시제의 구분

## A 다음 괄호 안에서 알맞은 것을 고르시오.

1 Everything (is / are / am) going to be all right.

2 I (make / made / will make) dinner for you tomorrow.

3 Jennifer is (go to / to go / going to) play the violin after Eric.

4 They (will / be going / are going) to travel to Paris this summer.

5 It (is / will / will be) rainy next Monday.

6 Mia (will be / will is / is going to) there soon.

7 Andy and I are going to meet (at the moment / last year / next weekend).

8 He (breaks / broke / will break) the world record next year.

9 She's going (watch / watches / to watch) the movie *Mamma Mia* tonight.

everything 모든 것, 모두
travel 여행하다
break 깨다, 부수다
world record 세계기록

## B 주어진 말을 이용하여 미래 시제로 문장을 완성하시오.

1 He ________ ________ a special party. (plan)

2 We are ________ to ________ camping this weekend. (go camping)

3 I ________ ________ for Olivia at the library. (wait)

4 She ________ ________ to ________ a new computer next month. (buy)

5 They ________ ________ at home this Christmas. (stay)

6 You're ________ to be very ________ this year. (lucky)

7 Jason and I ________ ________ to ________ badminton on Saturdays. (play)

8 My family ________ ________ to ________ out every weekend. (eat out)

9 Kelly ________ ________ off the television in an hour. (turn off)

special 특별한
plan 계획하다
stay 머무르다, 그대로 있다
lucky 운이 좋은, 행운의
badminton 배드민턴
eat out 외식하다
turn off 끄다

STEP 2
# Grammar PRACTICE

## A 밑줄 친 부분을 바르게 고쳐 쓰시오.

1 My aunt are going to move to Toronto. ➡ ______

2 James will to clean his room today. ➡ ______

3 You and I will playing basketball tomorrow. ➡ ______

4 It is go to be sunny tomorrow. ➡ ______

5 We go will camping on Saturday. ➡ ______

6 I be going to go to the museum. ➡ ______

7 She is to going cook chicken soup. ➡ ______

8 He will is here for the game tomorrow. ➡ ______

9 Leo and I will be eat lunch together. ➡ ______

go camping 캠핑을 가다
chicken soup 닭고기 수프

## B 주어진 우리말을 이용하여 빈칸에 알맞은 말을 쓰시오.

1 내 남동생은 야구 선수가 될 것이다.
➡ My brother ______ ______ a baseball player.

2 나는 매주 수요일에 수영하러 갈 것이다.
➡ I ______ ______ to ______ for a swim every Wednesday.

3 그녀는 백화점에 쇼핑을 갈 것이다.
➡ She ______ ______ shopping at the department store.

4 나는 주말마다 많은 종류의 책을 읽을 것이다.
➡ I'm ______ to ______ many kinds of books on weekends.

5 Ethan은 그의 실수에 대해 그녀에게 사과할 것이다.
➡ Ethan ______ ______ for his mistake to her.

6 Tom Cruise는 6시에 서울에 도착할 것이다.
➡ Tom Cruise ______ ______ to ______ in Seoul at 6 o'clock.

go for a swim 수영하러 가다
go shopping 쇼핑을 가다
department store 백화점
apologize 사과하다
arrive 도착하다

## C 다음 문장을 will 또는 be going to를 이용하여 미래 시제로 쓰시오.

1 He starts to learn Spanish today.

will ➡ ______________________

2 I leave for Australia on Sunday.

be going to ➡ ______________________

3 Andrea was very tired this weekend.

will ➡ ______________________

4 We visit our grandparents on Saturday.

be going to ➡ ______________________

5 You and she went to bed at 9 o'clock.

will ➡ ______________________

6 The sun comes out every day.

be going to ➡ ______________________

7 They shouted, "Happy new year!" at midnight.

will ➡ ______________________

8 My dad rides a bicycle at the park.

be going to ➡ ______________________

Spanish 스페인어, 스페인의
go to bed 자다
come out 나오다
shout 외치다, 소리치다
midnight 자정, 밤 12시

## D 우리말과 같은 뜻이 되도록 주어진 단어를 바르게 배열하시오.

1 Amy는 내년에 열네 살이 될 것이다. (be, next year, will, Amy, fourteen years old)

➡ ______________________

2 오늘 날씨는 맑을 것이다. (to, is, going, today, it, be, sunny)

➡ ______________________

3 나는 점심으로 샌드위치를 먹을 것이다. (will, a sandwich, have, I, for lunch)

➡ ______________________

4 그녀는 방과 후에 피아노를 칠 것이다. (going, play the piano, is, she, after school, to)

➡ ______________________

STEP 3
# Upgrade TEST

**1** 빈칸에 들어갈 수 없는 것을 고르시오.

Britney will move to Spain ________.

① tomorrow ② in December
③ this evening ④ last night
⑤ next year

**2** 빈칸에 들어갈 말이 바르게 짝지어진 것을고르시오.

The students ________ plant trees this Arbor Day.
= They ________ to plant trees this Arbor Day.

① will, is going ② will, are going
③ is going to, will ④ are going to, will
⑤ was going to, will

**3** 밑줄 친 말과 바꿔 쓸 수 있는 것을 고르시오.

We are going to visit the orphanage every Saturday.

① will ② might ③ can
④ ought to ⑤ are able to

**4** 빈칸에 들어갈 알맞은 것을 고르시오.

A What are you going to do on the weekend?
B I ________ soccer with my friends.

① played ② was playing
③ am playing ④ will going to
⑤ am going to play

**5** 밑줄 친 부분의 쓰임이 나머지와 다른 것을고르시오.

① Steve is going to meet Sandra.
② Are you going to school?
③ Ann is going to the dentist.
④ I am going to the Seoul Art Center.
⑤ They are going to the movies.

**6** 밑줄 친 부분이 바르지 못한 것을 고르시오.

① Kevin will beat you in the game.
② We're go skiing tomorrow.
③ I'm going to play badminton this evening.
④ Samuel is going to visit you tonight.
⑤ They're going to go to the concert this Saturday.

**7** 다음 중 어법상 올바른 문장을 고르시오.

① Will she plays the violin at the concert?
② Ryan is going to watches a movie.
③ I will not am in Korea this Friday.
④ They are going to attacked the enemy to the last moment.
⑤ You're going to have a great time at the amusement park tomorrow.

**8** 밑줄 친 부분 중 어법상 어색한 것을 고르시오.

Dominic and I ① are ② going ③ to ④ plays online games ⑤ tonight.

plant 심다 Arbor 수목, 나무 Arbor Day 식목일 orphanage 고아원 badminton 배드민턴 attack 공격하다 enemy 적, 장애물 amusement park 놀이공원

**9** 다음 중 어법상 어색한 문장을 고르시오.

① Emily will go to Canada next year.
② Thomas is going to buy a new yacht.
③ We are going to participate in the contest last month.
④ They are going to study math in the evening.
⑤ She is going to hold a party tomorrow.

**10** 다음 우리말을 영어로 바르게 옮긴 것을 고르시오.

| Simpson 부인은 이번 여름에 가족과 함께 바하마로 여행을 갈 예정이다. |
|---|

① Mrs. Simpson will travels to the Bahamas with her family this summer.
② Mrs. Simpson be going to travel to the Bahamas with her family this summer.
③ Mrs. Simpson are going to travel to the Bahamas with her family this summer.
④ Mrs. Simpson will be going to travel to the Bahamas with her family this summer.
⑤ Mrs. Simpson is going to travel to the Bahamas with her family this summer.

**11** 다음 중 어법상 어색한 문장을 고르시오.

① He will doing the chores this Saturday.
② You will meet him soon.
③ She will take a trip to Europe.
④ She is going to go to Las Vegas next Monday.
⑤ Mr. Gibson will not complete his project by tomorrow.

## [12-15] 서술형 주관식

**[12-13]** 다음 우리말을 영어로 옮길 때 빈칸에 알맞은 말을 쓰시오.

**12**

David는 다음 달이면 열다섯 살이 될 것이다.

→ David ________ ________ fifteen years old next month.

**13**

나는 아내의 생일을 위해 깜짝 파티를 열 예정이다.

→ I ________ ________ ________ have a surprise party for my wife on her birthday.

**14** 어법상 어색한 부분을 찾아 바르게 고쳐 쓰시오.

| Many incredible things will be going to happen in the near future. Mike and I are going to be astronauts. |
|---|

________ → ________

**15** 주어진 단어를 이용하여 다음 우리말을 영어로 쓰시오.

네가 집에 도착하면 저녁이 준비되어 있을 것이다.

(dinner, ready)

→ ______________________________ when you come home.

take a trip 여행을 가다 complete 완료하다 project 프로젝트, 과제 incredible 놀랄 만한, 믿을 수 없는 astronaut 우주비행사 ready 준비된

Unit 02

# 미래 시제의 부정문과 의문문

## 1 미래 시제의 부정문

미래 시제의 부정문은 will 뒤에 not을 붙이거나, be동사 뒤에 not을 붙이며 다음과 같은 형태로 줄여서 쓸 수 있다.

| | will | be going to |
|---|---|---|
| 부정형 | will + not + 동사원형 = won't + 동사원형 | be동사 + not + going to + 동사원형 |
| 예문 | It will not snow tonight.<br>= It won't snow tonight.<br>오늘 밤에는 눈이 오지 않을 것이다.<br>She will not take the offer.<br>= She won't take the offer.<br>그녀는 그 제안을 받아들이지 않을 것이다. | I am not going to take the offer.<br>= I'm not going to take the offer.<br>나는 그 제안을 받아들이지 않을 예정이다.<br>They are not going to have a party tonight.<br>= They're not going to have a party tonight.<br>그들은 오늘 파티를 열지 않을 예정이다. |

**Tip**

미래 시제와 자주 쓰이는 부사에는 'soon 곧, tomorrow 내일, later 나중에, next time 다음에' 등이 있다.

## 2 미래 시제의 의문문

미래 시제의 의문문은 『Will + 주어 + 동사원형?』이나, 주어의 인칭에 따라 『Am / Are / Is + 주어 + going to + 동사원형?』의 형태이다. 각 질문의 유형에 따라 긍정과 부정의 대답은 다음과 같다.

| | will | be going to |
|---|---|---|
| 의문형 | Will + 주어 + 동사원형? | Am / Are / Is + 주어 + going to + 동사원형? |
| 예문 | Will you go there alone?<br>넌 혼자 거기에 갈 거니?<br>Yes, I will. 응, 그래.<br>No, I won't. 아니, 그렇지 않아.<br>Will he play computer games?<br>그는 컴퓨터 게임을 할 거니?<br>Yes, he will. 응, 그래.<br>No, he won't. 아니, 그렇지 않아 | Are you going to participate in the audition?<br>너는 그 오디션에 참가할 예정이니?<br>Yes, I am. 응, 그래.<br>No, I am not. 아니, 그렇지 않아.<br>Is she going to appear on *The Tonight Show*?<br>그녀는 오늘 *The Tonight Show*에 출연할 예정이니?<br>Yes, she is. 응, 맞아.<br>No, she isn't. 아니, 그렇지 않아. |

**Tip**

말하는 시점에 따라 과거, 현재, 미래 등 다양한 시제와 함께 쓸 수 있는 어구가 있다.
→ today, every day, tonight, this morning, on Saturday

I played baseball today. 나는 오늘 야구를 했다.
The supermarket opens today. 슈퍼마켓은 오늘 문을 연다.
He will have a sandwich today. 그는 오늘 샌드위치를 먹을 것이다.

STEP 1

# Grammar START

**Grammar on Target**

1. 미래 시제의 부정형의 두 가지 형태
2. 미래 시제의 의문문 만들기

## A 다음 문장에서 알맞은 것을 고르시오.

1 I am (going not / not going) to be at home today.

2 You won't (show / to show / showed) me your album.

3 He (not is / is not / will) going to run away from the enemy.

4 We (don't / didn't / won't) go to the party tomorrow.

5 Emily (will not / not will / be going to) drink water after dinner.

6 Your sister won't (to get up / get up / gets up) at 7 o'clock this morning.

7 She's not going to move to Boston (last week / next month / yesterday).

8 Jeremy won't (turn down / to turn down / turns down) the volume.

9 They're not going (talk / to talk / talking) to me anymore.

show 보여주다
run away 도망치다
enemy 적, 적군
volume 볼륨(음량)
anymore 이제는 더이상

## B 다음 문장을 의문문으로 바꿀 때, 빈칸에 들어갈 알맞은 말을 쓰시오.

1 You will send her flowers today.
➡ ________ ________ send her flowers today?

2 She is going to have a date with him.
➡ ________ ________ ________ to have a date with him?

3 Michael will wear blue jeans today.
➡ ________ ________ ________ blue jeans today?

4 We are going to study in the library on Thursday.
➡ ________ we ________ to ________ in the library on Thursday?

5 Noah is going to accept her apology in five minutes.
➡ ________ ________ ________ to ________ her apology in five minutes?

have a date with ~ ~와 데이트를 하다
accept 받아주다, 수락하다
apology 사과, 변명

STEP 2

# Grammar PRACTICE

## A 주어진 단어를 이용하여 미래 시제의 부정문을 완성하시오.

1 I ________ ________ ________ your secret to anyone. (tell)

2 Emily ________ ________ ________ to ________ late at night for her health. (eat)

3 We ________ ________ going to ________ ________ alone at night. (go out)

4 My little brothers ________ ________ ________ noise in the library. (make)

5 He's ________ ________ to ________ ________ next week. (busy)

6 They ________ ________ to New Zealand this weekend. (fly)

7 Amanda and Isabel ________ ________ ________ to ________ to music. (listen)

8 My dog ________ ________ the children in the park. (bite)

9 She'll ________ ________ me to her birthday party. (invite)

10 Brandon ________ ________ ________ climbing a tree. (give up)

anyone 아무도, 누구도 (부정문에서)
fly to ~ 비행기로 ~에 가다
make noise 떠들다, 소란을 피우다
give up 포기하다
bite 물다
invite 초대하다

## B 주어진 단어를 이용하여 미래 시제의 의문문을 완성하시오. (축약형으로)

1 A Are you ________ to ________ to Europe next year? (travel)
B Yes, ________ ________. I can't wait to go.

2 A ________ he ________ his homework today? (finish)
B No, ________ ________. He'll go skiing today.

3 A ________ your sister ________ to ________ a new coat? (buy)
B Yes, ________ ________. She'll go shopping at a department store soon.

4 A ________ they going to ________ the movie *Avengers*? (watch)
B No, ________ ________. They don't like action movies.

5 A ________ you ________ a bus to go there? (take)
B No, ________ ________. I'll take the subway.

travel 여행하다
wait 기다리다
take a bus 버스를 타다

## C 밑줄 친 부분을 바르게 고쳐 문장을 다시 쓰시오.

1 It's windy. It is go to rain soon.

➡ ______

2 Be she going to play the piano at the concert?

➡ ______

3 He won't stands for your rude behavior the next time.

➡ ______

4 Are you to going drink a cup of tea?

➡ ______

5 I'm going not to go camping this summer.

➡ ______

6 Will you are at home all day long today?

➡ ______

7 They will not to make the same mistake.

➡ ______

8 Is my dad going buys a cake on his way home?

➡ ______

9 She's not go to arrive in New York at 9 o'clock.

➡ ______

stand 참다, 견디다
rude 무례한
behavior 행동
mistake 실수, 오류
on one's way home 집에 오는 도중에

## D 우리말과 같은 뜻이 되도록 주어진 단어를 바르게 배열하시오.

1 Serena는 수영 클럽에 가입할 거니? (join, Serena, to, the swimming club, going, is)

➡ ______

2 나는 게으른 학생은 되지 않을 것이다. (not, am, I, be, going, a lazy student, to)

➡ ______

3 그 아기는 오늘밤 울지 않을 것이다. (the baby, cry, not, tonight, will)

➡ ______

4 그들은 곧 너의 컴퓨터를 고칠 거니? (going, soon, they, to, your computer, fix, are)

➡ ______

join 가입하다
lazy 게으른
fix 수리하다

STEP 3
# Upgrade TEST

**1 빈칸에 들어갈 말이 바르게 짝지어진 것을 고르시오.**

> It _________ rain tonight.
> = It _________ rain tonight.

① will - is ② will - won't
③ will not - isn't ④ won't - isn't
⑤ will not - won't

**2 다음 우리말을 영어로 바르게 옮긴 것을 고르시오.**

> 너는 친구들과 영화를 보러 갈 거니?

① Will you go the movies with your friends?
② Will you goes to the movies with your friends?
③ Will you go to the movies with your friends?
④ Will you going to the movies with your friends?
⑤ Will you be going to the movies with your friends?

**3 빈칸에 들어갈 알맞은 것을 고르시오.**

> A Are you going to join the club?
> B _______________________

① Yes, I do. ② No, I don't.
③ Yes, I am. ④ No, we won't.
⑤ No, I won't be

**4 빈칸에 공통으로 들어갈 말을 고르시오.**

> A Are you _______ study in library tomorrow?
> B No, I'm not. I'm _______ buy a backpack tomorrow.

① doing to ② go to ③ go
④ going to ⑤ being to

**5 다음 중 대화가 자연스럽지 않은 것을 고르시오.**

① A Will she come here today?
B Yes, she will.
② A Will John play baseball this afternoon?
B No, he won't. He will do his homework.
③ A Are you going to take a shower?
B No, I'm going to drink some water.
④ A Are you going to visit your grandma on vacation?
B Yes, I was. I can't wait.
⑤ A Will Sharon watch the movie *Kung Fu Panda*?
B No, she won't. She doesn't like animated films.

**6 다음 우리말을 영어로 바르게 옮긴 것을 고르시오.**

> 그녀는 그 제안을 받아들이지 않을 것이다.

① She will don't take the offer.
② She will not takes the offer.
③ She isn't going taking the offer.
④ She won't take the offer.
⑤ She won't be going to take the offer.

**7 다음 대화의 빈칸에 알맞은 대답을 고르시오.**

> A Will you come over to my house to play cards?
> B _______________________

① Yes, I will. ② No, I will.
③ Yes, I am. ④ No, I am not.
⑤ Yes, I won't

take a shower 샤워를 하다 offer 제안 join 가입하다, 합류하다 club 클럽, 동호회

**8** 밑줄 친 부분 중 어법상 어색한 것을 고르시오.

Marie ① is going ② to go to Paris this summer, and she is ③ going to attend an Art School. But she ④ won't be going to learn design there. She ⑤ will be a sculptor later.

**9** 다음 중 어법상 올바른 문장을 고르시오.

① We'rent going to take a tax in this city.
② Its not going to be on the desk.
③ The mission isn't be going easy.
④ The dog won't be big and black.
⑤ He and his brother is going to visit me this weekend.

**10** 다음 우리말을 영어로 바르게 옮긴 것을 고르시오.

| 그는 아직 그곳에 도착하지 못했을 거야. |
|---|

① He isn't there yet.
② He won't be there yet.
③ He isn't going be there yet.
④ He will not going to be there yet.
⑤ He isn't going to will be there yet.

**11** 빈칸에 들어갈 말이 나머지와 다른 것을 고르시오.

① He isn't ________ do chores this afternoon.
② They aren't ________ move to Chicago.
③ The idea isn't ________ work well.
④ He and I are ________ practice dribbling after school.
⑤ She ________ be just a good pianist, but a great one.

## [12-15] 서술형 주관식

**12** 다음 질문에 부정문으로 답하시오.

| Is Nicole going to appear on *The Tonight Show*? |
|---|

→ ______________________

**13** 어법상 어색한 곳을 모두 찾아 바르게 고쳐 쓰시오.

| A Are you going to climbing the mountain this Sunday?<br>B No, I am. I'm so tired. |
|---|

1) ________ → ________
2) ________ → ________

**[14-15]** 주어진 단어를 이용하여 다음 우리말을 영어로 쓰시오.

**14**

| 그는 부모님으로부터 도움을 받지 않을 것이다.<br>(will, take help from) |
|---|

→ ______________________

**15**

| 나는 그녀의 결혼식에 가지 않을 것이다.<br>(be going to, wedding ceremony) |
|---|

→ ______________________

attend 다니다, 출석하다 sculptor 조각가 yet (부정문, 의문문에서) 아직 work 효과가 나다, 작동되다 practice 연습하다 dribble (공을) 드리블하다 wedding ceremony 결혼식

**1** 다음 중 어법상 어색한 문장을 고르시오.

① I am walking to school.
② You are prettying.
③ They are counting the bottles.
④ She is looking for a red skirt.
⑤ He is taking vitamins.

**2** 다음 우리말을 영어로 바르게 옮긴 것을 고르시오.

| 그녀는 지금 머리를 빗는 중이다. |
|---|

① She combs her hair now.
② She is combs her hair now.
③ She combing her hair now.
④ She is combing her hair now.
⑤ She is combbing her hair now.

**[3-4] 다음 중 어법상 올바른 문장을 고르시오.**

**3** ① I am making not coffee.
② She not is telling you a lie.
③ You are doing not your homework.
④ We are not going to the movie theater.
⑤ They are watching not a baseball game.

**4** ① She is preferring pizza.
② He is believing in God.
③ I am thinking about moving out.
④ This book is belonging to the library.
⑤ They are wanting you to come here.

**5** 다음 중 어법상 어색한 문장을 고르시오.

① Is he coming tonight?
② Are you eating doughnuts?
③ Are they apologizing?
④ Is she enjoy learning French?
⑤ Are we checking the list?

**6** 다음 중 과거진행형이 틀린 문장을 고르시오.

① We were not eating hamburgers.
② Was she dancing on the stage?
③ We were senting the email.
④ Were they wiping the floor?
⑤ He was wrapping the gift.

**7** 밑줄 친 부분의 쓰임이 나머지와 다른 것을 고르시오.

① I am meeting my friend tonight.
② I am getting married next month.
③ We are taking a photo of the building.
④ We are going to go to Japan next week.
⑤ He is going to attend the meeting this afternoon.

**8** 다음 중 대화가 어색한 것을 고르시오.

① A Did you wake up early?
B Yes, I did. I am going to go jogging.
② A Are you going to go shopping today?
B No, I am going to rest today.
③ A It's so hot today.
B I will turn on the air conditioner.
④ A We are waiting for 30 minutes for food.
B Don't worry. We will get it soon.
⑤ A Will you go to the soccer training camp?
B Yes, I am. I'm going to the camp.

**9** **다음 중 문장을 지시대로 바르게 고친 것을 고르시오.**

① I will be a lawyer.
부정문 → I will be not a lawyer.

② Tom will wear a red tie.
부정문 → Tom will not wear a red tie.

③ Jenny is going to buy a house.
부정문 → Jenny is going not to buy a house.

④ Sara will pay for dinner.
부정문 → Sara not will pay for dinner.

⑤ They are going to leave soon.
부정문 → They are going to not leave soon.

**10** **다음 중 문장을 지시대로 고친 것이 틀린 것을 고르시오.**

① She will be back home by 9 p.m.
의문문 → Will be she back home by 9 p.m.?

② Mom will forget to water the plants.
의문문 → Will Mom forget to water the plants?

③ Tina will return the book for me.
의문문 → Will Tina return the book for me?

④ Steven will visit Korea this May.
의문문 → Will Steven visit Korea this May?

⑤ Jack will drink milk tonight.
의문문 → Will Jack drink milk tonight?

**[11-15] 주어진 단어를 이용하여 우리말을 영어로 쓰시오.**

**11**

나는 여름 휴가를 계획 중이다.
(plan, my summer vacation)

➡ ______________________________

**12**

나 오늘 재채기를 많이 하고 있어.
감기에 걸릴 것 같아. (get a cold)

⬇

I am sneezing a lot today.
______________________________

**13**

나는 친구와 커피를 마시고 있었다. 그리고 남자친구 사진을 보았다.
(drink coffee, see, boyfriend, photo)

➡ ______________________________
______________________________

**14**

나는 오전 8시쯤 사무실에 도착할 것 같아.
(arrive, at the office, around 8 a.m.)

➡ ______________________________

**15**

나 다이어트 중이야. 운동하고 나서 닭가슴살을 먹을 거야.
(eat, some chicken breast, after exercising)

⬇

I am on a diet.
______________________________

# 불규칙 동사표

• 원형과 과거형이 같은 경우

| 동사원형 | 과거형 |
|---|---|
| cost 비용이 들다 | cost |
| cut 자르다 | cut |
| hit 치다 | hit |
| hurt 다치다 | hurt |
| let ~하게 하다 | let |
| put 놓다 | put |
| read 읽다 | read |
| set 놓다 | set |
| shut 닫다 | shut |
| spread 퍼지다 | spread |

따라 써 보세요.

| 동사원형 | 과거형 |
|---|---|
| | |
| | |
| | |
| | |
| | |
| | |
| | |
| | |
| | |
| | |

• 원형과 과거형이 다른 경우

| 동사원형 | 과거형 |
|---|---|
| become 되다 | became |
| begin 시작하다 | began |
| bite 물다 | bit |
| blow 불다 | blew |
| break 깨뜨리다 | broke |
| bring 가져오다 | brought |
| build 짓다 | built |
| buy 사다 | bought |
| catch 잡다 | caught |
| choose 선택하다 | chose |
| come 오다 | came |
| do 하다 | did |
| draw 그리다 | drew |

따라 써 보세요.

| 동사원형 | 과거형 |
|---|---|
| | |
| | |
| | |
| | |
| | |
| | |
| | |
| | |
| | |
| | |
| | |
| | |
| | |

| 동사원형 | 과거형 |
| --- | --- |
| dream 꿈꾸다 | dreamt |
| drink 마시다 | drank |
| drive 운전하다 | drove |
| eat 먹다 | ate |
| fall 떨어지다 | fell |
| feed 먹이다 | fed |
| feel 느끼다 | felt |
| fight 싸우다 | fought |
| find 발견하다 | found |
| fly 날다 | flew |
| forget 잊다 | forgot |
| get 얻다 | got |
| give 주다 | gave |
| go 가다 | went |
| grow 자라다 | grew |
| have 가지고 있다 | had |
| hear 듣다 | heard |
| hold 지니다 | held |
| keep 유지하다 | kept |
| know 알다 | knew |
| lay 놓다, 낳다 | laid |
| lead 인도하다 | led |
| leave 떠나다 | left |
| lend 빌려주다 | lent |
| lose 잃어버리다 | lost |
| make 만들다 | made |
| mean 의미하다 | meant |
| meet 만나다 | met |

| 동사원형 | 과거형 |
| --- | --- |
| | |
| | |
| | |
| | |
| | |
| | |
| | |
| | |
| | |
| | |
| | |
| | |
| | |
| | |
| | |
| | |
| | |
| | |
| | |
| | |
| | |
| | |
| | |
| | |
| | |
| | |
| | |
| | |

| 동사원형 | 과거형 |
|---|---|
| pay 지불하다 | paid |
| ride 타다 | rode |
| ring 울리다 | rang |
| rise 오르다 | rose |
| run 달리다 | ran |
| say 말하다 | said |
| see 보다 | saw |
| sell 팔다 | sold |
| send 보내다 | sent |
| shine 빛나다 | shone |
| sing 노래하다 | sang |
| sit 앉다 | sat |
| sleep 자다 | slept |
| slide 미끄러지다 | slid |
| speak 말하다 | spoke |
| spend 소비하다 | spent |
| stand 서다 | stood |
| swim 수영하다 | swam |
| take 가지고 가다 | took |
| teach 가르치다 | taught |
| tell 말하다 | told |
| think 생각하다 | thought |
| throw 던지다 | threw |
| understand 이해하다 | understood |
| wake 깨다 | woke |
| wear 입다 | wore |
| win 이기다 | won |
| write 쓰다 | wrote |

| 동사원형 | 과거형 |
|---|---|

# 기초탄탄 GRAMMAR

## Workbook

# 1

Happy House

# 기초탄탄 GRAMMAR 1

## Workbook

Happy House

# Contents

Unit 01

# 주격 인칭대명사와 be동사

## A 다음 표의 빈칸에 알맞은 말을 쓰시오.

| 주어 | be동사 | 축약형 |
|---|---|---|
| I | am | ⓒ |
| You | ⓐ | You're |
| He | is | ⓓ |
| She | is | She's |
| It | ⓑ | It's |
| We | are | We're |
| They | are | ⓔ |

## B 밑줄 친 주어를 대신하는 인칭대명사를 고르시오.

1 The girl is under the tree. (He / She)

2 My friends are in the library. (They / It)

3 Mr. Brown is a good speaker. (It / He)

4 Ms. Scott is a famous writer. (She / You)

5 He and I are twins. (They / We)

6 The airplane is at the airport. (It / She)

## C 빈칸에 알맞은 be동사를 쓰시오.

1 I __________ on the subway.

2 My dogs __________ very smart.

3 It __________ a horse.

4 We __________ at the shopping mall.

5 You __________ quiet and shy.

speaker 말하는 사람, 연설가 writer 작가 twins 쌍둥이 airport 공항 subway 지하철 quiet 조용한 shy 수줍어하는

## D 다음 문장을 줄여서 다시 쓰시오.

1 You are free after school. ➡ ____________________

2 He is friendly and popular. ➡ ____________________

3 We are the same age. ➡ ____________________

4 I am at the bus stop. ➡ ____________________

5 They are baseball players. ➡ ____________________

6 It is next to the bed. ➡ ____________________

## E 밑줄 친 부분을 바르게 고쳐 축약형으로 쓰시오.

1 My name is Jessi. You are a good swimmer. ➡ ____________

2 Kali is my cat. They are on the sofa. ➡ ____________

3 John and I are classmates this year. He is close. ➡ ____________

4 My father is an engineer. She is busy on weekends. ➡ ____________

5 Sean and Mia are at a theater. We are in line. ➡ ____________

6 Lily and you are very creative. They are great artists. ➡ ____________

## F 우리말과 같은 뜻이 되도록 주어진 단어를 바르게 배열하시오.

1 그는 용감한 군인이다. (brave, soldier, a, is, he)

➡ ______________________________

2 그들은 지금 매우 화가 나 있다. (angry, are, now, they, very)

➡ ______________________________

3 우리는 박물관 가까이에 있다. (near, are, the museum, we)

➡ ______________________________

4 너희는 정직한 학생들이다. (you, honest, are, students)

➡ ______________________________

---

after ~한 후에 next to ~ 바로 옆에 friendly 친절한 popular 인기 있는 swimmer 수영하는 사람 engineer 기술자 on weekends 주말에 theater 극장

Unit 02

# be동사의 부정문과 의문문

## A 다음 표의 빈칸에 알맞은 말을 쓰시오.

| 주어 | be동사의 부정형 | 『be동사 + not』의 축약형 | 『주어 + be동사』의 축약형 |
|---|---|---|---|
| I | am not | 없음 | ⓓ |
| You | are not | ⓐ | You're not |
| He | is not | isn't | He's not |
| She | is not | ⓑ | She's not |
| It | is not | isn't | ⓔ |
| We | are not | ⓒ | We're not |
| They | are not | aren't | ⓕ |

## B 주어진 우리말을 이용하여 빈칸에 알맞은 말을 쓰시오.

1 Baker 씨는 부자이다. 그는 가난하지 않다.
➡ Mr. Baker is rich. __________ __________ __________ poor.

2 Jessica와 나는 사촌이다. 우리는 자매가 아니다.
➡ Jessica and I are cousins. __________ __________ __________ sisters.

3 Susan은 빙벽등반을 잘한다. 그녀는 초보자가 아니다.
➡ Susan is good at climbing the ice wall. __________ __________ __________ a beginner.

4 Jack과 Hector는 숙적이다. 그들은 친한 친구가 아니다.
➡ Jack and Hector are old enemies. __________ __________ __________ close friends.

5 그 임무는 달성하기가 어렵다. 그것은 전혀 쉽지 않다.
➡ The mission is hard to accomplish. __________ __________ __________ easy at all.

6 나의 부모님은 그들의 일을 하느라 바쁘다. 그들은 지금 한가하지 않다.
➡ My parents are busy doing their work. __________ __________ __________ free now.

poor 가난한 climb 등반하다 ice wall 빙벽 beginner 초보자 old enemy 숙적, 오래된 적 mission 임무, 사명 accomplish 성취하다 be busy -ing ~하느라 바쁘다 free 한가한

Chapter 1

## C 다음 문장을 부정문과 의문문으로 바꾸어 쓰시오.

1 It is difficult to master English in a year.

➡ ______________________________

➡ ______________________________

2 Jim is concerned about the audition.

➡ ______________________________

➡ ______________________________

3 Korea is abundant in minerals.

➡ ______________________________

➡ ______________________________

4 They are intelligent and ambitious.

➡ ______________________________

➡ ______________________________

## D 우리말과 같은 뜻이 되도록 주어진 단어를 바르게 배열하시오.

1 그는 뉴욕 출신이니? (from, is, New York, he)

➡ ______________________________

2 우리는 목이 마르지 않다. (not, we, thirsty, are)

➡ ______________________________

3 나는 호랑이가 무섭지 않다. (afraid of, I'm, tigers, not)

➡ ______________________________

4 그녀는 나에게 화가 났니? (angry, she, is, with, me)

➡ ______________________________

5 당신들은 이 프로젝트에 관심이 있습니까? (interested, you, in this project, are)

➡ ______________________________

---

difficult 어려운 master 숙달하다, 터득하다 concerned 걱정하는 audition 오디션, 심사 abundant 풍부한 mineral 광물 intelligent 영리한 ambitious 야심적인, 야망이 있는 thirsty 목이 마른 angry 화난

Unit 01
# 일반동사의 긍정문

## A 다음 표의 빈칸에 알맞은 말을 쓰시오.

| 동사원형 | 주어가 3인칭 단수 | 동사원형 | 주어가 3인칭 단수 |
|---|---|---|---|
| live | lives | jump | jumps |
| walk | walks | push | ⓓ |
| teach | teaches | go | ⓔ |
| write | writes | fly | ⓕ |
| move | ⓐ | have | ⓖ |
| carry | ⓑ | miss | misses |
| fix | ⓒ | run | runs |

## B 주어진 동사를 알맞게 바꿔 현재 시제로 문장을 완성하시오.

1 I __________ in the river. (swim)

2 The sun __________ in the east. (rise)

3 He often __________ sneakers. (wear)

4 My mom __________ flour and milk. (mix)

5 She __________ her teeth after breakfast. (brush)

6 We __________ organic food for our health. (eat)

7 Harry and I __________ at night. (study)

8 The early bird __________ the worm. (catch)

9 Mr. Robinson __________ a cup of coffee every morning. (drink)

10 Jennifer __________ a powerful voice. (have)

11 Max __________ his homework at 8 o'clock. (do)

the east 동쪽 rise 뜨다, 떠오르다 organic food 유기농 식품 early 빠른, 이른 worm 벌레 a cup of coffee 한 잔의 커피 powerful 강력한, 강렬한

## C 다음 문장의 주어를 바꿔, 동사에 유의하여 다시 쓰시오.

1 My uncle often buys us chocolate and candy.
➡ My parents ______

2 We always work as a team.
➡ Brian and Jack ______

3 Gilbert and I enjoy catching fish on weekends.
➡ Lina ______

4 The girl worries about the weather.
➡ They ______

5 Spiders make webs to trap its food.
➡ A spider ______

6 She goes to work five times a week.
➡ I ______

## D 우리말과 같은 뜻이 되도록 주어진 단어를 바르게 배열하시오. 단, 필요에 따라 동사를 변형시켜 쓰시오.

1 수업은 5시에 끝난다. (finish, the class, at 5 o'clock)
➡ ______

2 그는 불어를 아주 잘한다. (very well, speak, French, he)
➡ ______

3 아빠는 일요일마다 빨래를 하신다. (do the laundry, on Sundays, dad)
➡ ______

4 우리 할아버지는 오늘 화가 난 것처럼 보인다. (angry, today, look, my grandfather)
➡ ______

5 엄마는 식사 후에 설거지를 하신다. (the dishes, wash, mom, after meals)
➡ ______

---

buy 사다, 사주다 team 팀, 단체 worry 걱정하다 weather 날씨 web 거미줄, 직물 trap 가두다, 덫으로 잡다 week 일주일 five times 다섯 번
meal 식사, 끼니

Unit 02

# 일반동사의 부정문과 의문문

## A 주어진 동사를 알맞게 바꿔 현재 시제 부정문을 완성하시오. (축약형으로)

1 They _________ _________ a big dog. (have)

2 I _________ _________ eggplant. (eat)

3 The pasta _________ _________ good. (smell)

4 He _________ _________ English at a middle school. (teach)

5 You _________ _________ beans and nuts. (like)

6 Amy _________ _________ her clothes online. (buy)

7 We _________ _________ baseball on weekends. (play)

## B 주어진 동사를 이용하여 대화를 완성하시오.

1 A _________ he _________ spicy food? (enjoy)
B Yes, _________ _________. He's good at eating spicy food.

2 A _________ you _________ a lot of water? (drink)
B Yes, _________ _________. It's good for health.

3 A _________ it _________ in July in your country? (rain)
B Yes, _________ _________. July is the rainy season in my country.

4 A _________ Lynn and Dylan _________ happy? (seem)
B Yes, _________ _________. They love each other.

5 A _________ she _________ her room every day? (clean)
B No, _________ _________. I clean her room.

6 A _________ they _________ a school bus to school? (take)
B Yes, _________ _________. They take it at 8 o'clock.

7 A _________ Ethan _________ a sandwich every morning? (have)
B No, _________ _________. He drinks milk.

---

eat 먹다 eggplant 가지 smell 냄새가 나다 pasta 파스타 bean 콩 nut 견과 clothes 옷, 의복 rain 비가 오다 online 온라인의, 온라인으로
spicy 매운, 양념 맛이 강한 July 7월 rainy season 장마철 seem ~ ~처럼 보이다

## C 다음 괄호 안에서 알맞은 것을 고르고, 부정문과 의문문으로 바꿔 쓰시오.

1 He (work / works) from 9 a.m. to 6 p.m.

➡ ______________________________

➡ ______________________________

2 Jake and you (take / takes) a walk on weekends.

➡ ______________________________

➡ ______________________________

3 My grandma (need / needs) a person to talk with.

➡ ______________________________

➡ ______________________________

4 Cindy and Leo (remember / remembers) their first day at school.

➡ ______________________________

➡ ______________________________

## D 우리말과 같은 뜻이 되도록 주어진 단어를 이용하여 문장을 완성하시오.

1 우리 아빠는 우리 가족에게 거짓말을 하지 않으신다. (lie)

➡ My dad __________ __________ to my family.

2 너의 개는 아침마다 널 깨워주니? (wake)

➡ __________ your dog __________ you up in the morning?

3 그들은 너와 네 남동생을 아니? (know)

➡ __________ they __________ you and your brother?

4 너는 영어 실력을 향상시키고 싶니? (want, improve)

➡ __________ you __________ to __________ your English?

5 Robin과 Elin은 패스트푸드를 먹지 않는다. (eat, fast food)

➡ Robin and Elin __________ __________ __________.

---

remember 기억하다 lie 거짓말하다 wake 깨우다 improve 개선하다, 향상시키다

Unit 01

# 셀 수 있는 명사

## A 다음 표의 빈칸에 알맞은 말을 쓰시오.

| 명사의 단수 | 명사의 복수 | 명사의 단수 | 명사의 복수 |
|---|---|---|---|
| cat | cats | hero | heroes |
| kangaroo | ⓐ | bus | ⓔ |
| baby | babies | city | ⓕ |
| foot | ⓑ | leaf | leaves |
| life | ⓒ | mouse | mice |
| day | days | child | ⓖ |
| deer | ⓓ | zoo | zoos |

## B 주어진 명사를 알맞은 형태로 바꿔 문장을 완성하시오.

1 There are ten __________ in this book. (story)

2 The farmer buys three __________. (sheep)

3 Do you need two __________ to cook? (potato)

4 The five __________ go outside on a sunny day. (ox)

5 Many __________ visit Korea for the long vacation. (Chinese)

6 Santorini is famous for whitewashed houses with blue __________. (roof)

7 People camp in the __________ in the summer. (wood)

8 The two __________ are friends, and they work together. (man)

9 There are many __________ on the lake. (boat)

10 Spiders have eight __________. (leg)

11 The boy has two __________ and five loaves of bread. (fish)

farmer 농부 outside 밖, 겉 tourist 관광객 whitewashed 하얗게 칠한 lake 호수 together 함께, 같이 boat 배, 보트 loaf 빵 한 덩이

**C** **밑줄 친 부분을 바르게 고쳐 문장을 다시 쓰시오.**

1 There are two pianoes on the stage.
➡ ______________________________

2 The baby has only two tooth.
➡ ______________________________

3 They see kangarooes and monkeies at the zoo.
➡ ______________________________

4 A lot of goose are in the pond.
➡ ______________________________

5 There are many wolfs in the wood.
➡ ______________________________

6 My grandma needs a new pairs of glasses.
➡ ______________________________

**D** **우리말과 같은 뜻이 되도록 주어진 단어를 바르게 배열하시오. 단, 필요에 따라 단어를 변형시켜 쓰시오.**

1 생쥐들이 도망가기 시작한다. (to, begin, the mouse, run away)
➡ ______________________________

2 그 여자들은 양말 세 켤레가 필요하다. (a pair of, need, the woman, socks)
➡ ______________________________

3 아이들은 우리의 미래이고 희망이다. (and, future, are, hope, child, our)
➡ ______________________________

4 기차 안에 사람들이 많다. (person, on the train, a lot of, there are)
➡ ______________________________

5 신사 숙녀 여러분, 조용히 해주시기 바랍니다. (be quiet, lady and gentleman, please)
➡ ______________________________

---

pond 연못 run away 달아나다 future 미래 hope 희망 gentleman 신사 person 개인, 사람

Unit 02

# 셀 수 없는 명사

## A 보기에서 알맞은 말을 골라 빈칸에 쓰시오.

| 보기 | information | orange juice | cheese | cup of | loaves of | bags of |
|---|---|---|---|---|---|---|

1 The bakery uses four __________ __________ flour a week.

2 One bottle of __________ __________ is in the plastic bag.

3 Does he have three __________ __________ fresh bread?

4 She puts five slices of __________ on the plate.

5 The book has a lot of useful __________.

6 He has some cookies with a __________ __________ tea every afternoon.

## B 주어진 우리말을 이용하여 빈칸에 알맞은 말을 쓰시오.

1 그녀는 파란 눈에 긴 금발 머리이다.
➡ She has blue eyes and long blond __________.

2 그 아이들은 한 달에 쌀 한 자루가 필요하다.
➡ The children need a __________ of __________ a month.

3 우리는 일주일에 시리얼 두 상자를 먹는다.
➡ We eat two __________ of cereal a week.

4 Kimberly는 점심으로 콜라 한 잔과 피자 두 조각을 먹는다.
➡ Kimberly has a __________ of coke and two __________ of pizza for lunch.

5 Smith 씨는 언제나 우리에게 숙제를 많이 내주신다.
➡ Mr. Smith always gives us a lot of __________.

6 나는 컴퓨터를 살만큼 많은 돈을 가지고 있지 않다.
➡ I don't have much __________ to buy a computer.

bakery 제과점 flour 밀가루 plastic bag 비닐 봉지 fresh 신선한 plate 접시, 그릇 afternoon 오후 rice 쌀

## C 틀린 부분을 바르게 고쳐 문장을 다시 쓰시오.

1 Her parents live in a Seoul.
➡ ______________________________

2 She needs a pair of scissor.
➡ ______________________________

3 Robin sends olivia a present for her birthday.
➡ ______________________________

4 There are two pieces of sugars on the table.
➡ ______________________________

5 An air is essential to human life.
➡ ______________________________

6 I want some breads and a sheet of milk.
➡ ______________________________

Chapter 3

## D 우리말과 같은 뜻이 되도록 주어진 단어를 바르게 배열하시오. 단, 필요에 따라 형태를 변형시켜 쓰시오.

1 그는 거기에 소금을 약간 넣고 싶어한다. (some, add, to it, salt)
➡ He wants to ______________________________

2 나는 색종이 일곱 장과 가위가 필요하다. (scissors, colored paper, seven, and, a sheet of)
➡ I need ______________________________

3 그 개는 입에 고기 한 덩어리를 물고 있다. (meat, in his mouth, a piece of)
➡ The dog holds ______________________________

4 그녀는 파티를 위해 열두 잔의 와인을 준비한다. (a glass of, for the party, wine, twelve)
➡ She prepares ______________________________

5 선인장은 줄기 안에 많은 물을 저장한다. (its stem, water, a lot of, inside)
➡ A cactus stores ______________________________

air 공기 essential 중요한, 필수적인 human 인간의, 인류의 life 생명, 삶 prepare 준비하다 cactus 선인장 store 저장하다, 보관하다
inside ~ ~ 안에 stem 줄기 its 그것의

Unit 01

# 인칭대명사와 재귀대명사

## A 다음 표의 빈칸에 알맞은 말을 쓰시오.

| 수 | 인칭 | 인칭대명사 | | | 소유대명사 (~의 것) | 재귀대명사 (~ 자신) |
|---|---|---|---|---|---|---|
| | | 주격 (~은/는/이/가) | 소유격 (~의) | 목적격 (~을/를) | | |
| 단수 | 1 | I | my | ⓑ | mine | myself |
| | 2 | You | your | you | ⓓ | yourself |
| | 3 | He<br>She<br>It | his<br>her<br>its | him<br>ⓒ<br>it | his<br>hers<br>- | ⓕ<br>herself<br>itself |
| 복수 | 1 | We | ⓐ | us | ours | ourselves |
| | 2 | You | your | you | yours | yourselves |
| | 3 | They | their | them | ⓔ | themselves |

## B 주어진 대명사를 알맞은 형태로 바꿔 문장을 완성하시오.

1 I don't know __________ at all. (he)

2 I __________ clean my room every day. (I)

3 Does he buy __________ new computer? (he)

4 Is that __________ family in the picture? (you)

5 Look at the flowers. I love __________ so much. (they)

6 She introduces __________ to them. (she)

7 The movie is not boring. __________ is exciting. (it)

8 We try to understand __________. (we)

9 Heather and Jake don't lie to __________ parents. (they)

10 The watch is not __________, but it is __________. (she, he)

11 __________ wife is a cook. __________ name is Jessica. (he, she)

at all (부정문에서) 전혀 picture 사진, 그림 boring 지루한 exciting 신나는, 흥미진진한 understand 이해하다 lie 거짓말하다 watch 손목시계 wife 아내 cook 요리사

## C 밑줄 친 부분을 바르게 고쳐 문장을 다시 쓰시오.

1 Is the blue dress <u>your</u>?
➡ ______________________________

2 Do you remember <u>theirs</u> names?
➡ ______________________________

3 An elephant has a long nose. <u>It's</u> ears are large.
➡ ______________________________

4 Emma meets <u>his</u> at church every Sunday.
➡ ______________________________

5 My backpack is big, but <u>her</u> is bigger.
➡ ______________________________

6 After school, Daniel and I play basketball. <u>Our</u> are good at <u>them</u>.
➡ ______________________________

Chapter 4

## D 우리말과 같은 뜻이 되도록, 주어진 단어를 이용하여 문장을 완성하시오.

1 우리 아빠는 나에게 과학을 가르쳐 주신다. (science)
➡ My dad ________ ________ ________.

2 그는 모든 파티에서 즐거운 시간을 보낸다. (enjoy)
➡ He ________ ________ at every party.

3 이 책은 너의 것이다. Sam의 것은 책상 위에 있다. (on the desk)
➡ This book is ________. ________ ________ ________ ________ ________.

4 그녀는 매우 지쳐 보인다. 그녀는 그의 도움이 필요하다. (tired, help)
➡ She looks very ________. She ________ ________ ________.

5 그들은 정직하다. 그래서 우리는 그들을 믿는다. (honest, trust)
➡ They are ________, so ________ ________ ________.

---

remember 기억하다 large 큰 church 교회 backpack 배낭 (등에 메는 가방) bigger 더 큰 (big의 비교급) basketball 농구 honest 정직한 trust 믿다, 신뢰하다

Unit 02

# 지시대명사와 부정대명사

## A 보기에서 알맞은 말을 골라 빈칸에 쓰시오.

| 보기 | this | those | ones | cake | one | it | cats | he |
|---|---|---|---|---|---|---|---|---|

1 These __________ are so cute.

2 __________ are my mother's necklaces.

3 Is __________ your brother's camera?

4 That __________ is very delicious.

5 My shoes are too old. I want new __________.

6 Look at that dog. __________ looks very dangerous.

7 This is Chris. __________ is my best friend.

8 He likes his white shirt. He wants to buy the same __________.

## B 다음 문장에서 알맞은 것을 고르시오.

1 Can you show me (other / another) scarf?

2 One is science fiction, and (the other / others) is comedy.

3 Is (that / those) a giraffe? (It / They) has a long neck.

4 (These / Some) are their caps. Those are yours.

5 I put a red pencil in my pencil case, but I can't find (one / it).

6 I have four sisters. One has brown hair, and (others / the others) have blond hair.

7 One is green, another is pink, and (other / the other) is blue.

8 (Those / Some) are strawberries, and the others are oranges.

9 There are two muffins. (One / Some) is mine, and (another / the other) is Emma's.

---

necklace 목걸이 delicious 맛있는 old 낡은, 오래된 dangerous 위험한 science fiction (영화, 소설) 공상 과학 comedy 코미디 giraffe 기린 neck 목 cap 모자 strawberry 딸기 muffin 머핀

## C 우리말과 같은 뜻이 되도록 주어진 단어를 이용하여 문장을 완성하시오.

1 나는 이 꽃들을 사고, 그녀는 저 꽃들을 산다. (buy, flower)
➡ I buy _________ _________, and she _________ _________ _________.

2 한 명은 의사이고, 나머지 한 명은 간호사이다. (doctor, nurse)
➡ _________ is a _________ , and _________ _________ _________ _________ _________.

3 어떤 사람들은 커피를 좋아하고, 다른 사람들은 차를 좋아한다. (coffee, tea)
➡ _________ _________ _________, _________ _________ _________.

4 한 명은 독일인이고, 나머지는 전부 이탈리아인들이다. (Italian)
➡ _________ is German, and _________ _________ _________ _________.

5 저 여자들은 배우들이다. 그들은 아름답다. (woman, actress)
➡ _________ _________ are _________. _________ are beautiful.

6 하나는 개, 다른 하나는 고양이, 나머지 하나는 햄스터이다. (hamster)
➡ One is a dog, _________ is a cat, and _________ _________ _________ _________ _________.



## D 우리말과 같은 뜻이 되도록 주어진 단어를 바르게 배열하시오.

1 저 고양이들은 뚱뚱하다. 그들은 귀엽다. (they, those, are, cats, fat, cute, are)
➡ ______________________________________________

2 이것은 그녀의 것이 아니라, 그녀의 언니의 것이다. (is, her, hers, this, it's, but, sister's, not)
➡ ______________________________________________

3 하나는 튤립이고, 나머지 하나는 장미이다. (is, the other, a rose, and, a tulip, is, one)
➡ ______________________________________________

4 어떤 이들은 산을 좋아하고, 다른 이들은 바다를 좋아한다. (others, like, some, and, seas, mountains, like)
➡ ______________________________________________

5 하나는 Ethan의 것이고, 나머지는 전부 Olivia의 것이다. (Olivia's, is, Ethan's, one, the others, are, and)
➡ ______________________________________________

---

nurse 간호사 tea (마시는) 차 German 독일인, 독일의 Italian 이탈리아인, 이탈리아의 actress 여배우 hamster 햄스터 tulip 튤립 rose 장미 mountain 산 sea 바다

Unit 01

# be동사의 과거 긍정문

## A 다음 문장에서 알맞은 것을 고르시오.

1 My jeans (is / was / were) in the closet two days ago.

2 Last Sunday, my dad and I (am / was / were) at the stadium.

3 You (are / was / were) an elementary school student last year.

4 Sandra (is / was / were) sick with a cold yesterday.

5 We (are / was / were) friends a week ago, but now we are not.

6 Andy and Paul (are / was / were) on the playground 10 minutes ago.

7 Today, the weather (is / are / were) sunny, but yesterday it (is / was / were) rainy.

8 I (am / was / were) in Canada 2 years ago, and now I (am / was / were) here.

9 People (are / was / were) happy a while ago, but they (are / was / were) sad now.

## B 빈칸에 알맞은 be동사를 쓰시오.

1 Yesterday __________ Sunday. Today __________ Monday.

2 The clothes __________ wet last night. They __________ dry now.

3 Last week, he __________ very busy. Now, he __________ free.

4 My hair __________ curly at that time, but now it __________ straight.

5 The cookies __________ soft two hours ago, but they __________ hard now.

6 Jessica __________ lazy last year, but she __________ diligent this year.

7 Those balloons __________ so tiny 2 minutes ago. They __________ giant now.

8 My puppy __________ light a month ago, but it __________ heavy now.

9 It __________ dark 5 minutes ago, but now it __________ bright.

10 The shoes __________ clean yesterday, but they __________ too dirty now.

11 Alice __________ poor at English last year, but this year she __________ good at English.

---

closet 벽장 stadium 경기장 elementary school 초등학교 a while ago 조금 전에 wet 젖은 dry 마른, 건조한 curly 곱슬곱슬한 straight 곧은, 일직선의 soft 부드러운 hard 단단한 diligent 부지런한 light 가벼운 heavy 무거운 dark 어두운 bright 밝은

## C 밑줄 친 부분을 바르게 고쳐 문장을 다시 쓰시오.

1 My aunt is in Singapore last month.
➡ ______________________________

2 We was at the bus stop an hour ago.
➡ ______________________________

3 The street is safe for children to play on at that time.
➡ ______________________________

4 The glasses was twenty dollars last week.
➡ ______________________________

5 Ryan were just a friend a year ago, but now he was my husband.
➡ ______________________________

6 They are at the beach last summer during vacation.
➡ ______________________________



## D 우리말과 같은 뜻이 되도록 주어진 단어를 이용하여 문장을 완성하시오.

1 우리는 지난 겨울에 토론토에 있었다. (in Toronto)
➡ ______________________________

2 그 진주 목걸이는 서랍 안에 있었다. (pearl necklace, in the drawer)
➡ ______________________________

3 오래 전에, 그 마을들은 조용하고 매우 작았다. (a long time ago, town, quiet)
➡ ______________________________

4 지난 밤에 그 창문을 열려 있었다. (open)
➡ ______________________________

5 그들은 한 시간 전에 꼭대기층에 있었다. (on the top floor)
➡ ______________________________

safe 안전한 husband 남편 beach 해변 vacation 방학 pearl necklace 진주 목걸이 drawer 서랍 a long time ago 오래 전에 open 열려 있는

Unit 02

# be동사의 과거 부정문과 의문문

## A 다음 문장을 be동사의 과거 부정문으로 완성하시오. (축약형으로)

1 They __________ in London 3 years ago.

2 I __________ surprised to see him there.

3 My grades __________ good, except for English.

4 You __________ really interested in math at that time.

5 Just a year ago, my grandpa __________ bald.

6 The shoes __________ expensive. They were cheap.

7 We __________ here on time this morning.

## B 인칭대명사와 be동사를 이용하여 대화를 완성하시오.

1 A __________ __________ shy and quiet at that time?
B Yes, he was. But now he is very confident and friendly.

2 A Was it rainy last weekend?
B No, __________ __________. It was sunny.

3 A __________ __________ the class president at school last year?
B Yes, I was. It was a hard time for me.

4 A __________ __________ Emma's best friend?
B Yes, she was. But now she is my best friend.

5 A Last vacation, were they in Long Beach, California?
B No, __________ __________. They were in New York.

6 A __________ __________ in the same class last year?
B No, we weren't. But she and I are in the same class this year.

7 A Were my glasses next to the lamp?
B No, __________ __________. They were in the drawer.

---

surprised 놀란 grade 성적, 등급 bald 대머리의 on time 시간대로, 정각에 confident 자신감 있는 friendly 친근한, 다정한
class president 반장 hard 어려운, 단단한 lamp 램프, 조명

## C 다음 괄호 안에서 알맞은 것을 고르고, 부정문과 의문문으로 바꿔 쓰시오.

1 She (was / were) eleven years old at that time.
➡ ______________________________
➡ ______________________________

2 My dad and I (was / were) very close a year ago.
➡ ______________________________
➡ ______________________________

3 It (was / were) your first Christmas in New York.
➡ ______________________________
➡ ______________________________

4 They (was / were) at the museum last Saturday.
➡ ______________________________
➡ ______________________________

Chapter 5

## D 우리말과 같은 뜻이 되도록 주어진 단어를 이용하여 문장을 완성하시오.

1 10년 전에 내 개는 하얀색이 아니었다. 그것은 검은색이었다. (black)
➡ My dog ________ white 10 years ago. ________ ________ ________.

2 그것은 너에게 너무 맵고 자극적이었니? (hot, spicy)
➡ ________ ________ ________ ________ and ________ for you?

3 그녀의 팔찌들은 그곳에 없었다. 그것들은 그녀의 침대 밑에 있었다. (bracelet)
➡ Her ________ ________ there. ________ ________ ________ her bed.

4 Lily와 Olivia는 집에 가는 길에 피곤해 했니? (tired)
➡ ________ ________ and ________ ________ on the way home?

5 그는 축구를 잘 하지 못했다. 그는 작년에 야구팀에 있었다. (be good at)
➡ He ________ ________ ________ soccer. He ________ on the baseball team last year.

hot 매운 spicy 양념 맛이 강한 bracelet 팔찌

Unit 01

# 일반동사의 과거 긍정문

## A 다음 표의 빈칸에 알맞은 말을 쓰시오.

| 일반동사 | 과거형 | 일반동사 | 과거형 |
|---|---|---|---|
| enjoy | enjoyed | jump | ⓓ |
| cry | ⓐ | like | liked |
| arrive | arrived | play | ⓔ |
| build | built | sleep | ⓕ |
| cut | ⓑ | put | put |
| walk | ⓒ | read | read |
| worry | worried | leave | ⓖ |

## B 주어진 동사를 알맞게 바꿔 과거 시제로 문장을 완성하시오.

1 Mia __________ happy yesterday. (look)

2 He __________ to live here in 2018. (begin)

3 We __________ umbrellas in the morning. (carry)

4 My dad __________ fishing last weekend. (go)

5 Daniel and I __________ our bikes at the park. (ride)

6 The boy __________ a blue shirt and white shorts. (wear)

7 Jennifer __________ chocolate cookies for him. (make)

8 Your sister __________ English very hard. (study)

9 Kate and her mom __________ lunch together yesterday. (eat)

10 They __________ an important lesson last week. (learn)

11 I __________ various foreigners at Gyeongbok Palace on Saturday. (see)

---

enjoy 즐기다 arrive 도착하다 build 짓다 put 놓다, 두다 leave 떠나다 look ~처럼 보이다, ~한 것 같다 begin 시작하다 umbrella 우산 go fishing 낚시하러 가다 shorts 반바지 important 중요한 lesson 수업, (교과서의) 과 various 다양한 foreigner 외국인

## C 다음 문장을 과거 시제로 바꿔 쓰시오

1 I think about the accident.
➡ ______________________________

2 Olivia lends him the *Harry Potter* books.
➡ ______________________________

3 My brother chooses the honest way.
➡ ______________________________

4 The actor gives people a lot of pleasure.
➡ ______________________________

5 You want to become friends with Joe.
➡ ______________________________

6 She speaks Japanese very well.
➡ ______________________________

## D 우리말과 같은 뜻이 되도록 주어진 단어를 바르게 배열하시오. 단, 필요에 따라 동사를 변형시켜 쓰시오.

1 그는 그 게임의 규칙을 이해했다. (the rules, he, of the game, understand)
➡ ______________________________

2 어젯밤에 비가 심하게 왔다. (last night, heavily, rain, it)
➡ ______________________________

3 그들은 사탕을 낱개로 팔았다. (sell, by the piece, candy, they)
➡ ______________________________

4 경찰은 그곳에서 커다란 발자국을 발견했다. (big, there, find, the police, footprints)
➡ ______________________________

5 그녀는 중학교에서 역사를 가르쳤다. (history, she, at a middle school, teach)
➡ ______________________________

---

think 생각하다 lend 빌려주다 accident 사고 way 방법 choose 선택하다 a lot of 많은 pleasure 기쁨, 즐거움 become ~이 되다
heavily 심하게, 아주 많이 footprint 발자국

Unit 02
# 일반동사의 과거 부정문과 의문문

## A 주어진 동사를 알맞게 바꿔 과거 시제 부정문을 완성하시오. (축약형으로)

1 I __________ __________ with them. (agree)

2 You __________ __________ in your diary. (write)

3 She __________ __________ her father. (understand)

4 They __________ __________ the red button. (push)

5 Harry __________ __________ playing the computer game. (stop)

6 We __________ __________ to wake up early in the morning. (want)

7 My family __________ __________ in Incheon in 2017. (live)

## B 주어진 동사를 이용하여 대화를 완성하시오.

1 A __________ he __________ late last night? (work)
B Yes, __________ __________. He looks so tired.

2 A __________ she __________ her alarm for 7 o'clock? (set)
B No, __________ __________. She was late for school today.

3 A __________ you __________ a good time on your vacation? (have)
B Yes, __________ __________. It was so wonderful.

4 A __________ Sandy and William __________ your birthday? (forget)
B No, __________ __________. They prepared a surprise party for me.

5 A __________ your dad __________ you to school? (drive)
B Yes, __________ __________. So I arrived early.

6 A __________ they __________ to go jogging? (start)
B Yes, __________ __________. They started doing it today.

7 A __________ Heather __________ a doctor? (become)
B No, __________ __________. She is an artist.

---

agree with ~ ~에 동의하다 diary 일기 wake up 일어나다 button 단추, 버튼 set 설정하다, 맞추다 forget 잊다 prepare 준비하다 drive 운전하다, 태워 주다 surprise party 깜짝 파티 go jogging 조깅하다 artist 예술가

## C 다음 문장을 과거 시제의 부정문과 의문문으로 바꿔 쓰시오.

1 She covered the table with a cloth.

➡ ______________________________

➡ ______________________________

2 You planned a trip to China yesterday.

➡ ______________________________

➡ ______________________________

3 James repeated the same mistakes.

➡ ______________________________

➡ ______________________________

4 Emma met him two weeks ago.

➡ ______________________________

➡ ______________________________

## D 우리말과 같은 뜻이 되도록 주어진 단어를 바르게 배열하시오.

1 그녀는 간밤에 잠을 잘 못 잤다. (very well, sleep, didn't, last night, she)

➡ ______________________________

2 그 농구 선수가 공을 던졌니? (the ball, throw, the basketball player, did)

➡ ______________________________

3 너는 어제 가족과 외식했니? (eat out, did, with your family, yesterday, you)

➡ ______________________________

4 Tina는 오늘 머리를 감지 않았다. (today, wash, Tina, didn't, her hair)

➡ ______________________________

5 그들은 10시 반에 집에 돌아왔니? (they, home, did, at ten thirty, come back)

➡ ______________________________

Chapter 6

---

cover 덮다, 가리다 cloth 옷감, 천 plan 계획하다 trip 여행 repeat 반복하다 mistake 실수 eat out 외식하다

# Unit 01 현재진행형

## A 다음 표의 빈칸에 알맞은 말을 쓰시오.

| 동사원형 | 진행형 | 동사원형 | 진행형 |
|---|---|---|---|
| come | coming | run | ⓓ |
| look | ⓐ | eat | eating |
| go | going | write | ⓔ |
| learn | learning | study | studying |
| get | ⓑ | take | ⓕ |
| wait | ⓒ | sit | sitting |
| sleep | sleeping | fly | flying |
| give | giving | clean | ⓖ |

## B 주어진 동사를 알맞게 바꿔 현재진행형으로 문장을 완성하시오.

1 The cat __________ __________ on the wall. (lie)

2 I __________ __________ breakfast. (have)

3 We __________ __________ pictures. (draw)

4 Olivia __________ __________ online. (shop)

5 My cell phone __________ __________ now. (ring)

6 Mr. Duke and I __________ __________ on the phone. (talk)

7 Jennifer __________ __________ the flowers. (water)

8 He __________ __________ the door. (open)

9 Sue and Daniel __________ __________ sunglasses. (wear)

10 Your sister __________ __________ her teeth. (brush)

11 Kelly and Danny __________ __________ in the pool. (swim)

wait 기다리다 give 주다 run 달리다 sit 앉다 clean 청소하다 lie 누워 있다 wall 담, 벽 shop 사다, 쇼핑하다 ring (전화가) 울리다 draw 그리다 water 물을 주다 brush 빗질을 하다 pool 수영장

**C** 다음 문장을 부정문과 의문문으로 바꾸어 쓰시오.

1 I am sending him a text message.
➡ ____________________
➡ ____________________

2 Amy is writing a letter to her grandparents.
➡ ____________________
➡ ____________________

3 George and Lily are going to the airport.
➡ ____________________
➡ ____________________

4 They are wearing white sneakers today.
➡ ____________________
➡ ____________________

**D** 우리말과 같은 뜻이 되도록 주어진 단어를 바르게 배열하시오. 단, 필요에 따라 동사를 변형시켜 쓰시오.

1 그녀는 지금 저녁을 만들고 있나요? (dinner, is, at this moment, make, she)
➡ ____________________

2 Olivia와 Brian은 탄산음료를 마시고 있지 않다. (are, soda, drink, Olivia and Brian, not)
➡ ____________________

3 Jason은 그의 방에서 자고 있지 않다. (sleep, not, is, in his bedroom, Jason)
➡ ____________________

4 그들은 그 노래를 함께 부르고 있니? (together, sing, they, the song, are)
➡ ____________________

5 너희들은 모래성을 만들고 있니? (a sandcastle, are, you, build)
➡ ____________________

text message 문자 메시지 at this moment 바로 지금 sneakers 운동화 wear (옷, 신발, 모자 등) 입다, 신다, 쓰다 together 함께
sandcastle 모래성

Unit 02

# 과거진행형

## A 주어진 동사를 알맞게 바꿔 과거진행형으로 문장을 완성하시오.

1 I __________ __________ for the bus. (wait)

2 The giraffes __________ __________ water. (drink)

3 We __________ __________ a fashion magazine. (read)

4 Mia __________ __________ to school. (run)

5 Carl and I __________ __________ our pet dogs. (walk)

6 People __________ __________ at the beach. (surf)

7 It __________ __________ at that time. (rain)

## B 주어진 동사를 이용하여 대화를 완성하시오.

1 A Were you __________ for a bus stop? (look)
B Yes, __________ __________. I was on my way home.

2 A __________ she __________ the piano? (play)
B Yes, __________ __________. She was preparing for a concert.

3 A __________ the babies __________ two hours ago? (cry)
B No, they weren't. They were sleeping.

4 A __________ Jenny __________ her mom? (help)
B No, she wasn't. She was watching TV.

5 A Was he __________ attention to the history teacher? (pay)
B No, __________ __________. He was sending a text message.

6 A Were they __________ a good time? (have)
B No, __________ __________. They looked bored.

7 A Was she __________ at me a while ago? (smile)
B Yes, __________ __________. She is looking at you now.

---

fashion magazine 패션 잡지 surf 파도타기를 하다 look for 찾다 on one's way ~에 가는 도중에 prepare 준비하다
pay attention to ~ ~에 주목하다 bored 지루한 smile at ~ ~에게 미소 짓다

## C 밑줄 친 부분을 바르게 고쳐 문장을 다시 쓰시오.

1 My aunt were liveing in Sydney then.
➡ ______________________________

2 I not was planning to travel to Alaska.
➡ ______________________________

3 Was they drawing pictures of animals?
➡ ______________________________

4 Ryan is playing baseball on the field at that time.
➡ ______________________________

5 Were Emily and you pray for me?
➡ ______________________________

6 Were your dad driveing on the highway?
➡ ______________________________

## D 우리말과 같은 뜻이 되도록 주어진 단어를 이용하여 영어로 쓰시오.

1 한 아이가 꽃을 꺾고 있었다. (a kid, pick, a flower)
➡ ______________________________

2 Daniel은 문을 당기고 있지 않았다. (pull, the door)
➡ ______________________________

3 그 소년이 그때 고함을 지르고 있었니? (the boy, shout, then)
➡ ______________________________

4 그들이 너의 개를 만지고 있었니? (touch)
➡ ______________________________

5 너는 너의 생일 케이크를 자르고 있지 않았다. (cut, your birthday cake)
➡ ______________________________

Sydney 시드니 pray 기도하다 highway 고속도로 pick 뽑다 touch 만지다

Unit 01

# will, be going to

## A 주어진 단어와 will을 이용하여 미래 시제로 문장을 완성하시오.

1 buy, for Eric, a birthday present, I

➡ ______________________________

2 the bus, Alice and I, miss

➡ ______________________________

3 she, next year, fourteen years old, be

➡ ______________________________

4 brush, we, our teeth, tonight

➡ ______________________________

5 in the future, a baseball player, Tony, become

➡ ______________________________

## B 주어진 우리말과 단어를 이용하여 빈칸에 알맞은 말을 쓰시오.

1 Harry는 오늘밤에 영화를 보러 갈 것이다. (watch)

➡ Harry __________ __________ to __________ a movie tonight.

2 나는 지하철역까지 걸어 갈 것이다. (walk)

➡ I __________ __________ to __________ to the subway station.

3 경찰이 그 도둑을 잡을 것이다. (catch)

➡ The police __________ __________ to __________ the thief.

4 우리는 이번 주말에 청바지를 빨 것이다. (wash)

➡ We __________ __________ to __________ the blue jeans this weekend.

5 그는 다음 주에 바쁠 것이다. (be busy)

➡ He __________ __________ __________ __________ busy next week.

present 선물 miss 놓치다 in the future 미래에 subway station 지하철역 the police 경찰 (복수) thief 도둑

## C 밑줄 친 부분을 바르게 고쳐 문장을 다시 쓰시오.

1 She going to cook this evening.

➡ ______

2 They are go to have fun.

➡ ______

3 Heather going is to move next month.

➡ ______

4 Kelly and I will going to bed early.

➡ ______

5 The train will arrives soon.

➡ ______

6 He will is a great musician someday.

➡ ______

## D 우리말과 같은 뜻이 되도록 주어진 단어를 바르게 배열하시오.

1 그는 나에게 편지를 보낼 것이다. (is going to, a letter, me, he, send)

➡ ______

2 나는 내년에 열세 살이 될 것이다. (will, thirteen years old, be, next year, I)

➡ ______

3 그녀는 오늘 그 시험에 합격할 것이다. (the exam, she, today, pass, will)

➡ ______

4 우리는 점심을 먹고 쇼핑을 갈 것이다. (go shopping, are going to, after lunch, we)

➡ ______

5 그 영화는 재미있을 것이다. (be, interesting, is going to, the movie)

➡ ______

musician 음악가 someday 언젠가, 훗날 send 보내다, 발송하다 pass 합격하다, 통과하다 exam 시험

Unit 02

# 미래 시제의 부정문과 의문문

## A 빈칸에 알맞은 말을 넣어 미래 시제의 부정문을 완성하시오. (축약형으로)

1 I am not hungry. I ________ have lunch.

2 We're ________ ________ ________ go to school.

3 Noah is bad at singing. He ________ become a singer.

4 You ________ come back at ten o'clock.

5 She's ________ ________ ________ eat anything at night.

6 Sam and Jack are too late. They ________ get there on time.

7 They're ________ ________ ________ play soccer together.

## B 주어진 동사를 이용하여 대화를 완성하시오.

1 A ________ the exam ________ easy?
B No, ________ ________. It will be difficult.

2 A ________ you ________ to go to the doctor tomorrow? (go)
B Yes, ________ ________. I feel bad.

3 A ________ he ________ to leave here tomorrow?
B No, ________ ________. He is going to leave here this weekend.

4 A ________ Lily and Noel clean their house?
B Yes, ________ ________. They will begin at ten o'clock.

5 A ________ you ________ to spend your vacation in Vietnam?
B No, ________ ________. I'm going to stay home.

6 A ________ they ________ the guitars in the band?
B No, ________ ________. They will sing.

7 A ________ Emily ________ to wait for him at the library?
B No, ________ ________. She is going to go home at six.

anything (부정문, 의문문에서) 아무것 go to the doctor 의사의 진찰을 받다, 병원에 가다 difficult 어려운 leave 떠나다 spend (시간을) 보내다 stay 머물다

## C 다음 문장을 부정문과 의문문으로 바꾸어 쓰시오.

1 He will buy a new smartphone.
➡ ______
➡ ______

2 You are going to be lucky next year.
➡ ______
➡ ______

3 They will join the book club.
➡ ______
➡ ______

4 Ryan is going to invite Juliet tomorrow.
➡ ______
➡ ______

## D 우리말과 같은 뜻이 되도록 주어진 단어를 바르게 배열하시오.

1 그녀는 그 기차를 탈 예정이니? (the train, to, take, going, she, is)
➡ ______

2 나는 오늘 너의 카메라를 쓰지 않을 것이다. (not, I, your camera, will, today, use)
➡ ______

3 내일은 날씨가 맑을 예정이니? (the weather, going, sunny, be, to, tomorrow, is)
➡ ______

4 그는 토요일에 테니스를 치지 않을 것이다. (not, is, on Saturday, going, he, play tennis, to)
➡ ______

5 그들이 내 생일 파티에 올까? (they, my birthday party, come to, will)
➡ ______

Chapter 8

smartphone 스마트폰 lucky 운이 좋은, 행운의 join 가입하다 weather 날씨 sunny 맑은

MEMO

MEMO

MEMO

MEMO

기초탄탄
GRAMMAR
Workbook

# Reading Skill로 끝내는 중학 내신 독해 1

Level

Happy House

# 구성 및 특징

지문 정보 요약
지문의 주제, 단어 수, 그리고 난이도를 쉽게 확인할 수 있습니다.
(상 ★★★, 중 ★★☆, 하 ★☆☆)

**다양한 소재의 독해 지문 학습**

챕터별로 리딩 스킬에 맞는 신선하고 흥미로운 소재의 4개의 지문이 레벨에 맞게 구성되어 있습니다.

**핵심 구문 분석 / 서술형 핵심 문법**

지문을 이해하는 데에 도움이 되는 핵심 구문 및 서술형 평가를 위한 중학 필수 문법을 분석하여 제시합니다.

**01**

Food | 140 words | ★★★

Most children love chocolate because it tastes delicious. However, most parents tell their children not to eat too much. The reason is that chocolate is high in calories. It also has a lot of sugar, so it is bad for the teeth. Fortunately, children have a good excuse for eating chocolate.

A recent study says that dark chocolate has some health benefits. ⓐ It has more cocoa than other types of chocolate. Cocoa contains *flavonoids. These provide several benefits for the body. ______________, they help prevent heart disease. They reduce the chances of a heart attack or a *stroke. They also increase blood flow to the brain. That improves a person's memory.

So feel free to enjoy chocolate each day. But scientists say people only need to eat around 85 grams of dark chocolate daily. So don't eat too much.

*flavonoids 플라보노이드 *stroke 뇌졸중

핵심 구문 분석

7행 ▸ These / **provide** / several / benefits / **for** / the body.
이것들은 / 제공한다 / 몇 가지 / 이점을 / ~를 위해 / 몸

〈provide A for B〉는 'B에게 A를 제공하다'는 의미로 〈provide B with A〉로 바꿔 쓸 수 있다.

8

**리딩 스킬 학습**

효과적인 독해를 위한 리딩 스킬을 선별하여 챕터별로 제시하였습니다.

- Step 01 리딩 스킬의 이론적인 이해를 위한 설명을 해 줍니다.
- Step 02 해당 리딩 스킬이 어떻게 유형화되어 문제에 출제되는지 알려줍니다.
- Step 03 해당 유형의 문제를 풀 수 있는 Tips를 제시합니다.
- Step 04 학습한 리딩 스킬을 적용한 내신 실전 문제를 제시합니다.

**내신 대비 실전 Test**

학습한 문법과 어휘를 확장해 평가할 수 있는 선다형 문제를 포함한 최신 서술형 문제를 수록하여 내신 시험에 대비하도록 하였습니다. 특히 같은 지문을 읽고, 본문과는 다른 심화한 유형의 문제를 수록하여 재확인할 수 있도록 구성하였습니다.

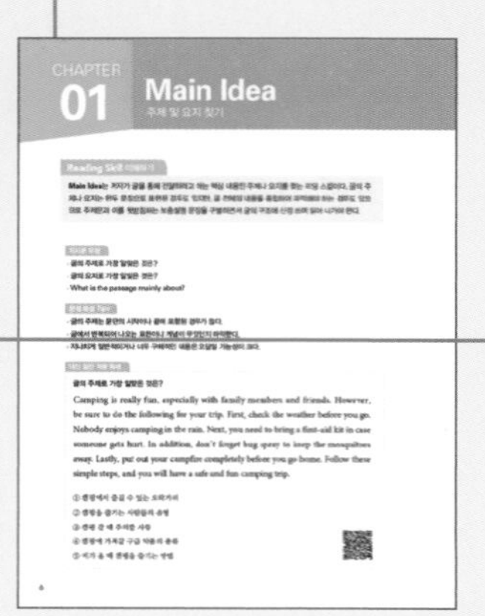


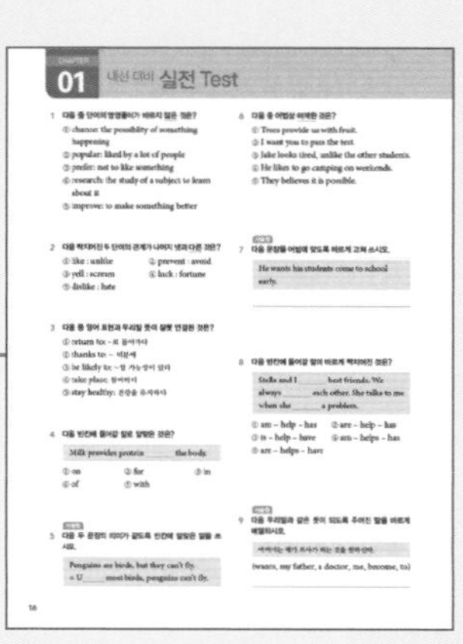

지문 QR코드
QR코드를 스캔하여 해당 지문의
MP3 파일을 바로 들을 수 있습니다.

Reading Skill | Main Idea

1 글의 요지로 가장 알맞은 것은?

① 초콜릿은 아이들의 대표적인 간식 중 하나이다.
② 초콜릿을 적당량 섭취하는 것은 건강에 도움이 된다.
③ 초콜릿에는 설탕이 많이 첨가되어 건강에 좋지 않다.
④ 초콜릿에는 몸에 좋은 플라보노이드 성분이 들어있다.
⑤ 초콜릿이 건강에 미치는 영향에 대한 연구가 활발하다.

2 글의 빈칸에 들어갈 말로 가장 알맞은 것은?

① However ② Therefore ③ On the other hand
④ For example ④ Moreover

3 글에서 cocoa의 효과로 언급되지 않은 것은?

① 심장질환 예방
② 뇌졸중 위험 감소
③ 심장 박동 수 증가
④ 뇌 혈류 증가
⑤ 기억력 증진

서술형

4 글의 밑줄 친 ⓐ It이 가리키는 것을 찾아 쓰시오.

ⓐ ____________________

Vocabulary

delicious 아주 맛있는
high in ~의 함량이 높은
fortunately 다행스럽게도
excuse 변명, 핑계
recent 최근의
benefit 이점, 혜택
contain 함유하다, 들어 있다
prevent 막다, 예방하다
disease 병, 질환
reduce 줄이다
chance 가능성
heart attack 심장마비
increase 증가시키다, 증가하다
improve 개선하다, 향상시키다

CHAPTER 01 | 9

지문 이해도 확인 문제

챕터에서 학습한 리딩 스킬을 활용한 내신 유형 문제 및 출제 빈도가 높은 지문 이해도 평가 문제를 수록하였습니다. 특히 내신 대비 서술형 평가를 위한 문제도 다수 수록하였습니다.

Vocabulary

지문에 나오는 핵심 어휘를 중학 영어 교과서의 필수 어휘로 선별하여 정리하였습니다.

CHAPTER 01 Main Idea

Workbook

챕터별 중요 어휘와 숙어를 다양한 문제와 새로운 예문으로 복습할 수 있도록 구성하였습니다. 또한 본문에 나온 문법을 활용하여 새로운 문장을 완성해 보는 서술형 연습 문제를 다수 수록하였습니다.

# Contents

## 목차

CHAPTER 01

## Main Idea

## Titles

## Cause and Effect

## Guessing Unknown Words

## Identifying Cohesive Devices: Pronoun

## Compare & Contrast

CHAPTER 01

# Main Idea

## 주제 및 요지 찾기

### Reading Skill 이해하기

**Main Idea**는 저자가 글을 통해 전달하려고 하는 핵심 내용인 주제나 요지를 찾는 리딩 스킬이다. 글의 주제나 요지는 한두 문장으로 표현된 경우도 있지만, 글 전체의 내용을 종합하여 파악해야 하는 경우도 있으므로 주제문과 이를 뒷받침하는 보충설명 문장을 구별하면서 글의 구조에 신경 쓰며 읽어 나가야 한다.

#### 지시문 유형

- 글의 주제로 가장 알맞은 것은?
- 글의 요지로 가장 알맞은 것은?
- What is the passage mainly about?

#### 문제 해결 Tips

- 글의 주제는 문단의 시작이나 끝에 포함된 경우가 많다.
- 글에서 반복되어 나오는 표현이나 개념이 무엇인지 파악한다.
- 지나치게 일반적이거나 너무 구체적인 내용은 오답일 가능성이 크다.

#### 내신 실전 적용 독해

**글의 주제로 가장 알맞은 것은?**

Camping is really fun, especially with family members and friends. However, be sure to do the following for your trip. First, check the weather before you go. Nobody enjoys camping in the rain. Next, you need to bring a first-aid kit in case someone gets hurt. In addition, don't forget bug spray to keep the mosquitoes away. Lastly, put out your campfire completely before you go home. Follow these simple steps, and you will have a safe and fun camping trip.

① 캠핑에서 즐길 수 있는 오락거리
② 캠핑을 즐기는 사람들의 유형
③ 캠핑 갈 때 주의할 사항
④ 캠핑에 가져갈 구급 약품의 종류
⑤ 비가 올 때 캠핑을 즐기는 방법

## 01 A Healthy or Unhealthy Food?

초콜릿 먹어도 될까요? | **Food**

## 02 The Naki Zumo Festival

이게 행운을 가져온다고요? | **Culture**

## 03 The Hulk's Secret

헐크에게 이런 비밀이? | **Entertainment**

## 04 Take It Easy on Mondays

월요일을 즐겨야 하는 이유 | **Science**

Food | 140 words | ★★★

Most children love chocolate because it tastes delicious. However, most parents tell their children not to eat too much. The reason is that chocolate is high in calories. It also has a lot of sugar, so it is bad for the teeth. Fortunately, children have a good excuse for eating chocolate.

A recent study says that dark chocolate has some health benefits. ⓐ It has more cocoa than other types of chocolate. Cocoa contains *flavonoids. These provide several benefits for the body. ________, they help prevent heart disease. They reduce the chances of a heart attack or a *stroke. They also increase blood flow to the brain. That improves a person's memory.

So feel free to enjoy chocolate each day. But scientists say people only need to eat around 85 grams of dark chocolate daily. So don't eat too much.

*flavonoids 플라보노이드 *stroke 뇌졸중

**핵심 구문 분석**

7행 ▸ These / **provide** / several / benefits / **for** / the body.
이것들은 / 제공한다 / 몇 가지 / 이점을 / ~를 위해 / 몸

⟨provide A for B⟩는 'B에게 A를 제공하다'는 의미로 ⟨provide B with A⟩로 바꿔 쓸 수 있다.

Reading Skill | Main Idea

**1** **글의 요지로 가장 알맞은 것은?**

① 초콜릿은 아이들의 대표적인 간식 중 하나이다.
② 초콜릿을 적당량 섭취하는 것은 건강에 도움이 된다.
③ 초콜릿에는 설탕이 많이 첨가되어 건강에 좋지 않다.
④ 초콜릿에는 몸에 좋은 플라보노이드 성분이 들어있다.
⑤ 초콜릿이 건강에 미치는 영향에 대한 연구가 활발하다.

**2** **글의 빈칸에 들어갈 말로 가장 알맞은 것은?**

① However ② Therefore ③ On the other hand
④ For example ④ Moreover

**3** **글에서 cocoa의 효과로 언급되지 않은 것은?**

① 심장질환 예방
② 뇌졸중 위험 감소
③ 심장 박동 수 증가
④ 뇌 혈류 증가
⑤ 기억력 증진

서술형

**4** **글의 밑줄 친 ⓐ It이 가리키는 것을 찾아 쓰시오.**

ⓐ ____________________

**Vocabulary**

**delicious** 형 아주 맛있는
**high in** ~의 함량이 높은
**fortunately** 부 다행스럽게도
**excuse** 명 변명, 핑계
**recent** 형 최근의
**benefit** 명 이점, 혜택
**contain** 동 함유하다, 들어 있다
**prevent** 동 막다, 예방하다
**disease** 명 병, 질환
**reduce** 동 줄이다
**chance** 명 가능성
**heart attack** 명 심장마비
**increase** 동 증가시키다, 증가하다
**improve** 동 개선하다, 향상시키다

Most parents never want to hear their babies cry. But Japanese parents sometimes want their babies to cry. In fact, they want their babies to yell and scream loudly.

Each year, the Naki Zumo festival takes place in Japan. Parents take their babies to the festival 5 and give them to sumo wrestlers. Then, the sumo wrestlers hold the babies up in the air. Most of the babies start crying. However, some babies do not cry. Then, men in scary masks ____________ the babies to make them cry loudly. 10

Why do they do ⓐ this? The Japanese believe if a baby cries in a wrestler's hands, it will bring good luck to the child. This is an old tradition in Japan. So Japanese parents pay around 10,000 yen to make their babies cry. What an interesting tradition!

**서술형 핵심 문법**

1행 ▸ **want + 목적어 + to부정사:** want 뒤에 〈목적어 + to부정사〉가 와서 '~가 …하는 것을 원하다'라고 해석한다.
Japanese parents sometimes **want** their babies **to cry**. 일본인 부모들은 가끔 그들의 아기들이 우는 것을 원한다.

**우리말과 같은 뜻이 되도록 주어진 말을 바르게 배열하시오.**

나는 당신이 그 축제에 오길 원한다. (want / come / to / I / to / you / the festival)

______________________________________________

Reading Skill Main Idea

## 1

**글의 주제로 가장 알맞은 것은?**

① the popular Japanese sport of sumo wrestling
② the most common reasons why babies cry
③ how to make babies cry loudly
④ interesting traditions around the world
⑤ an old Japanese tradition for good luck

## 2

**글의 빈칸에 들어갈 말로 가장 알맞은 것은?**

① frighten ② please ③ satisfy
④ tickle ④ shake

## 3

**Naki Zumo 축제에 관한 글의 내용과 일치하지 않는 것은?**

① 부모가 그들의 아기를 데리고 축제에 참여한다.
② 가면을 쓴 사람이 축제의 행사를 돕는다.
③ 울음을 참는 아기에게 행운이 온다고 믿는다.
④ 일 년에 한 번 열린다.
⑤ 축제에 참여하기 위해 비용을 내야 한다.

서술형

## 4

**글의 밑줄 친 ⓐ this가 의미하는 내용을 우리말로 쓰시오.**

______________________________

서술형

## 5

**다음 영영풀이에 해당하는 단어를 글에서 찾아 쓰시오.**

a custom passed from generation to generation

______________

**in fact** 사실은, 실은
**yell** 동 소리 지르다
**scream** 동 악을 쓰다
**loudly** 부 큰 소리로
**festival** 명 축제
**take place** 열리다, 개최되다
**sumo wrestler** 명 스모선수
**in the air** 공중에서
**scary** 형 무서운
**luck** 명 행운, 좋은 운
**interesting** 형 흥미로운
**tradition** 명 전통
**pay** 동 (비용 등을) 지불하다, 내다 (pay - paid - paid)

Entertainment | 131 words | ★★☆

Nowadays, movies with superheroes are popular. Superman, Batman, and the Incredible Hulk are some famous superheroes. They all started as comic book characters. The Hulk is a big, powerful superhero with green skin. But the original Hulk was not green. Instead, his skin was gray. ①

Stan Lee created the Hulk in 1962. ② He wanted the Hulk to look unlike anyone on the Earth. ③ So he drew the Hulk gray. ④ The Hulk was not just gray in the book. ⑤ He was green on some pages. The readers of the comic book preferred the green color. So Stan Lee made the Hulk green. ⓐ That was a smart decision. Thanks to his green color, people can easily recognize the Incredible Hulk.

**핵심 구문 분석**

5행 ▸ He / wanted / the Hulk / to look / **unlike** / anyone / on the Earth.
그는 / 원했다 / 헐크가 / 보이기를 / ~와 다르게 / 누구 / 지구상의

unlike는 '~와 다르게/닮지 않은'이라는 의미의 전치사로 뒤에 명사가 온다.

Reading Skill | Main Idea

1 What is the passage mainly about?

① problems printing comic books
② a change in the Hulk's color
③ the origins of famous superheroes
④ Stan Lee, the creator of the Hulk
⑤ why people like superheroes

2 다음 문장이 들어갈 위치로 가장 알맞은 곳은?

| But there was a problem with the printing of the first comic book. |
|---|

① ② ③ ④ ⑤

3 글의 밑줄 친 ⓐ That이 의미하는 것은?

① 헐크의 피부색을 처음에 회색으로 그린 것
② 헐크의 첫 번째 만화책 인쇄과정에 문제가 있었던 것
③ 헐크의 피부색을 초록색으로 바꾼 것
④ 헐크의 피부색을 두 가지 색으로 인쇄한 것
⑤ 독자들이 헐크의 초록색 피부색을 더 선호한 것

서술형

4 글의 내용과 일치하도록 다음 질문에 답하시오.

Q: Why did Stan Lee draw the Hulk gray at first?
A: Because he wanted ____________________

**popular** 형 인기 있는
**famous** 형 유명한
**comic book** 만화책
**character** 명 (책 등의) 등장인물
**instead** 부 대신에
**skin** 명 피부
**create** 동 만들어 내다, 창작하다
**reader** 명 독자, 읽는 사람
**prefer** 동 선호하다
**decision** 명 결정 *v.* decide 결정하다
**thanks to** ~ 덕분에
**recognize** 동 인식하다, 알아보다

# 04

Science | 132 words | ★★★

Which day of the week do you dislike the most? Most people say Monday. The fun, relaxing weekend is over. 그리고 사람들은 직장 혹은 학교로 되돌아가야 한다. Mondays are stressful for most people. Surprisingly, stress on Mondays threatens our health.

Some new research from Sweden studied when people have heart attacks. (a) The researchers learned something surprising. (b) People are 11% more likely to have a heart attack on Mondays than on other days. (c) Heart attacks usually occur in the early morning. (d) A person's stress level can cause a heart attack. (e) People have lots of stress every Monday. So they have many heart attacks on Mondays.

Unfortunately, it is not possible to avoid stress on Mondays. But you can lower your stress level by exercising, deep breathing, and watching funny movies. Then, you can avoid heart attacks and stay healthy.

서술형 핵심 문법

2·4행 ▸ **주어와 동사의 수 일치:** 주어가 단수일 때는 단수 동사, 주어가 복수일 때는 복수 동사로 일치시켜 써야 한다.
The fun, relaxing weekend is over. 재미있고, 편안한 주말은 끝난다.
Mondays are stressful for most people. 월요일은 대부분의 사람에게 스트레스를 준다.

**우리말과 같은 뜻이 되도록 주어진 말을 바르게 배열하시오.**

Jake는 낚시 가는 것을 좋아하지만, 그의 부모님은 하이킹 가는 것을 좋아하신다.

(likes / his parents / going hiking / Jake / going fishing / but / like)

______________________________

Reading Skill Main Idea

1 **글의 요지로 가장 알맞은 것은?**

① Most people dislike Mondays.
② It is hard to avoid stress on Mondays.
③ There are some helpful ways to lower your stress level.
④ Stress on Mondays can cause a heart attack.
⑤ People should get some rest on weekends.

2 **글의 (a)~(e) 중, 전체 흐름과 관계 없는 문장은?**

① (a) ② (b) ③ (c) ④ (d) ⑤ (e)

3 **글의 내용과 일치하면 T, 그렇지 않으면 F를 쓰시오.**

(1) 월요일은 다른 요일보다 심장마비를 일으킬 가능성이 적다. ________
(2) 스트레스는 심장마비를 일으키게 할 수 있다. ________

서술형

4 **밑줄 친 우리말과 같은 뜻이 되도록 주어진 말을 바르게 배열하시오.**

(have to, and, to work, return, people, or school)

________________________________________

서술형

5 **다음 빈칸에 공통으로 들어갈 단어를 글에서 찾아 쓰시오.**

| You cannot avoid ________ on Mondays. But you can reduce your ________ level. Exercising, deep breathing, and watching funny movies can lower your ________ level. |
|---|

Vocabulary

**dislike** 동 싫어하다
**return to** ~로 되돌아가다
**stressful** 형 스트레스가 많은
**threaten** 동 위협하다
**research** 명 연구, 조사
**surprising** 형 놀라운
**be likely to** ~할 가능성이 있다
**avoid** 동 피하다, 방지하다
**lower** 동 낮추다
**exercise** 동 운동하다
**funny** 형 재미있는, 웃기는
**stay healthy** 건강을 유지하다

# 내신 대비 실전 Test

1 다음 중 단어의 영영풀이가 바르지 않은 것은?

① chance: the possiblity of something happening
② popular: liked by a lot of people
③ prefer: not to like something
④ research: the study of a subject to learn about it
⑤ improve: to make something better

2 다음 짝지어진 두 단어의 관계가 나머지 넷과 다른 것은?

① like : unlike
② prevent : avoid
③ yell : scream
④ luck : fortune
⑤ dislike : hate

3 다음 중 영어 표현과 우리말 뜻이 잘못 연결된 것은?

① return to: ~로 돌아가다
② thanks to: ~ 덕분에
③ be likely to: ~할 가능성이 있다
④ take place: 참여하다
⑤ stay healthy: 건강을 유지하다

4 다음 빈칸에 들어갈 말로 알맞은 것은?

Milk provides protein _______ the body.

① on
② for
③ in
④ of
⑤ with

서술형

5 다음 두 문장의 의미가 같도록 빈칸에 알맞은 말을 쓰시오.

Penguins are birds, but they can't fly.
= U_____ most birds, penguins can't fly.

6 다음 중 어법상 어색한 것은?

① Trees provide us with fruit.
② I want you to pass the test.
③ Jake looks tired, unlike the other students.
④ He likes to go camping on weekends.
⑤ They believes it is possible.

서술형

7 다음 문장을 어법에 맞도록 바르게 고쳐 쓰시오.

He wants his students come to school early.

______________________________

8 다음 빈칸에 들어갈 말이 바르게 짝지어진 것은?

Stella and I _______ best friends. We always _______ each other. She talks to me when she _______ a problem.

① am – help – has
② are – help – has
③ is – help – have
④ am – helps – has
⑤ are – helps – have

서술형

9 다음 우리말과 같은 뜻이 되도록 주어진 말을 바르게 배열하시오.

아버지는 내가 의사가 되는 것을 원하신다.

(wants, my father, a doctor, me, become, to)

______________________________

[10-12] 다음 글을 읽고 물음에 답하시오.

Most children love chocolate because it tastes delicious. However, most parents ___(a)___ their children not to eat too much. The reason is that chocolate is high in calories. It also has a lot of sugar, so it is bad for the teeth. Fortunately, children ___(b)___ a good excuse for eating chocolate.

(A) For example, they help prevent heart disease. They reduce the chances of a heart attack or a stroke. They also increase blood flow to the brain. That improves a person's memory.

(B) So feel free to enjoy chocolate each day. But scientists say people only need to eat around 85 grams of dark chocolate daily. So don't eat too much.

(C) A recent study ___(c)___ that dark chocolate has some health benefits. It has more cocoa than other types of chocolate. Cocoa contains flavonoids. ⓐ These provide several benefits for the body.

서술형

**10** 글의 밑줄 친 ⓐ These가 가리키는 것을 찾아 쓰시오.

______________________

**11** (A)~(C)를 글의 흐름에 알맞게 배열한 것은?

① (A) – (B) – (C)
② (B) – (A) – (C)
③ (B) – (C) – (A)
④ (C) – (A) – (B)
⑤ (A) – (C) – (B)

**12** (a)~(c)에 들어갈 말로 가장 적절한 것은?

① tell – has – says
② tells – have – say
③ tell – have – say
④ tells – has – says
⑤ tell – have – says

[13-15] 다음 글을 읽고 물음에 답하시오.

Which day of the week do you dislike the most? Most people say Monday. The fun, relaxing weekend is over. And people have to return to work or school. Mondays are stressful for most people. Surprisingly, stress on Mondays threatens our health. ①

Some new research from Sweden studied when people have heart attacks. ② The researchers learned something surprising. ③ A person's stress level can cause a heart attack. ④ People have lots of stress every Monday. ⑤ So they have many heart attacks on Mondays.

______________, it is not possible to avoid stress on Mondays. But there are some ways to ⓐ reduce it. You can lower your stress level by exercising, deep breathing, and watching funny movies. Then, you can avoid heart attacks and stay healthy.

**13** 글의 빈칸에 들어갈 말로 가장 알맞은 것은?

① Thankfully
② Unfortunately
③ Happily
④ Importantly
⑤ Luckily

**14** 다음 문장이 들어갈 위치로 가장 알맞은 곳은?

People are 11% more likely to have a heart attack on Mondays than on other days.

① ② ③ ④ ⑤

서술형

**15** 밑줄 친 ⓐ reduce와 바꿔 쓸 수 있는 단어를 글에서 찾아 쓰시오.

______________________

CHAPTER

# 02 Titles

제목 찾기

## Reading Skill 이해하기

**Titles**는 글의 중심 내용을 표현하고 있는 제목을 찾는 리딩스킬이다. 제목은 글의 주제나 요지를 잘 요약하여 포괄적으로 나타낸 것으로 글의 주제와 밀접한 관련이 있으므로 글의 주제나 요지를 파악해야 찾을 수 있다.

### 지시문 유형

- 글의 제목으로 가장 알맞은 것은?
- What is the best title for the passage?

### 문제 해결 Tips

- 글에서 반복되는 핵심어가 무엇인지 파악한다.
- 글의 주제나 요지를 가장 잘 표현한 선택지를 찾는다.
- 제목의 범위는 글의 내용보다 지나치게 포괄적이거나 한정적이지 않아야 한다.

### 내신 실전 적용 독해

**글의 주제로 가장 알맞은 것은?**

Eating breakfast is very important. When you skip breakfast, your brain does not get enough energy. Then, you will not be able to pay attention during class. So you will not learn much. Skipping breakfast will also make you hungry before lunchtime. You might eat a snack during your break. As a result, you will not be hungry at lunch. This will upset your meal cycle. And it will lead to an unhealthy lifestyle.

① Ways to Provide Energy to Your Brain
② An Unhealthy Lifestyle
③ A Good Diet: Eating Breakfast
④ The Effects of Skipping Breakfast
⑤ How to Pay Attention during Class

## 05 How Google and Yahoo! Got Their Names

별난 이름 Google과 Yahoo! | **Origins**

## 06 Unhealthy Food Combinations

음식에도 궁합이 있어요 | **Food**

## 07 Time in Ethiopia

에티오피아에서는 12시에 해가 진다? | **Culture**

## 08 The Ecofriendly Poo Bus

영국에는 똥 버스가 있다! | **Environment**

Origins | 140 words | ★★★

Millions of people visit Google and Yahoo! to search for information daily. Have you ever wondered how they got their names? The stories behind them are interesting.

Larry Page and Sergey Brin founded Google. First, they wanted to use the name Googolplex. A googolplex is a very large number. They liked the name because their website could handle large amounts of data. However, Page wanted to shorten it to Googol. But Sean Anderson, Page's friend, *misspelled the name and used Google. Both Page and Brin liked the ______________ spelling, so they named their company Google.

The history of Yahoo! is also fun. In the book *Gulliver's Travels*, Yahoos are wild, rude creatures. Founders Jerry Yang and David Filo thought they were like Yahoos. So they changed their website's name to Yahoo! Originally, they planned to use Dave and Jerry's Guide to the World Wide Web.

*misspell 철자를 잘못 쓰다

핵심 구문 분석

7행 ▸ But / Sean Anderson, / Page's friend, / **misspelled** / the name / **and** / **used** / Google.
하지만 / Sean Anderson은 / Page의 친구인 / 철자를 잘못 썼다 / 그 이름을 / 그리고 / 사용했다 / Google을

and는 단어와 단어, 구와 구, 절과 절을 대등하게 연결하는 등위 접속사이다.

Reading Skill | Titles

**1** 글의 제목으로 가장 알맞은 것은?

① The Way That Google Got Its Name
② The First Names of Google and Yahoo!
③ The Meanings of Google and Yahoo!
④ How People Name Their Websites
⑤ How Two Websites Got Their Names

**2** 글의 빈칸에 들어갈 말로 가장 알맞은 것은?

① long ② short ③ incorrect
④ important ④ large

**3** 글을 읽고 Yahoo!에 관해 답할 수 없는 질문은?

① Who are the two founders of Yahoo!?
② What is the original name of Yahoo!?
③ Where does the name Yahoo! come from?
④ Why do people visit Yahoo! daily?
⑤ What do people think about the name Yahoo!?

서술형

**4** 글의 내용과 일치하도록 다음 질문에 답하시오.

Q: Why did the founders of Google like the name Googolplex?
A: Because ______________________________

**millions of** 수백만의 ~
**search for** ~을 찾다
**information** 명 정보
**wonder** 동 궁금해하다
**found** 동 설립하다 *n.* founder 설립자
**handle** 동 처리하다
**shorten** 동 짧게 하다
**incorrect** 형 틀린, 맞지 않는
**wild** 형 야생의, 거친
**rude** 형 무례한, 거친
**creature** 명 생물, 창조물
**plan to** ~할 계획이다

Food | 134 words | ★★☆

Some foods like bacon and eggs go well together. However, when you eat certain foods together, they can harm your body.

Tea and milk are both healthy. Many people pour milk in their tea. ① *Proteins in the milk make the *antioxidants in tea useless. ② And the caffeine in the tea prevents your body from absorbing the calcium in the milk. 5

③ White bread and jam are another bad combination. ④ When you eat them together, the sugar in your blood rises quickly. ⑤ Then, your body needs to release lots of insulin to bring your blood sugar down. ⓐ <u>That</u> can cause *diabetes. 10

Nowadays, people love eating salads with fat-free dressing. But the nutrients in plants are not absorbed well with fat-free dressing. Instead, olive oil and vinegar are good on salads.

*protein 단백질 *antioxidant 항산화제 *diabetes 당뇨병

**서술형 핵심 문법**

8행 ▸ **접속사 when:** 시간을 나타내는 접속사 when은 '~할 때'라는 뜻으로 뒤에 주어, 동사가 온다. when이 이끄는 절이 문장 앞에 올 경우에는 절 뒤에 콤마(,)를 쓴다.
<u>When you eat them together,</u> the sugar in your blood rises quickly.
당신이 그것들을 함께 먹을 때, 혈당이 급격하게 올라간다.

**우리말과 같은 뜻이 되도록 주어진 말을 바르게 배열하시오.**

나는 슬플 때, 약간의 초콜릿을 먹는다. (feel sad / I / eat / when / some / I / chocolate)

______________________________

Reading Skill | Titles

1 What is the best title for the passage?

① What Foods Go Well Together
② The Bad Habit of Drinking Tea
③ The Role of Caffeine in the Body
④ What Can Cause Diabetes
⑤ Don't Eat These Foods Together

2 다음 문장이 들어갈 위치로 가장 알맞은 곳은?

| But they are an unhealthy combination. |
| --- |

① ② ③ ④ ⑤

3 다음 중 글의 내용과 일치하지 않는 것은?

① 많은 사람이 차에 우유를 넣어 마신다.
② 차에는 항산화제와 카페인이 함유되어 있다.
③ 흰 빵에 잼을 발라 먹으면 혈당이 급격하게 올라간다.
④ 혈당이 올라가면 우리 몸에서는 인슐린이 분비된다.
⑤ 무지방 드레싱을 곁들인 샐러드는 다이어트에 효과적이다.

서술형

4 글의 밑줄 친 ⓐ That이 의미하는 내용을 우리말로 쓰시오.

______________________________

서술형

5 샐러드와 함께 먹으면 좋은 음식 두 가지를 글에서 찾아 우리말로 쓰시오.

______________________________

Vocabulary

**go well together** 잘 어울리다
**harm** 동 해치다, 해를 끼치다
**pour** 동 붓다, 따르다
**useless** 형 쓸모 없는
**absorb** 동 흡수하다
**combination** 명 조합
*v.* combine 합치다
**blood** 명 피, 혈액
**rise** 동 증가하다, 오르다
(rise - rose - risen)
**quickly** 부 빠르게
**release** 동 방출하다
**fat-free** 형 무지방의
**nutrient** 명 영양분

# 07

Around the world, most people tell time the same way. But the African country Ethiopia is different. Ethiopia is close to the *equator. So the amount of daylight is almost the same throughout the year. As a result, many Ethiopians use a twelve-hour clock. One cycle of 1 to 12 is from dawn to sunset. The other cycle is from sunset to dawn.

So when it is 7 A.M. in other places, it is 1 o'clock in Ethiopia. At 6 o'clock Ethiopian time, Ethiopians usually eat lunch. When the sun sets at 6 P.M. in other countries, it is 12 o'clock in Ethiopia.

This twelve-hour clock confuses many foreigners. _______ ⓐ it makes sense to Ethiopians, and they are proud of their unique ways. So if you visit Ethiopia, remember their way of telling time.

*equator 적도

**핵심 구문 분석**

4행 ▸ One cycle / of 1 to 12 / is / **from** dawn / **to** sunset.
하나의 주기는 / 1에서 12까지의 / 이다 / 새벽부터 / 해질 때까지

〈from A to B〉는 'A부터 B까지'라는 뜻으로 범위를 나타낼 때 사용되며, 전치사 from과 to 뒤에는 명사가 온다.

Reading Skill | Titles

## 1 글의 제목으로 가장 알맞은 것은?

① The Amount of Daylight in Ethiopia
② Why Ethiopian Clocks Cannot Be Trusted
③ When the Sun Rises and Sets in Ethiopia
④ Where Ethiopia Is Located
⑤ The Way to Tell Time in Ethiopia

## 2 글에 따르면, 에티오피아에서 twelve-hour clock을 사용하는 이유는?

① 많은 외국인을 혼란스럽게 만들기 위해
② 12시에 일조량이 가장 많기 때문에
③ 적도 가까이에 위치해 있기 때문에
④ 일조량이 일 년 내내 거의 같기 때문에
⑤ 그들의 독특한 시간을 구분하는 방식을 자랑스러워해서

## 3 글의 빈칸에 들어갈 말로 가장 알맞은 것은?

① And ② Because ③ But
④ So ④ When

서술형

## 4 글의 밑줄 친 ⓐ it이 가리키는 것을 찾아 쓰시오.

______________________

**country** 명 국가, 나라
**daylight** 명 (낮의) 햇빛, 일조량
**throughout** 전 ~동안 죽, 내내
**cycle** 명 주기, 순환
**dawn** 명 새벽
**sunset** 명 일몰
**confuse** 동 혼란스럽게 만들다
**foreigner** 명 외국인
**make sense** 일리가 있다, 타당하다
**be proud of** ~을 자랑스럽게 여기다
**unique** 형 독특한
**remember** 동 기억하다

# 08

Have you ever heard of *biomethane? It is a type of gas made from human and household waste. People can use it as fuel in their homes and vehicles. Then, they do not have to use *fossil fuels like gasoline. Biomethane is a form of *renewable energy.

In England, there is a bus called the Bio-Bus. It looks normal, but its engine burns biomethane made from human poo and food waste. So people call it the poo bus.

(a) The poo bus is an ecofriendly bus. (b) It uses the waste from more than 32,000 households in the local area. (c) There are over 100 bus routes in the area. (d) By turning poo into energy, it is reducing waste. (e) It also produces less pollution than gasoline engines do. It is receiving attention around the world. Someday, maybe you will take a poo bus in your country.

*biomethane 바이오 메탄
*fossil fuel 화석 연료 *renewable 재생 가능한

**서술형 핵심 문법**

7행 ▸ **there is/are + 명사:** '~이 있다'라고 할 때 쓰는 표현으로, there는 뜻이 없이 문장을 유도하는 역할을 한다. There is 뒤에는 단수명사가, there are 뒤에는 복수명사가 온다.
In England, **there is** a bus called the Bio-Bus. 영국에는 '바이오 버스'라고 불리는 버스가 있다.

**다음 문장을 어법에 맞도록 바르게 고쳐 쓰시오.**

There is hundreds of cars on the street. 길에는 수백 대의 자동차가 있다.

______________________________

Reading Skill | Titles

**1** What is the best title for the passage?

① What Biomethane Is and What It Is For
② How to Reduce Household Waste
③ A New Form of Renewable Energy
④ How to Save the Environment
⑤ A Bus That Helps the Environment

**2** 글의 (a)~(e) 중, 전체 흐름과 관계 없는 문장은?

① (a)　② (b)　③ (c)　④ (d)　⑤ (e)

**3** 글의 내용과 일치하면 T, 그렇지 않으면 F를 쓰시오.

(1) 바이오 메탄은 교통수단의 연료로 사용될 수 있다. ________
(2) 똥 버스가 전 세계적으로 운행되고 있다. ________

서술형

**4** 다음 영영풀이에 해당하는 단어를 글에서 찾아 쓰시오.

not causing damage to the environment

________________

서술형

**5** 다음 빈칸에 알맞은 단어를 글에서 찾아 쓰시오.

__________ is a form of renewable energy, and it is made from human and food __________. An English bus uses it as fuel, and it is called the poo bus.

**Vocabulary**

**household** 명 가정
**waste** 명 쓰레기, 폐기물
**fuel** 명 연료
**vehicle** 명 차량, 탈 것
**form** 명 형태, 종류
**normal** 형 평범한, 보통의
**burn** 동 태우다
**ecofriendly** 형 친환경적인
**local** 형 지역의, 현지의
**area** 명 지역
**produce** 동 배출하다, 생산하다
**pollution** 명 오염 (물질)
*v.* pollute 오염시키다
**receive attention** 주목을 받다

# 내신 대비 실전 Test

서술형

**1** 다음 영영풀이가 의미하는 단어를 넣어 문장을 완성하시오.

to have a wish to know something

I ___________ if he will come to the party or not.

**2** 다음 빈칸에 들어갈 말로 알맞은 것은?

incorrect : correct = benefit : ___________

① rise ② burn ③ absorb
④ harm ⑤ found

**3** 다음 중 영어 표현과 우리말 뜻이 잘못 연결된 것은?

① be proud of: ~을 자랑스럽게 여기다
② make sense: 감지하다
③ milions of: 수백만의 ~
④ go well together: 잘 어울리다
⑤ receive attention: 주목을 받다

**4** 다음 빈칸에 들어갈 말로 알맞은 것은?

Mexicans like to sing and ___________.

① danced ② dancing ③ dancer
④ to dance ⑤ dances

**5** 다음 빈칸에 공통으로 들어갈 말로 알맞은 것은?

• Here's a list of everything _______ A to Z.
• Warm tea prevents you _______ getting a cold.

① in ② on ③ from
④ by ⑤ about

**6** 다음 밑줄 친 부분의 쓰임이 나머지 넷과 다른 것은?

① There are two people in the room.
② Are there any questions?
③ There is not a picture on the wall.
④ Please look over there.
⑤ No, there is nothing in the fridge.

서술형

**7** 다음 우리말과 같은 뜻이 되도록 주어진 단어를 이용해 영작하시오.

나는 기분이 안 좋을 때, 재미있는 비디오를 본다.

(funny videos)

___________________________

**8** 다음 중 어법상 어색한 것은?

① She lost her watch and buying a new one.
② We go to school from Monday to Friday.
③ When the sun sets, the sky is beautiful.
④ There are trees and flowers in the park.
⑤ He drinks coffee when he feels tired.

서술형

**9** 다음 우리말과 같은 뜻이 되도록 주어진 말을 바르게 배열하시오.

뉴욕에는 많은 높은 빌딩들이 있다.

(tall, in, New York, are, many, buildings, there)

___________________________

[10-12] 다음 글을 읽고 물음에 답하시오.

Larry Page and Sean Anderson founded Google. ① First, they wanted to use the name Googolplex. ② A googolplex is a very large number. ③ They liked the name because their website could handle large amounts of data. ④ But Anderson misspelled the name and used Google. ⑤ Both men liked the incorrect spelling, so they named their company Google.

The history of Yahoo! is also fun. In the book *Gulliver's Travels*, ⓐ Yahoos are wild, rude creatures. ⓑ Founders Jerry Yang and David Filo thought ⓒ they were like Yahoos. So they changed ⓓ their website's name to Yahoo! Originally, ⓔ they planned to use Dave and Jerry's Guide to the World Wide Web.

서술형

10 다음 영영풀이에 해당되는 단어를 글에서 찾아 쓰시오.

to start something such as a company

______________________

11 다음 문장이 들어갈 위치로 가장 알맞은 곳은?

However, Page wanted to shorten it to Googol.

① ② ③ ④ ⑤

12 글의 밑줄 친 ⓐ~ⓔ 중, 가리키는 대상이 나머지 넷과 다른 것은?

① ⓐ ② ⓑ ③ ⓒ ④ ⓓ ⑤ ⓔ

[13-15] 다음 글을 읽고 물음에 답하시오.

(A) White bread and jam are another bad combination. When you eat them together, the sugar in your blood rises quickly. Then, your body needs to release lots of insulin to bring your blood sugar down. That can cause diabetes.

(B) Some foods like bacon and eggs go well together. However, when you eat certain foods together, ______________________.

(C) Tea and milk are both healthy. Many people pour milk in their tea. But ⓐ they are an unhealthy combination. Proteins in the milk make the antioxidants in tea useless. And the caffeine in the tea prevents your body from absorbing the calcium in the milk.

13 글의 빈칸에 들어갈 말로 가장 알맞은 것은?

① they are good for you
② they go well together
③ they can be helpful
④ they can harm your body
⑤ they change surprisingly

14 (A)~(C)를 글의 흐름에 알맞게 배열한 것은?

① (A) – (B) – (C)
② (B) – (A) – (C)
③ (B) – (C) – (A)
④ (C) – (A) – (B)
⑤ (A) – (C) – (B)

서술형

15 글의 밑줄 친 ⓐ they가 가리키는 것을 찾아 쓰시오.

______________________

# CHAPTER 03 Cause and Effect
원인과 결과

## Reading Skill 이해하기

**Cause and Effect**는 어떤 상황이나 사건이 일어난 원인과 그로 인해 발생한 결과를 파악하는 리딩 스킬이다. 원인과 결과를 이해하는 것은 사건들의 연관성을 분석하여 글의 내용을 파악하는 데 꼭 필요하다.

### 지시문 유형

- 글에 따르면, 사람들이 잠을 충분히 자야 하는 이유는?
- 글에 따르면, 밑줄 친 ⓐ의 이유로 알맞은 것은?

### 문제 해결 Tips

- 원인(because, since)과 결과(so, therefore)를 나타내는 접속사의 종류와 의미를 익힌다.
- 접속사 앞뒤 문장에 원인과 결과를 나타내는 내용이 있을 가능성이 크다.
- 일련의 사건을 원인과 결과로 나누어 보고 내용이 자연스러운지 확인한다.

### 내신 실전 적용 독해

**글에 따르면, 동물들이 겨울잠을 자는 이유는?**

Winter is often cold and snowy. It is hard for animals to find food then. Therefore, many animals sleep during winter. This is called *hibernation. During hibernation, the animals seem to be dead. They breathe very slowly, and their body temperature drops. So the animals do not need much energy. Therefore, they can stay alive without eating food during winter. However, when the warm spring comes, they wake up. And they eat a lot of food because they are so hungry.

*hibernation 겨울잠

① 봄이 오면 많은 에너지를 필요로 하기 때문에
② 겨울에는 체온이 떨어져 움직이기 힘들기 때문에
③ 가을에 많은 영양분을 몸속에 비축해 놓았기 때문에
④ 겨울에는 춥고 눈이 와서 먹이를 찾기 힘들기 때문에
⑤ 겨울잠을 자는 동안 쉴 수 있기 때문에

Food | 134 words | ★☆☆

Have you ever cut an onion? What happened after you did that? You probably started crying. There is a reason for this. Cutting an onion releases chemicals called *amino acid sulfoxides. When these chemicals go into the air, they make a gas. When the gas touches your eyes, it forms an acid. Then, the acid burns and makes your eyes sting. So ⓐ tears flow to stop the stinging.

Fortunately, there are some ways to avoid crying when you cut an onion. First, put the onion into water or the freezer before cutting it. ⓑ This prevents the gas from spreading and reaching your eyes. Second, light a candle. It will burn the gas away. Finally, put a spoon into your mouth. The gas will stick to the spoon, so it will not reach your eyes.

*amino acid sulfoxides 아미노산 술폭시드 (휘발성 유기화합물)

핵심 구문 분석

10행 ▸ This / **prevents** / the gas / **from** spreading / and / reaching / your eyes.
이것은 / 막는다 / 기체가 / 퍼지는 것을 / 그리고 / 닿는 것을 / 당신의 눈에
〈prevent + 목적어 + from + v-ing〉는 '~가 …하는 것을 막다/방지하다'라는 뜻으로 전치사 from 뒤에 동명사가 온다.

## 1 글의 제목으로 가장 알맞은 것은?

① The Secret of Onions
② How to Cut Onions
③ Why Onions Make You Cry
④ What Chemicals Onions Have
⑤ Ways to Stop Your Eyes from Stinging

**Reading Skill** **Cause and Effect**

## 2 글에 따르면, 밑줄 친 ⓐ의 이유로 알맞은 것은?

① 기체가 산화되는 것을 막기 위해서
② 공중에 퍼진 화학 물질이 기체를 생성하는 것을 막기 위해서
③ 양파에서 방출되는 화학 물질이 눈에 들어오는 것을 막기 위해서
④ 기체가 눈에 들어와서 산성 물질을 형성하는 것을 막기 위해서
⑤ 눈이 따끔거리는 것을 멈추기 위해서

## 3 양파를 자를 때 눈물을 흘리지 않는 방법으로 언급되지 않은 것은?

① 양파를 자르기 전에 물에 넣어두기
② 양파를 자르기 전에 얼려 두기
③ 양파를 자를 때 보호 안경 쓰기
④ 양파를 자를 때 촛불 켜기
⑤ 양파를 자를 때 숟가락을 입에 물기

서술형

## 4 글의 밑줄 친 ⓑ This가 의미하는 내용을 우리말로 쓰시오.

_______________________________________________

**happen** 동 발생하다, 일어나다
**reason** 명 이유, 까닭
**chemical** 명 화학 물질
**touch** 동 닿다, 접촉하다
**form** 동 형성하다
**sting** 동 따끔거리다
**flow** 동 흐르다
**freezer** 명 냉동고
**spread** 동 퍼지다
(spread - spread - spread)
**reach** 동 이르다, 닿다
**light** 동 불을 비추다
**stick to** ~에 들러붙다

# 10

Animals | 135 words | ★★☆

Dogs and cats are two popular pets. But look closely at them. Most cat *breeds look similar. But dog breeds look quite different in their sizes, shapes, faces, and colors. There is a reason for this.

Humans tamed dogs and cats a long time ago. They kept cats to catch mice. ______________, humans kept dogs for several reasons. For example, they used dogs for hunting, herding animals, protecting places, and pulling sleds. So humans created new breeds of dogs because dogs had to do different tasks. This resulted in many different ⓐ types of dogs.

In addition, humans started breeding dogs hundreds of years ago. But they only started breeding cats around 75 years ago. As a result, there are 340 breeds of dogs today. But there are only 42 breeds of cats.

*breed (가축의) 품종, (품종을) 개량하다

**서술형 핵심 문법**

1행 ▸ **감각동사 + 형용사:** 감각을 나타내는 감각동사 look, feel, sound, taste, smell 뒤에 형용사가 와서 '~하게 보이다/느끼다/들리다/맛이 나다/냄새가 나다'라는 뜻이다.
Most cat breeds look similar. 대부분의 고양이 품종은 비슷하게 보인다.

**우리말과 같은 뜻이 되도록 주어진 말을 바르게 배열하시오.**

이 강아지는 귀여워 보이고, 부드러운 느낌이 난다. (this puppy / and / feels / cute / soft / looks)

______________________________________________

Reading Skill | Cause and Effect

1 글에 따르면, 개의 품종이 고양이보다 다양한 이유는?

① 사람들이 고양이보다 개를 반려동물로 선호하기 때문에
② 고양이의 품종은 개량시키는 것은 어렵기 때문에
③ 원래부터 개가 고양이보다 크기, 모양 등이 다양했기 때문에
④ 개의 품종을 개량시키는 것이 훨씬 더 수월했기 때문에
⑤ 다양한 일에 적합하도록 오랜 기간 개의 품종을 개량해왔기 때문에

2 글의 빈칸에 들어갈 말로 가장 알맞은 것은?

① As a result ② Moreover ③ In spite of
④ On the other hand ⑤ As well as

3 글에서 사람들이 개를 길러온 이유로 언급되지 않는 것은?

① hunting ② pulling sleds ③ catching mice
④ herding animals ⑤ protecting places

서술형
4 밑줄 친 ⓐ types와 바꿔 쓸 수 있는 단어를 글에서 찾아 쓰시오.

______________________

서술형
5 글의 내용과 일치하도록 다음 질문에 답하시오.

Q: How many breeds of dogs and cats are there today?
A: There are ______________________ today.

Vocabulary

**similar** 형 비슷한 (≠ different 다른)
**human** 명 인간, 사람
**quite** 부 꽤, 상당히
**shape** 명 모양, 형태
**tame** 동 길들이다
**keep** 동 기르다, 유지하다
**catch** 동 잡다
**herd** 동 (짐승을) 몰다
**protect** 동 보호하다, 지키다
**pull** 동 끌다
**task** 명 일, 작업
**result in** 동 결과적으로 ~을 낳다

Science | 121 words | ★☆☆

Everyone yawns. Even babies in their mothers' bodies yawn. Why do we yawn? Scientists are not sure. But they have a couple of ideas.

According to one theory, breathing affects yawning. (a) When we are bored or tired, we do not breathe deeply. (b) So our bodies get less oxygen. (c) A lack of oxygen makes us feel tired. (d) The body needs oxygen, so it makes us yawn. (e) Don't forget to cover your mouth when you yawn. This brings in oxygen and removes *carbon dioxide from the body.

Another theory is that yawning is contagious. In other words, one person can make another person yawn. What happens when you see someone yawn? You probably feel like yawning, too. Try it right now. Look at someone and then yawn. Did that person also yawn?

*carbon dioxide 이산화탄소

핵심 구문 분석

13행 ▸ You / probably / **feel like** / yawning, / too.
당신은 / 아마도 / ~하고 싶은 생각이 들다 / 하품을 / 또한

feel like는 '~하고 싶은 생각이 들다'라는 뜻으로 뒤에 명사나 동명사 또는 문장이 온다.

Reading Skill | Cause and Effect

## 1

**글에서 우리가 하품하는 이유로 언급된 것을 모두 고르시오.**

① 몸 안에 이산화탄소가 부족해서
② 몸 안에 산소가 부족해서
③ 몸 밖으로 산소를 배출하기 위해서
④ 하품은 전염성이 있어서
⑤ 갑자기 하품하고 싶은 생각이 들어서

## 2

**글의 (a)~(e) 중, 전체 흐름과 관계 없는 문장은?**

① (a) ② (b) ③ (c) ④ (d) ⑤ (e)

## 3

**글의 내용과 일치하면 T, 그렇지 않으면 F를 쓰시오.**

(1) Babies yawn when they are in their mothers' bodies. ________
(2) When you yawn, oxygen is removed from your body. ________

서술형

## 4

**다음 빈칸에 알맞은 단어를 글에서 찾아 쓰시오.**

Everyone yawns. A lack of oxygen makes us yawn to bring in more ________ to our bodies. Yawning is also ________. So we yawn when another person yawns.

### Vocabulary

**yawn** 동 하품하다
**according to** ~에 따르면
**theory** 명 이론, 생각
**breathe** 동 호흡하다 *n.* breath 호흡
**affect** 동 영향을 주다
**bored** 형 지루한
**oxygen** 명 산소
**a lack of** ~의 부족(결핍)
**remove** 동 없애다
**contagious** 형 전염성의, 전염되는
**in other words** 다시 말해서
**probably** 부 아마
**right now** 지금 당장

# 12

Measure your height in the morning. Then measure it again at night. You are about one centimeter taller in the morning. Surprised?

Soft, stretchy tissue covers two body parts. ① They are the knees and the spine. ② While we walk during the day, the tissue in both places gets squeezed. ③ This makes the spaces between the bones grow smaller. ④ However, when we go to sleep, the soft tissue in the knees and spine goes back to its original form. ⑤

Gravity also affects our height. While we are standing, it pushes out the water between the *discs in the spine. <u>그것은 우리가 더 작아지게 하는 원인이 된다.</u> But when we sleep, our bodies are horizontal. Therefore, gravity does not affect our height.

For these two reasons, our height changes during the day and night.

*disc 추간판 (척추 마디 사이에 들어있는 물렁뼈)

**서술형 핵심 문법**

6행 ▸ **비교급 만들기:** 대부분의 형용사나 부사는 뒤에 -er를 붙이거나 앞에 more를 써서 비교급을 만들며, '더 ~한'이라는 뜻이다.
This makes the spaces between the bones grow **smaller**. 이것은 뼈 사이의 공간을 더 작게 만든다.

**우리말과 같은 뜻이 되도록 주어진 말을 바르게 배열하시오.**

나는 이전보다 더 행복하고 더 쾌활해졌다. (I / than / before / happier / and / became / more cheerful)

______________________________

1 **글의 내용과 일치하면 T, 그렇지 않으면 F를 쓰시오.**

(1) 신축성 있는 연조직은 낮 동안 원래의 형태로 되돌아간다. ________

(2) 우리 몸이 수평일 때 중력은 키에 영향을 미치지 못한다. ________

2 **다음 문장이 들어갈 위치로 가장 알맞은 곳은?**

| As a result, we get shorter during the day. |
|---|

① ② ③ ④ ⑤

Reading Skill Cause and Effect

3 **다음 빈칸에 알맞은 원인을 두 가지 고르시오.**

| Cause | | Effect |
|---|---|---|
| ________________ | ➡ | We get smaller during the day. |

① Gravity does not affect our height.
② When we sleep, our bodies are horizontal.
③ The soft tissue in the knees and spine gets squeezed.
④ The soft tissue in the knees returns to its original form.
⑤ Gravity pushes out the water between the discs in the spine.

서술형

4 **밑줄 친 우리말과 같은 뜻이 되도록 주어진 말을 바르게 배열하시오.**

(causes, smaller, get, that, us, to)

________________________________

서술형

5 **다음 영영풀이에 해당하는 단어를 글에서 찾아 쓰시오.**

| to find the size of something using a special tool |
|---|

________________

**Vocabulary**

**measure** 동 측정하다
**height** 명 키, 신장
**surprised** 형 놀란, 놀라는
**stretchy** 형 신축성이 있는
**tissue** 명 조직
**cover** 동 덮다
**spine** 명 척추
**squeeze** 동 압착하다
**go back to** ~로 돌아가다
**original** 형 원래의
**gravity** 명 중력
**horizontal** 형 수평의
**change** 동 변하다, 달라지다

CHAPTER 03 내신 대비 **실전 Test**

1 다음 중 단어의 영영풀이가 바르지 않은 것은?

① contagious: spreading from one person to another
② bored: not interested in something
③ original: parallel to the ground
④ flow: to move continuously in one direction
⑤ protect: to keep something from harm

2 다음 빈칸에 들어갈 말로 알맞은 것은?

The giraffe can ______ leaves on tall trees.

① squeeze ② spread ③ keep
④ reach ⑤ remove

3 다음 중 영어 표현과 우리말 뜻이 잘못 연결된 것은?

① stick to: ~에 들러붙다
② result in: ~로부터 야기되다
③ go back to ~로 돌아가다
④ according to: ~에 따르면
⑤ in other words: 다시 말해서

4 다음 빈칸에 들어갈 말로 알맞은 것은?

The hurricane prevented us from ______ outside.

① go ② to go ③ goes
④ going ⑤ gone

5 다음 빈칸에 공통으로 들어갈 말로 알맞은 것은?

• I ______ like going home now.
• The silk scarf ______s soft.

① look ② taste ③ sound
④ feel ⑤ smell

6 다음 중 어법상 어색한 것은?

① You look beautiful in that dress.
② Come closer to look at this.
③ I feel like I am a princess!
④ This shirt is more bigger.
⑤ The dentist prevented me from eating candy.

7 다음 빈칸에 들어갈 말로 알맞지 않은 것은?

What happened? You look ______ today.

① happy ② lovely ③ tiredly
④ busy ⑤ sleepy

서술형

8 다음 문장을 어법에 맞도록 바르게 고쳐 쓰시오.

Korean food is becoming popularer around the world.

______________________________

______________________________

서술형

9 다음 우리말과 같은 뜻이 되도록 주어진 말을 바르게 배열하시오.

이것은 그 병이 퍼지는 것을 막아줄 것이다.

(from, the disease, will, this, prevent, spreading)

______________________________

[10-12] 다음 글을 읽고 물음에 답하시오.

Dogs and cats are two popular pets. But look closely at ⓐ them. Most cat breeds look similar. But dog breeds look quite different in their sizes, shapes, faces, and colors. ① There is a reason for this.

② Humans tamed dogs and cats a long time ago. ⓑ They kept cats to catch mice. On the other hand, ⓒ they kept dogs for several reasons. ③ For example, ⓓ they used dogs for hunting, herding animals, protecting places, and pulling sleds. ④ So humans created new breeds of dogs because dogs had to do different tasks. ⑤

In addition, humans started breeding dog hundreds of years ago. But ⓔ they only started breeding cats around 75 years ago. As a result, there are 340 breeds of dogs today. But there are only 42 breeds of cats.

**10** 글의 밑줄 친 ⓐ~ⓔ 중, 가리키는 대상이 나머지 넷과 다른 것은?

① ⓐ ② ⓑ ③ ⓒ ④ ⓓ ⑤ ⓔ

서술형

**11** 다음 영영풀이에 해당하는 단어를 글에서 찾아 쓰시오.

to make something easier to control

______________

**12** 다음 문장이 들어갈 위치로 가장 알맞은 곳은?

This resulted in many different types of dogs.

① ② ③ ④ ⑤

[13-15] 다음 글을 읽고 물음에 답하시오.

(A) For these two reasons, our height changes during the day and night.

(B) Soft, stretchy tissue covers two body parts. They are the knees and the spine. While we walk during the day, the tissue in both places gets squeezed. This makes the spaces between the bones grow ___(a)___. As a result, we get shorter during the day. However, when we go to sleep, the soft tissue in the knees and spine goes back to its original form.

(C) Gravity also affects our height. While we are standing, it pushes out the water between the discs in the spine. That causes us to get ___(b)___ But when we sleep, our bodies are horizontal. ______________, gravity does not affect our height.

**13** 글의 빈칸에 들어갈 말로 가장 알맞은 것은?

① For example ② Therefore
③ In addtion ④ However
⑤ In other words

**14** (A)~(C)를 글의 흐름에 알맞게 배열한 것은?

① (A) – (B) – (C) ② (B) – (A) – (C)
③ (B) – (C) – (A) ④ (C) – (A) – (B)
⑤ (A) – (C) – (B)

서술형

**15** 글의 빈칸 (a)와 (b)에 공통으로 들어갈 알맞은 말을 쓰시오. (1단어)

______________

CHAPTER
# 04 Guessing Unknown Words
## 어휘 추론

### Reading Skill 이해하기

**Guessing Unknown Words**는 모르는 단어의 의미를 문맥을 이용하여 추측하는 리딩 스킬이다. 대부분 단어 앞뒤에 그 뜻을 짐작할 수 있는 어구들이 제시되어 있으므로 이를 종합하여 단어의 의미를 파악하는 훈련이 필요하다.

#### 지시문 유형

- 밑줄 친 ⓐ의 의미로 알맞은 것은?
- 밑줄 친 ⓐ와 바꿔 쓸 수 있는 단어를 글에서 찾아 쓰시오.

#### 문제 해결 Tips

- 문맥상 그 단어가 어떤 뜻이어야 글의 흐름이 자연스러운지 짐작해 본다.
- 모르는 단어가 있는 문장의 앞뒤 문장에서 다른 표현으로 되풀이되는 단어의 설명을 찾는다.
- 접속사(although, however, etc.)를 통해 단어의 뜻이 긍정적인지 부정적인지를 유추할 수 있다.

#### 내신 실전 적용 독해

**밑줄 친 ⓐ hesitate의 의미로 알맞은 것은?**

You wake up in the middle of the night and smell smoke. Your house is on fire! What should you do? Should you call the fire department first? Or should you find a safe place in the house? You need to get out of the house at once. Do not ⓐ hesitate. Do not take anything with you either. If there is smoke, get close to the floor. Smoke rises, so there is more fresh air near the floor. After you get outside, you can call the fire department.

① wake up
② leave
③ hurry
④ pause
⑤ breathe

# 13

Body & Food | 137 words | ★★☆

You eat some beans for lunch. A while later, you are sitting in class. You get a strange feeling in your body. Suddenly, it ⓐ happens: you fart out loud. It smells terrible, and everyone ⓑ laughs at you. You are embarrassed, but you should not be. Farting is actually a good sign.

Foods such as beans, bananas, and apples have lots of *resistant starch. All people have bacteria inside their *intestines. When the bacteria break down the resistant starch, they ⓒ release smelly gas. Then, your body removes this gas as a fart. At the same time, the bacteria release a *molecule. It ⓓ helps blood flow to the intestines and ⓔ gets rid of sick *cells.

So do not avoid eating foods rich in resistant starch. Sure, you will fart. But the resistant starch can help you avoid getting sick.

*resistant starch 저항성 전분 *intestine 장, 창자
*molecule 분자 *cell 세포

핵심 구문 분석

13행 ▸ So / do not **avoid** / eating foods / rich in / resistant starch.
그러므로 / 피하지 말아라 / 음식을 먹는 것을 / ~이 풍부한 / 저항성 전분

avoid는 '~을 피하다, 방지하다'라는 뜻으로 뒤에 명사나 동명사가 온다.

1 **글의 요지로 가장 알맞은 것은?**

① Some foods make your farts smell bad.
② Beans and apples are rich in resistant starch.
③ Foods that make you fart can be good for you.
④ Bacteria play an important role in our bodies.
⑤ You should not be embarrassed when you fart.

Reading Skill | Guessing Unknown Words

2 **글의 ⓐ~ⓔ 중, 밑줄 친 remove와 의미가 같은 것은?**

① ⓐ ② ⓑ ③ ⓒ ④ ⓓ ⑤ ⓔ

3 **글에 따르면, 방귀에서 냄새가 나는 이유는?**

① 냄새가 강한 음식을 먹었기 때문에
② 박테리아가 분자를 방출하기 때문에
③ 분자가 혈액이 내장으로 가는 것을 돕기 때문에
④ 병든 세포를 제거하는 과정에서 냄새가 발생하기 때문에
⑤ 박테리아가 저항성 전분을 분해할 때 냄새가 발생하기 때문에

서술형

4 **다음 빈칸에 알맞은 단어를 글에서 찾아 쓰시오.**

When __________ break resistant starch down in your intestines, they release smelly gas. Then, it is removed from your body. This is why your __________ smell bad.

**strange** 형 이상한
**suddenly** 부 갑자기
**fart** 명 방귀 동 방귀를 뀌다
**terrible** 형 끔찍한
**laugh at** ~을 비웃다
**embarrassed** 형 당황스러운
**actually** 부 실제로, 사실은
**sign** 명 신호, 징조
**inside** 전 ~의 안에
**break down** 분해하다
**smelly** 형 냄새 나는
**get rid of** ~을 없애다
**rich in** ~이 풍부한
**get sick** 병에 걸리다

# 14

Culture | 139 words | ★★★

Weddings are important events in people's lives. People celebrate them by singing, dancing, and eating delicious food. But there are ______________ in some countries. 5

In Scotland, friends sometimes throw garbage at the bride and groom. They are helping the bride and groom prepare for difficult times in their marriage. In Korea, wedding guests beat the groom's bare feet after the ceremony ends. They tie his feet together and ⓐ slap them with dried 10 fish. They are testing the groom's strength for married life.

Perhaps the strangest one of all is a Tujia tradition from China. Brides are expected to cry at their weddings. As a result, they practice for many hours before ⓑ the big day. After getting married, the brides cry in front of the guests. They think the more beautifully they cry, the luckier they 15 will be.

**서술형 핵심 문법**

11행 ▸ **현재진행형:** 〈am/are/is + v-ing〉의 형태로 지금 진행 중인 동작을 나타낼 때 쓰며, '~하고 있다, ~하는 중이다'라는 뜻이다.

They **are testing** the groom's strength for married life. 그들은 결혼생활을 위한 신랑의 힘을 시험하고 있다.

**우리말과 같은 뜻이 되도록 주어진 말을 바르게 배열하시오.**

그녀는 저녁으로 스파게티를 요리하고 있다. (spaghetti / is / for dinner / cooking / she)

______________________________

1 글의 내용과 일치하면 T, 그렇지 않으면 F를 쓰시오.

(1) 스코틀랜드의 결혼식에서 친구들은 신랑 신부에게 쓰레기를 던진다. ________

(2) 한국에서는 결혼식 후에 신랑의 발을 대나무로 때린다. ________

2 글을 읽고 답할 수 없는 질문은?

① How do people celebrate weddings?
② What do people throw at weddings in Scotland?
③ Why do people beat a Korean groom's feet?
④ How long do brides cry at Chinese weddings?
⑤ Why do Chinese brides cry at weddings?

3 글의 빈칸에 들어갈 말로 가장 알맞은 것은?

① some similar ceremonies
② typical ways to celebrate
③ unusual wedding traditions
④ tests for brides and grooms
⑤ many wedding ceremonies

Reading Skill | Guessing Unknown Words

4 밑줄 친 ⓐ slap과 바꿔 쓸 수 있는 단어를 글에서 찾아 쓰시오.

________________

서술형

5 글의 밑줄 친 ⓑ the big day가 의미하는 것을 우리말로 쓰시오.

________________

**Vocabulary**

**important** 형 중요한
**life** 명 삶 *pl.* lives
**celebrate** 동 기념하다, 축하하다
**unusual** 형 특이한, 독특한
**garbage** 명 쓰레기
**bride** 명 신부
**groom** 명 신랑
**throw** 동 던지다 (throw - threw - thrown)
**prepare** 동 준비하다, 대비하다
**bare** 형 벌거벗은
**ceremony** 명 의식, 식
**strength** 명 힘, 기운
**expect** 동 기대하다
**practice** 동 연습하다
**get married** 결혼하다

# 15

Origins | 140 words | ★★☆

Visit a park, and you will probably see a flying saucer. Is it a UFO? No, it is an *IFO: a frisbee. The Frisbee is popular because it is easy to carry and play with. But its beginning was humble.

In 1871, William Frisbie sold pies on thin metal plates. Students would throw the empty plates and yell, "Frisbie!" Later, Walter Morrison and Warren Franscioni ⓐ invented a plastic disc. It flew better than metal ones. They called it the Frisbee.

The Frisbee flies well thanks to its design. With its curved top, the Frisbee is shaped like an airplane wing. As it flies, air travels more quickly above it than below it. This creates lift, so it flies while spinning. The spinning motion of the Frisbee gives it *momentum. This lets it fly in the air for a long time.

*IFO (identified flying object) 확인 비행 물체 *momentum 가속도

10행 ▸ **As** / it flies, / air travels / more quickly / above it / than / below it.
~할 때 / 그것은 난다 / 공기는 이동한다 / 더 빨리 / 그것 위에서 / ~보다 / 그것 아래에서

as는 시간을 나타내는 접속사로 '~할 때, ~함에 따라'의 의미로 동시에 일어나는 상황을 나타낼 때 쓰인다.

1 What is the best title for the passage?

① How to Play with a Frisbee
② The Reasons Why the Frisbee Is Popular
③ How Fast the Frisbee Is
④ The Origin of the Frisbee and How It Flies
⑤ The Life of the Frisbee Inventor

Reading Skill | Guessing Unknown Words

2 밑줄 친 ⓐ invented의 의미로 알맞은 것은?

① flew ② created ③ sold ④ called ⑤ spun

3 Frisbee에 관한 글의 내용과 일치하지 않는 것은?

① Frisbee는 누구나 쉽게 가지고 놀 수 있다.
② 비행할 때 Frisbee의 위 아래 공기의 속도가 다르다.
③ Frisbee는 William Frisbie에 의해 만들어졌다.
④ 파이를 담아 팔던 철판 접시에서 시작되었다.
⑤ Frisbee의 윗부분은 비행기의 날개처럼 곡선 모양이다.

서술형

4 Frisbee가 오랫동안 공중에서 날 수 있는 이유를 우리말로 쓰시오.

______________________________

**saucer** 명 받침 접시
**carry** 동 운반하다, 나르다
**play with** ~을 가지고 놀다
**humble** 형 초라한, 겸손한
**thin** 형 얇은
**metal plate** 명 철판
**empty** 형 빈, 비어 있는
**disc** 명 원반
**design** 명 디자인, 설계
**curved** 형 곡선 모양의, 굽은
**spin** 동 회전하다 (spin - spun - spun)
**motion** 명 운동, 움직임
**for a long time** 오랫동안

# 16

Space | 140 words | ★☆☆

Some planets are easy to identify. Earth is blue, Mars is red, and Saturn has beautiful rings. And Jupiter is the big planet with the Great Red Spot.

What is the Great Red Spot in Jupiter? It is a ⓐ gigantic storm. In fact, it has winds blowing more than 640 kilometers per hour. The storm has been on Jupiter for at least 150 years and maybe for more than 400 years. How is that possible? 목성은 대부분 기체로 이루어져 있다. So it has no solid ground to weaken storms.

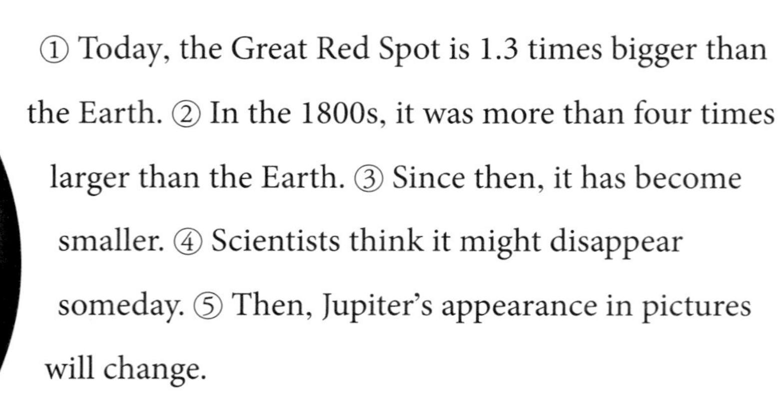

① Today, the Great Red Spot is 1.3 times bigger than the Earth. ② In the 1800s, it was more than four times larger than the Earth. ③ Since then, it has become smaller. ④ Scientists think it might disappear someday. ⑤ Then, Jupiter's appearance in pictures will change.

**서술형 핵심 문법**

13행 ▸ **접속사 that**: think, say, believe 등의 동사 뒤에 오는 접속사 that은 목적절을 이끈다. 이때 that은 생략할 수 있다.
Scientists think (**that**) it might disappear someday. 과학자들은 그것이 언젠가 사라질 수 있다고 생각한다.

**우리말과 같은 뜻이 되도록 주어진 말을 바르게 배열하시오.**

나는 네가 진실을 말하고 있다고 믿는다. (are telling / you / believe / I / the truth / that)

______________________________

1 **다음 중 글의 내용과 일치하지 않는 것은?**

① 토성은 아름다운 고리를 가지고 있다.
② 목성은 대부분 기체로 이루어져 있다.
③ 목성의 대적점은 거대한 폭풍이다.
④ 1800년대에 대적점의 크기는 지구의 1.3배였다.
⑤ 과학자들은 대적점이 사라질 수도 있다고 생각한다.

Reading Skill | Guessing Unknown Words

2 **밑줄 친 ⓐ gigantic의 의미로 알맞은 것은?**

① colorful ② beautiful ③ large ④ small ⑤ fantastic

3 **다음 문장이 들어갈 위치로 가장 알맞은 곳은?**

| But it used to be bigger. |
|---|

① ② ③ ④ ⑤

서술형

4 **밑줄 친 우리말과 같은 뜻이 되도록 주어진 말을 바르게 배열하시오.**

(mostly, Jupiter, of, made, is, gas)

______________________________

서술형

5 **글의 내용과 일치하도록 다음 질문에 답하시오.**

Q: Why has Jupiter had a gigantic storm for a long time?
A: Because ______________________________

### Vocabulary

**planet** 명 행성
**identify** 동 확인하다, 알아보다
**Mars** 명 화성
**Saturn** 명 토성
**ring** 명 고리, 고리 모양의 것
**Jupiter** 명 목성
**spot** 명 점
**gigantic** 형 거대한
**storm** 명 폭풍
**blow** 동 바람이 불다
**be made of** ~로 이루어지다
**solid** 형 고체의, 단단한
**weaken** 동 약하게 하다
**disappear** 동 사라지다
**appearance** 명 모습, 외모

CHAPTER
# 04 내신 대비 실전 Test

1 다음 영영풀이가 가리키는 단어로 알맞은 것은?

feeling ashamed or shy

① terrible ② solid ③ bare
④ embarassd ⑤ humble

2 다음 중 나머지 넷을 모두 포함할 수 있는 단어는?

① planet ② Mars ③ Jupiter
④ Earth ⑤ Saturn

3 다음 빈칸에 들어갈 말로 알맞은 것은?

Water ______ oxygen and hydrogen.

① gets rid of ② is made of
③ laughs at ④ plays with
⑤ breaks down

4 다음 빈칸에 공통으로 들어갈 말로 알맞은 것은?

• People become wise ______ they get old.
• You will become healthy ______ you exercise.

① so ② because ③ as
④ until ⑤ after

5 다음 빈칸에 들어갈 말로 알맞은 것은?

I think ______ the movie is wonderful.

① and ② but ③ so
④ that ⑤ or

6 다음 중 어법상 어색한 것은?

① If you can't avoid it, enjoy it.
② Mom is listening to music now.
③ As the sun sets, the sky is beautiful.
④ I think that I am good at math.
⑤ They is talking to each other.

7 다음 빈칸에 들어갈 말이 바르게 짝지어진 것은?

• Dave ______ a sandwich for lunch now.
• Jenny and I ______ math now.

① has – studies
② is having – is studying
③ has – study
④ is having – are studying
⑤ had – studied

서술형
8 다음 문장을 어법에 맞도록 바르게 고쳐 쓰시오.

You can avoid get a cold if you get a flu shot.

______________________________

서술형
9 다음 우리말과 같은 뜻이 되도록 주어진 단어를 이용해 영작하시오.

그 공은 공중에서 회전하고 있다.

(spin, in the air)

______________________________

[10-12] 다음 글을 읽고 물음에 답하시오.

Weddings are important events in people's lives. People celebrate them by singing, dancing, and eating delicious food. But there are unusual wedding traditions in some countries.

(A) In Scotland, friends sometimes throw garbage at the bride and groom. They are helping the bride and groom prepare for difficult times in their marriage.

① Perhaps the strangest one of all is a Tujia tradition from China. ② Brides are expected to cry at their weddings. ③ After getting married, the brides cry in front of the guests. ④ They think the more beautifully they cry, the luckier they will be. ⑤

서술형

**10** 밑줄 친 (A)와 같이 하는 이유를 우리말로 쓰시오.

______________________________

______________________________

**11** 다음 문장이 들어갈 위치로 가장 알맞은 곳은?

> As a result, they practice for many hours before the big day.

① ② ③ ④ ⑤

**12** Tujia 전통에 관한 글의 내용과 일치하지 않는 것은?

① 중국의 한 소수민족의 전통이다.
② 신부는 결혼식에서 울어야 한다.
③ 신부는 결혼식 전에 우는 연습을 한다.
④ 신부는 결혼식 날 신랑 앞에서 울어야 한다.
⑤ 신부가 아름답게 울수록 운이 더 좋아진다고 믿는다.

[13-15] 다음 글을 읽고 물음에 답하시오.

(A) Foods such as beans, bananas, and apples have lots of resistant starch. All people have bacteria inside their intestines. When the bacteria break down the resistant starch, they release smelly gas. Then, your body removes this gas as a fart. At the same time, the bacteria release a molecule. ⓐ It helps blood flow to the intestines and gets rid of sick cells.

(B) So do not avoid eating foods rich in resistant starch. Sure, you will fart. But the resistant starch can help you avoid getting sick.

(C) You eat some beans for lunch. A while later, you are sitting in class. You get a strange feeling in your body. Suddenly, it happens: you fart out loud. It smells terrible, and everyone laughs at you. You are embarrassed, but you should not be. Farting is actually a good sign.

**13** 글의 밑줄 친 ⓐ It이 가리키는 것은?

① your body ② resistant starch
③ smelly gas ④ fart
⑤ molecule

**14** (A)~(C)를 글의 흐름에 알맞게 배열한 것은?

① (A) – (B) – (C) ② (C) – (A) – (B)
③ (B) – (C) – (A) ④ (B) – (A) – (C)
⑤ (A) – (C) – (B)

서술형

**15** 다음 영영풀이에 해당하는 단어를 글에서 찾아 쓰시오. (2단어)

> to separate something into smaller parts

______________________________

CHAPTER 05

# Identifying Cohesive Devices: Pronoun 지칭 추론: 대명사

## Reading Skill 이해하기

대명사는 사람이나 사물을 가리키는 말로 보통 앞에서 언급된 명사를 대신하여 사용된다.
**Identifying Cohesive Devices: Pronoun**은 대명사가 가리키는 대상이 무엇인지 파악하여 글을 정확하게 이해할 수 있도록 돕는 리딩 스킬이다.

### 지시문 유형

- 글의 밑줄 친 ⓐ It이 가리키는 것은?
- 글의 밑줄 친 ⓐ~ⓔ 중, 가리키는 대상이 나머지 넷과 다른 것은?

### 문제 해결 Tips

- 대명사가 가리키는 대상은 단어뿐만 아니라 구, 절, 또는 문장 전체일 수 있다.
- 대명사의 종류에 따라 지칭하는 대상이 단수인지 복수인지 알 수 있다.
- 대명사 자리에 그것이 지칭하는 것을 넣어서 내용이 자연스러운지 확인한다.

### 내신 실전 적용 독해

**글의 밑줄 친 ⓐ it이 가리키는 것은?**

Matt used to spend more than 5 hours a day playing on his mobile phone. He lost interest in other activities. His mom was upset, so she took ⓐ it away from him. Matt had a hard time at first. He was bored and did not know what to do. But he slowly changed his lifestyle. He read more books. He did outdoor activities. He also spent more time with his friends and family. Living without his phone was not so bad after all.

① a day
② his mobile phone
③ interest
④ a hard time
⑤ his lifestyle

# 17

Origins | 137 words | ★★☆

Mom: Wake up! It's time for school.

Sam: Mom, I feel ⓐ under the weather.

What does Sam mean? Is the weather above him? He is saying he is sick. Many people use ⓑ this expression when they are sick. But where does ⓒ it come from? 5

*Historians believe ⓓ it comes from the sea. In the past, there were no airplanes. So people traveled long distances by ship. Ships usually sailed in clear weather. But sometimes the weather turned bad. The wind blew, and rain fell. Ships moved back and forth. ⓔ It caused passengers to become seasick. 10

In bad weather, people could not stay on a ship's top deck. Instead, they went below deck as the rocking there was less *noticeable. Passengers had to go under the deck because of the weather. So the expression "under the weather" was born. 15

*historian 역사가 *noticeable 뚜렷한

**핵심 구문 분석**

10행 ▸ It / **caused** / passengers / **to become** seasick.
그것은 / 야기했다 / 승객들이 / 뱃멀미하는 것을

〈cause + 목적어 + to부정사〉는 '~가 …하는 것을 야기하다, ~가 …하는 원인이 되다'라는 뜻으로 목적격보어 자리에 to부정사가 온다.

1 글의 제목으로 가장 알맞은 것은?

① An Expression about Feeling Sick
② How to Travel Long Distances
③ The Relationship between the Weather and Sailing
④ When You Are Feeling under the Weather
⑤ The Ways People Traveled in the Past

Reading Skill | Identify Cohesive Devices: Pronoun

2 글의 밑줄 친 ⓐ~ⓔ 중, 가리키는 대상이 나머지 넷과 다른 것은?

① ⓐ ② ⓑ ③ ⓒ ④ ⓓ ⑤ ⓔ

서술형

3 날씨가 좋지 않을 때 사람들이 갑판 아래로 내려간 이유를 우리말로 쓰시오.

______________________________

서술형

4 밑줄 친 ⓐ under the weather와 바꿔 쓸 수 있는 단어를 글에서 찾아 쓰시오.

______________

# 18

Society | 134 words | ★★☆

You are going on vacation to a tropical island. But your plane crashes. You survive and swim to the closest island. But ⓐ it is a deserted island. You probably feel frightened. But calm down and think about what you need to survive. Here are some tips for survival. 5

- Look for a source of *fresh water like a stream. You can only live 3~4 days without water.
- Build a shelter to protect yourself from bad weather and animals.
- Make a fire to cook food and to signal for help. 10
- Spell H-E-L-P on the beach. Someone can see your SOS message and rescue you.
- Find some edible food like roots and fruits. You can fish in the ocean, too.

_______________, stay positive and relax. Someone on a passing plane or ship will save you. 15

*fresh water 담수, 식수

**서술형 핵심 문법**

7행 ▸ **명령문:** 무엇을 시키거나 지시할 때 쓰는 문장으로 동사원형으로 시작한다. 부정명령문은 Don't를 동사원형 앞에 쓴다.
**Look** for a source of fresh water like a stream. 시냇물과 같은 식수의 원천을 찾아라.

**우리말과 같은 뜻이 되도록 주어진 말을 바르게 배열하시오.**

집에 돌아온 후에는 손을 씻어라. (you / come back / after / your hands / home / wash)

_______________________________________________

1 **글의 내용과 일치하면 T, 그렇지 않으면 F를 쓰시오.**

(1) Deserted islands usually have no food sources. ________

(2) You need fresh water to survive more than 4 days. ________

2 **글에서 무인도에서 살아남기 위한 조언으로 언급되지 않은 것은?**

① 마실 수 있는 물 찾기
② 열매나 물고기 같은 식량 구하기
③ 동물들의 접근을 막을 불 지피기
④ 해변에 조난 신호 메시지 적어 두기
⑤ 궂은 날씨를 피할 은신처 만들기

3 **글의 빈칸에 들어갈 말로 가장 알맞은 것은?**

① As a result ② However ③ Nevertheless
④ Most of all ⑤ Instead

Reading Skill | Identify Cohesive Devices: Pronoun

4 **글의 밑줄 친 ⓐ it이 가리키는 것을 찾아 쓰시오.**

________________

서술형

5 **다음 영영풀이에 해당하는 단어를 글에서 찾아 쓰시오.**

to stay alive in a difficult or dangerous situation

________________

Vocabulary

**go on vacation** 휴가를 가다
**tropical** 형 열대 지방의
**crash** 동 추락하다
**survive** 동 생존하다 *n.* survival 생존
**deserted island** 무인도
**frightened** 형 무서워하는, 겁먹은
**calm down** 진정하다
**source** 명 근원, 원천
**stream** 명 개울, 시내
**shelter** 명 은신처
**signal** 동 신호를 보내다 명 신호
**rescue** 동 구하다 (= save)
**edible** 형 먹을 수 있는
**root** 명 (식물의) 뿌리
**positive** 형 긍정적인

# 19

Story | 140 words | ★★☆

Imagine finding a box full of treasure. Wouldn't that be exciting? ⓐ This could really happen. But first, you need to travel to the Rocky Mountains in the United States.

In 2010, Forrest Fenn filled a box with $2 million of treasure. Then, he buried it in the Rocky Mountains. He also wrote a poem with clues for finding the treasure. ① Every year, people search for it. ② They dream of becoming rich. ③ Three people have died while searching for it. ④ So the police asked Fenn to take his treasure. ⑤ He said no because he wanted people to enjoy nature and have adventures.

Some say the whole thing is a trick. Others say Fenn already took the box back. Despite these rumors, people still look for the treasure. Do you want to join this treasure hunt?

**핵심 구문 분석**

9행 ▸ So / the police / **asked** / Fenn / **to take** / his treasure.
그래서 / 경찰은 / 부탁했다 / Fenn에게 / 가져가 달라고 / 그의 보물을

〈ask + 목적어 + to부정사〉는 '~에게 …할 것을 부탁하다/요청하다'라는 뜻으로 목적격보어 자리에 to부정사가 온다.

Reading Skill | Identify Cohesive Devices: Pronoun

1 **글의 밑줄 친 ⓐ This가 가리키는 것은?**

① 보물상자를 상상하는 것
② 보물상자를 발견하는 것
③ 로키산맥을 여행하는 것
④ 자연과 모험하기를 즐기는 것
⑤ 로키산맥에 보물상자를 묻어두는 것

2 **보물상자에 관한 글의 내용과 일치하지 않는 것은?**

① 2010년 Fenn이 로키산맥에 묻었다.
② 2백만 달러의 보물로 채워져 있다.
③ 찾을 수 있는 단서가 시에 있다.
④ 부자가 되고자 하는 많은 사람이 찾아 나섰다.
⑤ 경찰의 요구에 의해 Fenn이 이미 회수했다.

3 **다음 문장이 들어갈 위치로 가장 알맞은 곳은?**

| However, the search is not easy. |
|---|

① ② ③ ④ ⑤

서술형

4 **글의 내용과 일치하도록 다음 질문에 답하시오.**

Q: Why did Fenn refuse to take back the treasure box?
A: Because ______________________________

**imagine** 동 상상하다
**full of** ~로 가득 찬
**treasure** 명 보물
**exciting** 형 흥미진진한
**bury** 동 묻다
**poem** 명 시
**clue** 명 단서, 실마리
**dream of** ~을 꿈꾸다
**enjoy** 동 즐기다
**adventure** 명 모험
**whole** 형 전부의, 모든
**trick** 명 속임수
**despite** 전 ~에도 불구하고
**rumor** 명 소문, 유언비어

# 20

Laws | 138 words | ★★☆

Nations around the world establish laws to protect people's rights. They want people to live together without conflict. So most countries have similar laws. However, some places have strange laws.

In Singapore, chewing gum cannot be imported. This law was passed to keep public places clean. Denmark has official guidelines for naming children. There are 7,000 approved names on a list. If parents want to use different names, they need to get approval from the government. (a) People who feed the pigeons in Venice, Italy, will get fined $700. (b) The city thinks they are bad for people's health. (c) So they do not want more pigeons. (d) Finally, don't wear high heels in Greece. (e) High heels were first worn by men. ⓐ It is illegal because they can cause damage at ancient *monuments.

If you visit these places, remember these strange laws. Then, you will not ______________.

*monument 유물, 유적

서술형 핵심 문법

10행 ▸ **조동사 will**: 미래의 일을 말할 때 쓰는 것으로 '~할 것이다'라고 해석된다. will은 be going to로 대신할 수 있으며, 뒤에는 동사원형이 온다.

People who feed the pigeons in Venice, Italy, **will** get fined $700.

이탈리아 베네치아에서 비둘기에게 먹이를 주는 사람들은 700달러의 벌금을 부과받게 될 것이다.

**우리말과 같은 뜻이 되도록 주어진 말을 바르게 배열하시오.**

우리는 내일 소풍을 갈 것이다. (go on / will / a picnic / we / tomorrow)

______________________________

1 글의 주제로 가장 알맞은 것은?

① the roles of laws in countries
② why laws are similar around the world
③ how nations establish laws
④ laws to protect people's rights
⑤ unusual laws around the world

2 글의 빈칸에 들어갈 말로 가장 알맞은 것은?

① harm any monuments
② be fined a lot of money
③ get in trouble
④ avoid any conflicts
⑤ protect your rights

3 글의 (a)~(e) 중, 전체 흐름과 관계 없는 문장은?

① (a) ② (b) ③ (c) ④ (d) ⑤ (e)

Reading Skill | Identify Cohesive Devices: Pronoun

4 글의 밑줄 친 ⓐ It이 의미하는 내용을 우리말로 쓰시오.

__________________

서술형

5 다음 빈칸에 알맞은 단어를 글에서 찾아 쓰시오.

> Most countries have __________ laws. However, some places have __________ laws. You need to know these laws before you visit these places.

Vocabulary

- **nation** 명 국가
- **establish** 동 제정하다
- **conflict** 명 갈등, 분쟁
- **import** 동 수입하다 (≠ export 수출하다)
- **pass** 동 통과하다, 지나가다
- **public place** 공공장소
- **official** 형 공인된
- **approval** 명 승인 *v.* approve 승인하다
- **government** 명 정부
- **feed** 동 먹이를 주다
- **illegal** 형 불법의 (≠ legal 합법적인)
- **ancient** 형 고대의
- **damage** 명 손상, 훼손
- **get in trouble** 곤란에 처하다

# 내신 대비 실전 Test

서술형

**1** 다음 영영풀이가 의미하는 단어를 넣어 문장을 완성하시오.

a collection of valuable things such as gold

You will become rich if you find the hidden ____________.

**2** 다음 짝지어진 두 단어의 관계가 나머지 넷과 다른 것은?

① import : export ② legal : illegal
③ conflict : peace ④ exciting : boring
⑤ rescue : save

**3** 다음 중 영어 표현과 우리말 뜻이 잘못 연결된 것은?

① go on vacation: 휴가를 가다
② calm down: 내리다
③ full of: ~로 가득 찬
④ get in trouble: 곤란에 처하다
⑤ become seasick: 뱃멀미를 하다

**4** 다음 빈칸에 들어갈 말로 알맞은 것은?

Mom asked me ______ home early today.

① to come ② come ③ coming
④ came ⑤ is coming

**5** 다음 빈칸에 들어갈 말이 바르게 짝지어진 것은?

- ______ chew gum in the classroom.
- ______ quiet in public places.

① Be – Don't ② Don't be – Be
③ Don't be – Do ④ Don't – Be
⑤ Don't – Do

**6** 다음 중 어법상 어색한 것은?

① Imagine a desert without water.
② Don't be angry at me.
③ She will believes your lie.
④ Mom asked me to do my homework.
⑤ Stress can cause you to get sick.

서술형

**7** 다음 두 문장의 의미가 같도록 빈칸에 알맞은 말을 쓰시오.

Look at the sky. The sun will rise soon.
= Look at the sky. The sun ____________ rise soon.

서술형

**8** 다음 문장을 어법에 맞도록 바르게 고쳐 쓰시오.

It can cause many problems happened.

______________________________

서술형

**9** 다음 우리말과 같은 뜻이 되도록 주어진 말을 바르게 배열하시오.

Tom은 나에게 내 책을 빌려 달라고 부탁했다.

(to, asked, my, borrow, me, Tom, book)

______________________________

[10-12] 다음 글을 읽고 물음에 답하시오.

What does Sam mean? Is the weather above him? He is saying he is sick. Many people use this expression when they are sick. But where does it come from?

Historians believe it comes from the sea. ① In the past, there were no airplanes. ② So people traveled long distances by ship. ③ Ships usually sailed in clear weather. ④ The wind blew, and rain fell. ⑤ Ships moved back and forth. ⓐ It caused passengers __________ seasick.

In bad weather, people could not stay on a ship's top deck. Instead, they went below deck as the rocking there was less noticeable under the deck. Passengers had to go under the deck because of the weather. So the expression "under the weather" was born.

10 글의 빈칸에 들어갈 말로 가장 알맞은 것은?

① becomes ② to become
③ become ④ became
⑤ are becoming

11 다음 문장이 들어갈 위치로 가장 알맞은 곳은?

But sometimes the weather turned bad.

① ② ③ ④ ⑤

서술형
8 글의 밑줄 친 ⓐ It이 의미하는 내용을 우리말로 쓰시오.

__________

[13-15] 다음 글을 읽고 물음에 답하시오.

(A) If you visit these places, remember these strange laws. Then, you will not ⓐ get in trouble.

(B) Nations around the world establish laws to protect people's rights. They want people ⓑ to live together without conflict. So most countries have similar laws. However, some places have strange laws.

(C) In Singapore, chewing gum cannot be imported. This law was passed to keep public places clean. Denmark ⓒ has official guidelines for naming children. ⓓ There are 7,000 approved names on a list. If parents want to use different names, they need to get approval from the government. Finally, ⓔ not wear high heels in Greece. It is illegal because they can cause damage at ancient monuments.

13 글의 밑줄 친 ⓐ~ⓔ 중, 어법상 어색한 것은?

① ⓐ ② ⓑ ③ ⓒ ④ ⓓ ⑤ ⓔ

14 (A)~(C)를 글의 흐름에 알맞게 배열한 것은?

① (B) – (C) – (A) ② (B) – (A) – (C)
③ (A) – (B) – (C) ④ (C) – (A) – (B)
⑤ (A) – (C) – (B)

서술형
15 다음 영영풀이에 해당하는 단어를 글에서 찾아 쓰시오.

a disagreement or fighting between people

__________

CHAPTER

# 06 Compare & Contrast

비교와 대조

## Reading Skill 이해하기

**Compare & Contrast**는 글에서 언급된 사람이나 사물, 상황 등을 비교, 대조하는 리딩 스킬이다. 두 가지 또는 그 이상의 대상을 분석하여 유사점이나 차이점을 파악함으로써 글을 효율적으로 이해할 수 있도록 해준다.

### 지시문 유형

- 글에서 목관악기와 현악기의 공통점으로 언급된 것은?
- 글에 따르면, 캥거루와 코알라의 차이점은?
- 쥐와 햄스터의 차이점에 대한 다음의 도표를 완성하시오.

### 문제 해결 Tips

- 공통점을 언급할 때는 and, both, also, alike, similar 등의 단어를 자주 사용한다.
- 차이점을 나타낼 때는 but, however, yet, unlike, different 등의 단어를 자주 사용한다.
- 도표나 벤다이어그램을 활용하여 공통점과 차이점을 분석해 본다.

### 내신 실전 적용 독해

**글에서 다양한 빵들의 공통점으로 언급된 것은?**

Bread is delicious and a good source of energy. So it is popular around the world. But it has many different shapes and tastes. In France, the baguette is popular. It is a long, thin loaf of white bread. It is hard on the outside and chewy on the inside. In India, naan is a popular flat, round bread. People usually eat naan with butter or curry. And bagels are chewy rolls with a hole in the middle. People in Poland enjoy them. They spread cream cheese on their bagels.

① 폴란드 사람들이 즐겨 먹는다.
② 가운데에 구멍이 뚫려 있다.
③ 겉은 딱딱하고, 속은 쫄깃하다.
④ 맛있으며, 훌륭한 에너지원이다.
⑤ 버터나 카레와 함께 먹는다.

## 21 On the Left or Right?

좌측통행? 우측통행? | **Culture**

## 22 Upcycling

리사이클링 말고 업사이클링 | **Environment**

## 23 Colors and Advertising

색깔이 판매에 미치는 영향 | **Marketing**

## 24 Twins Are Not Always the Same

쌍둥이라고 다 같은 건 아니에요! | **Science**

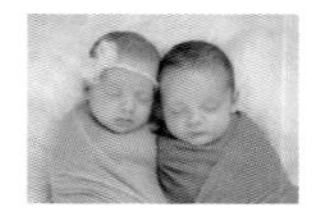

Culture | 140 words | ★★☆

Driving on the wrong side of the road is dangerous. In some countries, people drive on the left, but they drive on the right in other countries. Why are they different?

People often used to ride on horses in England. They rode to the left of others. So their right hand was closer to the people they passed. ⓐ That made it easier to wave or to draw a sword. Today, people in England and its former *colonies drive on the left.

However, wagons were popular in the USA. The drivers sat on the horse on the left. They drove the wagon with their left hand and whipped the horses with their right hand. They stayed on the right side of the road to see other wagons passing by. Today, the world's other countries, including the USA, drive on the right.

*colony 식민지

**핵심 구문 분석**

5행 ▸ People / often / **used to** ride / on horses / in England.
사람들은 / 종종 / 타곤 했다 / 말 위에 / 영국에서

used to는 '~하곤 했다'라는 뜻으로 과거의 반복적인 습관이나 상태를 나타낼 때 쓴다. 뒤에는 동사원형이 온다.

## 1 글의 내용과 일치하면 T, 그렇지 않으면 F를 쓰시오.

(1) 과거 영국의 식민지였던 국가에서는 차량이 우측통행을 한다. ________

(2) 미국에서는 운전자가 4륜 마차의 왼쪽 말에 탔다. ________

## 2 미국 사람들이 4륜 마차를 운전할 때 길의 오른쪽에 머문 이유는?

① 운전자가 왼쪽 말에 앉기 위해서
② 왼쪽 손으로 4륜 마차를 운전하기 위해서
③ 오른손으로 말에 채찍질하기 위해서
④ 우측통행을 해야 한다고 규정되어 있어서
⑤ 다른 마차들이 지나가는 것을 보기 위해서

Reading Skill | Compare & Contrast

## 3 다음 도표의 (A)에 들어갈 영국과 미국의 교통수단의 공통점은?

| England | | the USA |
|---|---|---|
| • People rode on horses.<br>• People drove on the left. | (A) | • Wagons were popular.<br>• People drove on the right. |

① People originally drove on the left.
② People originally drove on the right.
③ People used horses for transportation.
④ People preferred wagons to horses.
⑤ People whipped horses with their right hand.

서술형

## 4 글의 밑줄 친 ⓐ That이 의미하는 내용을 우리말로 쓰시오

________________________________________

**Vocabulary**

**wrong** 형 틀린, 잘못된
**dangerous** 형 위험한
**ride** 동 말을 타다
**wave** 동 (손을) 흔들다
**draw a sword** 칼을 뽑다
**former** 형 과거의, 예전의
**wagon** 명 4륜 마차
**whip** 동 채찍질하다
**side** 명 쪽, 편
**pass by** ~ 옆을 지나가다
**including** 전 ~을 포함하여

# 22

Environment | 137 words | ★★☆

Everyone knows recycling can help the environment. But few know about *upcycling. Both have positive impacts on the environment, but they have some differences.

When people recycle materials, they get broken down. Then, they are remade into new ⓐ products. It requires energy and water to break down the materials. And the quality of the new products is often worse than the original ones.

Upcycling does not break down items. ______________, people find different ways to use them. For example, someone might turn doors into tables. Another person might make vases from empty plastic bottles. Making upcycled items just requires creativity. And their quality is often better or the same as the originals.

Upcycling is nothing new. People used to make new goods from old items to save money. However, we can help the environment by upcycling nowadays.

*upcycling 업사이클링, 창조적 재활용

**서술형 핵심 문법**

1행 ▸ **조동사 can**: '~할 수 있다'라는 의미의 능력이나 가능을 나타낼 때 사용하며, 뒤에는 동사원형이 온다.
can은 be able to로 바꿔 쓸 수 있다.
Everyone knows recycling can help the environment. 모든 사람은 재활용이 환경에 도움이 될 수 있다고 알고 있다.

**우리말과 같은 뜻이 되도록 주어진 말을 바르게 배열하시오.**

모든 사람은 그 질문에 대답할 수 있다. (answer / question / everyone / the / can)

______________________________

1 What is the best title for the passage?

① Why Recycling Is Important
② When Upcycling Started
③ How to Help the Environment
④ What Can Be Upcycled
⑤ Upcycling for the Enviornment

2 글의 빈칸에 들어갈 말로 가장 알맞은 것은?

① So ② In other words ③ Instead
④ Besides ⑤ For example

Reading Skill Compare & Contrast

3 글에서 재활용과 업사이클링의 공통점으로 언급된 것은?

① 많은 사람들에게 잘 알려져 있는 활동이다.
② 돈을 절약하기 위해 예전부터 사용되어 왔다.
③ 오래된 것을 분해해 새로운 물건으로 만든다.
④ 새롭게 만들어지는 물건의 질이 본래의 것보다 좋지 않다.
⑤ 환경을 보호하는 데 도움이 된다.

서술형

4 다음 영영풀이에 해당하는 단어를 글에서 찾아 쓰시오.

believing that a situation will get better

______________________

서술형

5 다음 빈칸에 알맞은 단어를 글에서 찾아 쓰시오.

__________ does not break down old items. People use them in other ways. It just requires __________ and is a good way to help the __________.

Vocabulary

**recycling** 명 재활용
*v.* recycle 재활용하다
**environment** 명 환경
**impact** 명 영향, 효과
**difference** 명 차이, 다른 점
**material** 명 재료
**remake** 동 다시 만들다
(remake - remade -remade)
**product** 명 제품, 물건
**require** 동 필요하다
**quality** 명 품질
**creativity** 명 창의성, 독창력
**goods** 명 상품, 물건
**save** 동 절약하다, 아끼다

# 23

You go shopping at a store. But there are many things to buy. You do not know which one to get. How do you decide?

(A) In fact, about 90% of all purchases are based on colors. Companies want to make as much money as they can. (B) Researchers learned that most shoppers make sudden decisions. They also often choose items based on the colors of their packages. (C) So they tried to figure out which colors shoppers like. That way, they could use them in their *ads.

According to their research, men prefer dark colors. So packaging for men often includes the color black. Women, however, prefer softer colors. That is why packaging for women's products often includes white. However, both men and women like blue more than any other color. So ⓐ that color is common in packaging.

*ads (advertisements) 광고

핵심 구문 분석

5행 ▸ Companies / **want** / **to make** / as much money / as they can.
회사들은 / 원한다 / 벌기를 / 많은 돈을 / 가능한 한

want는 '~하기를 원하다'라는 뜻으로 뒤에 to부정사를 목적어로 취한다. 이처럼 to부정사를 목적어로 취하는 동사에는 hope, need, expect, decide, plan 등이 있다.

**1** 글의 요지로 가장 알맞은 것은?

① White is women's favorite color.
② Companies want to make much money.
③ Men and women both like the color blue.
④ Colors are important for marketing.
⑤ Many shoppers make sudden decisions.

**2** (A)~(C)를 글의 흐름에 알맞게 배열한 것은?

① (A) – (B) – (C)　② (B) – (A) – (C)　③ (B) – (C) – (A)
④ (C) – (A) – (B)　⑤ (A) – (C) – (B)

Reading Skill | Compare & Contrast

**3** 글에 따르면, 남자와 여자의 선호 색깔의 차이점은?

① 남자는 파란색을 선호하는 반면 여자는 파란색을 선호하지 않는다.
② 남자는 여자와 달리 특별히 선호하는 색이 없다.
③ 남자는 여자와 달리 파란색을 선호하지 않는다.
④ 남자는 연한 색을 선호하는 반면 여자는 짙은 색을 선호한다.
⑤ 남자는 짙은 색을 선호하는 반면 여자는 연한 색을 선호한다.

서술형

**4** 글의 밑줄 친 ⓐ that color가 가리키는 것을 찾아 쓰시오.

______________________

**learn** 동 배우다, 학습하다
**sudden** 형 갑작스러운
**choose** 동 선택하다
**item** 명 물품, 품목
**based on** ~에 근거하여
**package** 명 포장물 동 포장하다
**purchase** 명 구매 동 구매하다
**company** 명 회사
**figure out** 알아내다
**include** 동 포함하다
**common** 형 흔한, 공통의

# 24

When we see two identical boys or girls, we know they are twins. However, twins can be different in appearances and personalities. Let's look at the two most common types of twins.

*Identical twins look exactly alike. ① They are born when one egg in the mother divides into two when she is pregnant. ② Identical twins share the same DNA. ③ They also often act alike. ④ They may have the same personalities and likes and dislikes. ⑤

*ⓐ Fraternal twins do not look exactly alike. ⓑ They are born when two separate eggs develop into babies. Fraternal twins do not share the same DNA. ⓒ They share only about half of the same genes. Unlike ⓓ identical twins, fraternal twins are usually one boy and one girl. ⓔ They act like regular brothers and sisters.

*identical twins 일란성 쌍둥이 *fraternal twins 이란성 쌍둥이

**서술형 핵심 문법**

7행 ▸ **빈도부사:** always, usually, often, sometimes, never 등은 어떤 일이 얼마나 자주 일어나는지 나타낼 때 사용하는 빈도부사로, be동사 뒤, 일반동사 앞에 위치한다.
They also **often** act alike. 그들은 또한 종종 비슷하게 행동한다.

**다음 문장을 어법에 맞도록 바르게 고쳐 쓰시오.**

I go usually to school by bus. 나는 보통 버스를 타고 학교에 간다

______________________________

**1** **이란성 쌍둥이에 관한 글의 내용과 일치하는 것은?**

① 이란성 쌍둥이는 행동과 성격이 비슷하다.
② 이란성 쌍둥이는 대부분 같은 성별이다.
③ 이란성 쌍둥이는 유전자를 거의 공유하지 않는다.
④ 이란성 쌍둥이는 눈으로 구별할 수 없다.
⑤ 이란성 쌍둥이는 서로 다른 두 개의 난자에서 자란다.

**2** **다음 문장이 들어갈 위치로 가장 알맞은 곳은?**

| For that reason, they are almost always two boys or two girls. |
| --- |

① ② ③ ④ ⑤

**3** **글의 밑줄 친 ⓐ~ⓔ 중, 가리키는 대상이 나머지 넷과 다른 것은?**

① ⓐ ② ⓑ ③ ⓒ ④ ⓓ ⑤ ⓔ

서술형

**4** **밑줄 친 identical과 의미가 같은 단어를 글에서 찾아 쓰시오. (1단어)**

____________________

Reading Skill | Compare & Contrast

**5** **일란성 쌍둥이와 이란성 쌍둥이의 차이점에 대한 다음의 도표를 완성하시오.**

| Identical Twins | Fraternal Twins |
| --- | --- |
| • Developed from one egg<br>• (1) ____________<br>• Act alike<br>• (2) ____________ | • Developed from two separate eggs<br>• Look different<br>• Act differently<br>• Share half of the same genes |

Vocabulary
**identical** 형 똑같은, 동일한
**personality** 명 성격
**exactly** 부 정확히, 꼭
**alike** 형 비슷한, 같은
**divide into** ~으로 나뉘다
**pregnant** 형 임신한
**share** 동 공유하다
**separate** 형 서로 다른, 별개의
**develop** 동 발달하다, 성장하다
**gene** 명 유전자
**regular** 형 보통의

# 내신 대비 실전 Test

1 다음 중 단어의 영영풀이가 바르지 않은 것은?

① dangerous: likely to harm somebody
② share: to use something with others
③ common: not right or correct
④ creativity: the ability to make something new
⑤ sudden: happening or done quickly

2 다음 빈칸에 들어갈 말로 알맞은 것은?

goods : products = similar : _______

① former ② alike ③ regular
④ separate ⑤ wrong

3 다음 중 영어 표현과 우리말 뜻이 잘못 연결된 것은?

① figure out: 알아내다
② pass by: ~ 옆을 지나가다
③ divide into: ~으로 나뉘다
④ based on: ~에 근거하여
⑤ draw a sword: 칼을 그리다

4 다음 빈칸에 들어갈 말로 알맞지 않은 것은?

I _______ share things with my brother.

① usually ② often ③ always
④ not ⑤ sometimes

서술형
5 다음 두 문장의 의미가 같도록 빈칸에 알맞은 말을 쓰시오.

She is able to speak English and Chinese.
= She _______ speak English and Chinese.

6 다음 빈칸에 들어갈 말로 알맞지 않은 것은?

I _______ to meet her in the near future.

① want ② avoid ③ hope
④ plan ⑤ expect

서술형
7 다음 우리말과 같은 뜻이 되도록 주어진 단어를 이용해 영작하시오.

그들은 주말마다 낚시를 가곤 했다.

(go fishing)

_______________

8 다음 중 어법상 어색한 것은?

① He sometimes is late for school.
② I decided to go to the concert.
③ She can come to the party.
④ My parents never hit me.
⑤ The singer used to be famous.

서술형
9 다음 우리말과 같은 뜻이 되도록 주어진 말을 바르게 배열하시오.

나는 영어 선생님이 되기를 원한다.

(want, become, teacher, I, English, to, an)

_______________

[10-12] 다음 글을 읽고 물음에 답하시오.

Everyone knows recycling can help the environment. But few know about upcycling. ⓐ Both have positive impacts on the environment, but ____________________.

When people recycle materials, they get broken down. Then, they are remade into new products. It requires energy and water to break down the materials. And the quality of the new products is often worse than the original ones.

Upcycling does not break down items. ① Instead, people find different ways to use them. ② Another person might make vases from empty plastic bottles. ③ Making upcycled items just requires creativity. ④ And their quality is often better or the same as the originals. ⑤

**10** 글의 빈칸에 들어갈 말로 가장 알맞은 것은?

① people do not know about them
② they are quite similar
③ they have a lot of similarties
④ they have some differences
⑤ they can harm the enviroment

**11** 다음 문장이 들어갈 위치로 가장 알맞은 곳은?

> For example, someone might turn doors into tables.

① ② ③ ④ ⑤

서술형

**12** 글의 밑줄 친 ⓐ Both가 가리키는 것을 찾아 쓰시오.

____________________

[13-15] 다음 글을 읽고 물음에 답하시오.

You go shopping at a store. But there are many things to buy. You do not know which one to get. How do you decide?

Researchers learned that most shoppers make sudden decisions. ⓐ They also often choose items based on the colors of their packages. In fact, about 90% of all purchases are based on colors. Companies want __________ as much money as they can. So they tried to figure out which colors shoppers like. That way, they could use them in their ads.

According to their research, men prefer dark colors. So packaging for men often includes the color black. Women, however, prefer softer colors. That is why packaging for women's products often includes white.

**13** 글의 밑줄 친 ⓐ They가 가리키는 것은?

① Researchers ② Shoppers
③ Decisions ④ Companies
⑤ Products

**14** 글의 빈칸에 들어갈 말로 가장 알맞은 것은?

① make ② made ③ to make
④ makes ⑤ making

서술형

**15** 다음 영영풀이에 해당하는 단어를 글에서 찾아 쓰시오.

> one thing on a list of things to buy

____________________

# Reading Skill로 끝내는 중학 내신 독해 1

Level

저자 플라워에듀 · Michael A. Putlack

초판 1쇄 발행 2018년 10월 30일
초판 3쇄 발행 2023년 1월 17일

편집장 조미자
책임편집 김미경 · 정진희
표지디자인 김성희
디자인 김성희 · 임미영
마케팅 도성욱 · 문신영
인쇄 삼화 인쇄

펴낸이 정규도
펴낸곳 Happy House, an imprint of DARAKWON

경기도 파주시 문발로 211, 다락원 빌딩
전화 02-736-2031 (내선 250)
팩스 02-736-2037
출판등록 1977년 9월 16일 제406-2008-000007호



ISBN 978-89-6653-555-2 53740

값 11,000원

구성 본책 + Workbook + 정답 및 해설
무료 다운로드 MP3 파일, 단어 리스트, 단어 테스트, 정답 및 해설, Dictation Sheet, 녹음 대본 www.ihappyhouse.co.kr
*Happy House는 다락원의 임프린트입니다.

Laws

Architecture

Food

Space

Culture

Science

Story

Entertainment

Art

Animals

# Reading Skill로 끝내는 중학 내신 독해

Level 1

## 정답 및 해설

Happy House

# Reading Skill로 끝내는 중학 내신 독해 1

Level

## 정답 및 해설

Happy House

CHAPTER

# 01 Main Idea

## 내신 실전 적용 독해

p.06

정답 ③

날씨 확인, 구급상자 가져가기 등 캠핑 갈 때 주의할 여러 가지 사항에 관한 내용이므로 글의 주제는 ③이 가장 알맞다.

지문 해석 캠핑은 특히 가족이나 친구들과 함께하면 매우 즐겁다. 하지만 캠핑 여행을 위해서는 다음의 것들을 명심해라. 첫째, 가기 전에 날씨를 확인해라. 빗속에서 캠핑을 즐길 사람은 아무도 없다. 그 다음에, 누군가 다쳤을 경우를 대비하여 구급상자를 가져갈 필요가 있다. 덧붙여 모기를 쫓기 위한 벌레 퇴치 스프레이도 잊지 말아라. 마지막으로, 집으로 가기 전에 모닥불을 완전히 끄도록 해라. 이러한 간단한 방법을 따르면 당신은 안전하고 재미있는 캠핑 여행을 즐길 수 있을 것이다.

## 01

p.09

정답 **1** ② **2** ④ **3** ③ **4** dark chocolate

문제 해설

**1** 초콜릿에 들어있는 플라보노이드는 심장질환을 예방해주는 등 건강에 도움이 되지만, 너무 많은 양을 섭취하지는 말라는 내용이므로 글의 요지는 ②가 가장 알맞다.

**2** 빈칸 뒤에 플라보노이드가 건강에 주는 이점들을 예를 들어 설명하고 있으므로 ④ '예를 들어'가 가장 알맞다.
① 하지만 ② 그러므로 ③ 반면에 ⑤ 게다가

**3** 코코아는 심장질환을 예방하고, 심장마비의 위험을 줄여준다고 했지만, 심장 박동 수에 관한 내용은 언급되지 않았다.

**4** It은 바로 앞 문장에 있는 dark chocolate를 가리킨다.

구문 해설

01행 Most children love chocolate **because** it **tastes delicious**.
- because는 '~때문에'라는 접속사로 뒤에 〈주어 + 동사〉가 온다.
- 〈taste + 형용사〉는 '~한 맛이 나다'라는 뜻이다.

01행 However, most parents **tell** their children **not to eat** too much.
- 〈tell + 목적어 + to부정사〉는 '~에게 …하라고 말하다'라는 뜻인데, to부정사 앞에 not을 넣어 '…하지 말라고 말하다'라고 해석된다.

05행 A recent study **says that** dark chocolate has some health benefits.
- 〈say + that + 주어 + 동사〉는 '~라고 말하다'라는 뜻으로, that은 동사 says의 목적어로 쓰인 명사절을 이끄는 접속사이다.

11행 So **feel free to enjoy** chocolate each day.
- 〈feel free + to부정사〉는 '부담 없이 ~하다'라는 뜻으로, free 뒤에 to부정사가 온다.

지문 해석 대부분의 어린이는 맛이 좋다는 이유로 초콜릿을 아주 좋아한다. 그러나 대부분의 부모는 그들의 자녀들에게 너무 많이 먹지 말라고 말한다. 그 이유는 초콜릿은 열량이 높기 때문이다. 그것은 또한 많은 설탕을 함유하고 있어서, 치아에 좋지 않다. 다행스럽게도 아이들이 초콜릿을 먹기 위한 좋은 변명거리가 하나 있다.

최근의 연구는 다크 초콜릿이 건강에 몇 가지 이로운 점을 가지고 있다는 것을 밝혔다. 그것은 다른 종류의 초콜릿보다 더 많은 코코아 성분을 가지고 있다. 코코아는 플라보노이드를 함유하고 있다. 이것들은 우리 몸에 여러 가지 이점을 제공한다. 예를 들어, 그것들은 심장질환을 예방하는 데 도움을 준다. 그것들은 심장마비 혹은 뇌졸중의 위험성을 줄인다. 그것들은 또한 두뇌로 가는 혈류를 증가시킨다. 그것은 사람의 기억력을 향상시킨다.

그러니 매일 부담 없이 초콜릿 먹는 것을 즐겨라. 그러나 과학자들은 사람들은 하루에 대략 85g 정도의 다크 초콜릿만을 먹을 필요가 있다고 말한다. 그러니 너무 많이 먹지는 말아라.

## 02

pp.10~11

**서술형 핵심 문법** I want you to come to the festival.

| 정답 | 1 ⑤ | 2 ① | 3 ③ | 4 Naki Zumo 축제에서 아기를 울게 만드는 것 | 5 tradition |
|---|---|---|---|---|---|

**문제 해설**

1 아기에게 행운을 가져다주기 위한 일본의 전통을 소개하는 내용이므로 글의 주제는 ⑤ '행운을 얻기 위한 일본의 오래된 전통'이 가장 알맞다.
① 인기 있는 일본의 스포츠 스모
② 아기가 우는 가장 일반적인 이유
③ 아기를 큰 소리로 울게 만드는 방법
④ 세계의 흥미로운 전통들

2 빈칸에는 무서운 가면을 쓴 남자들이 아기들이 크게 울도록 '놀라게 하다'는 의미의 ① frighten이 들어가는 것이 가장 알맞다.
② 기쁘게 하다 ③ 만족시키다 ④ 간지럽히다 ⑤ 흔들다

3 일본인들은 스모선수의 손에서 아기가 울면, 그것이 아이에게 행운을 가져올 것이라고 믿는다고 했다. (11~12행)

4 앞 문단의 내용, 즉 'Naki Zumo 축제에서 아기를 울게 만드는 것'을 가리킨다.

5 '세대에서 세대로 전해지는 관습'이라는 뜻을 가진 단어는 tradition(전통)이다.

**구문 해설**

01행 Most parents never want to **hear** their babies **cry**.
- 〈hear + 목적어 + 동사원형〉은 '~가 …하는 것을 듣다'라는 뜻으로 지각동사의 목적격보어에는 동사원형이나 현재분사가 온다.

09행 Then, men in scary masks frighten the babies **to make** them **cry** loudly.
- to make는 to부정사의 부사적 용법의 목적으로 '~하기 위해서'라는 뜻이다.
- 〈make + 목적어 + 동사원형〉은 '~가 …하도록 만들다'라는 뜻이다.

14행 **What an interesting tradition!**
- 〈What + a/an + 형용사 + 명사 (+ 주어 + 동사)!〉는 '정말 …한 ~이다!'라는 뜻의 감탄문으로 이 문장에서는 〈주어 + 동사〉인 it is가 생략되어 있다.

**지문 해석**

대부분의 부모는 결코 그들의 아기들이 우는 소리를 듣는 것을 원치 않는다. 그러나 일본인 부모들은 가끔 그들의 아기들이 우는 것을 원한다. 사실 그들은 그들의 아기들이 소리 지르고 큰 소리로 악을 쓰는 것을 원한다.

매년 Naki Zumo 축제가 일본에서 열린다. 부모들은 그들의 아기들을 축제에 데려가서, 스모선수에게 건넨다. 그러면 스모선수들은 아기들을 공중으로 들어 올린다. 대부분의 아기는 울기 시작한다. 그러나 어떤

아기들은 울지 않는다. 그러면 무서운 가면을 쓴 남자들이 아기들을 크게 울리기 위해 놀라게 한다.

그들은 왜 이런 행동을 하는 것일까? 일본인들은 스모선수의 손에서 아기가 울면, 그것이 아이에게 행운을 가져올 것이라고 믿는다. 이것은 일본의 오래된 전통이다. 그래서 일본인 부모들은 그들의 아기들을 울리기 위해서 약 만 엔을 낸다. 정말 흥미로운 전통이다!

# 03

p.13

| 정답 | 1 ② | 2 ④ | 3 ③ | 4 the Hulk to look unlike anyone on the Earth |
|---|---|---|---|---|

**문제 해설**

1 Stan Lee가 헐크를 처음에 회색으로 그렸지만, 인쇄과정의 문제로 결국 초록색으로 바꾸게 된 내용이므로 ② '헐크 색깔의 변화'가 가장 알맞다.

[문제] 무엇에 관한 글인가?

① 만화책을 인쇄하는 것의 문제점

③ 유명한 슈퍼히어로의 기원

④ Stan Lee, 헐크의 창작자

⑤ 사람들이 슈퍼히어로를 좋아하는 이유

2 '그러나 첫 만화책 인쇄에 문제가 있었다'는 주어진 문장은 Stan Lee가 헐크를 회색으로 그렸다는 내용과 만화책에서 헐크의 색깔이 단지 회색만이 아니었다는 내용 사이인 ④에 오는 것이 가장 알맞다.

3 바로 앞 문장에 나온 내용, 즉 '헐크의 피부색을 초록색으로 바꾼 것'을 가리킨다.

4 Stan Lee는 헐크가 지구상의 어느 누구와도 다르게 보이기를 원해서 회색으로 그렸다고 했다. (5~6행)

Q: 왜 Stan Lee는 처음에 헐크를 회색으로 그렸는가?

A: 그는 헐크가 지구상의 어느 누구와도 다르게 보이기를 원했기 때문에

**구문 해설**

02행 They all **started as** comic book characters.

• as는 '~로서'라는 뜻의 자격을 나타내는 전치사로, started as는 '~로서 시작되었다'라고 해석된다.

09행 So Stan Lee **made** the Hulk **green**.

• 〈make + 목적어 + 형용사〉는 '~를 …하게 만들다'라는 뜻으로 형용사는 목적어를 설명해주는 목적격보어이다.

10행 **Thanks to** his green color, people can easily recognize the Incredible Hulk.

• thanks to는 '~ 덕분에'라는 뜻으로 뒤에 명사가 온다.

**지문 해석**

요즘에는 슈퍼히어로가 등장하는 영화들이 인기가 있다. 슈퍼맨, 배트맨, 그리고 인크레더블 헐크는 몇몇 유명한 슈퍼히어로들이다. 그들은 모두 만화책의 등장인물로서 시작되었다. 헐크는 초록색 피부를 가진 크고 힘이 센 슈퍼히어로이다. 그러나 최초의 헐크는 초록색이 아니었다. 대신에 그의 피부는 회색이었다.

Stan Lee는 1962년에 헐크를 만들었다. 그는 헐크가 지구상의 어느 누구와도 다르게 보이기를 원했다. 그래서 그는 헐크를 회색으로 그렸다. 그러나 첫 만화책 인쇄에 문제가 있었다. 만화책에서 헐크의 색깔이 단지 회색만이 아니었다. 일부 페이지에서 그는 초록색이었다. 그 만화책의 독자들은 초록색을 더 좋아했다. 그래서 Stan Lee는 헐크를 초록색으로 만들었다. 그것은 현명한 결정이었다. 그의 초록색 덕분에 사람들은 인크레더블 헐크를 쉽게 알아볼 수 있다.

## 04

pp.14~15

**서술형 핵심 문법** Jake likes going fishing but his parents like going hiking.

| 정답 | 1 ④ | 2 ③ | 3 (1) F (2) T | 4 And people have to return to work or school. | 5 stress |
|---|---|---|---|---|---|

**문제 해설**

1 월요일의 스트레스가 사람들의 건강을 위협하며, 월요일에 심장마비를 일으킬 확률이 더 높다는 내용이므로 글의 요지는 ④ '월요일의 스트레스는 심장마비를 일으킬 수 있다'가 가장 알맞다.
① 대부분의 사람은 월요일을 싫어한다.
② 월요일에 스트레스를 피하는 것은 어렵다.
③ 당신의 스트레스 수준을 낮추는 데 도움이 되는 몇 가지 방법이 있다.
⑤ 사람들은 주말에 약간의 휴식을 취해야 한다.

2 사람들이 월요일에 스트레스로 인해 심장마비에 걸릴 확률이 높다는 연구 결과를 설명하고 있는 내용 중에 (c) '심장마비는 보통 이른 아침에 발생한다'는 내용은 글의 흐름과 무관하다.

3 (1) 사람들은 다른 요일보다 월요일에 심장마비를 일으킬 확률이 11%나 더 높다고 했다. (8~9행)
(2) 사람의 스트레스 수준은 심장마비를 일으키게 할 수 있다고 했다. (10~11행)

4 '~해야 한다'는 〈have to + 동사원형〉 구문을 쓴다.

5 당신은 월요일의 스트레스를 피할 수 없다. 그러나 당신은 스트레스 수준을 줄일 수 있다. 운동, 심호흡, 그리고 재미있는 영화를 보는 것은 당신의 스트레스 수준을 낮출 수 있다.

**구문 해설**

08행 The researchers learned **something surprising**.
• 〈something + 형용사〉는 '~한 것'이라는 의미로, something을 수식하는 형용사는 뒤에 온다.

08행 People **are** 11% **more likely to** have a heart attack on Mondays **than** on other days.
• be likely to는 '~할 가능성이 있다'라는 뜻이다.
• 〈more ~ than …〉은 '…보다 더 ~한'이라는 뜻의 비교급 구문이다.

13행 Unfortunately, **it** is not possible **to avoid** stress on Mondays.
• to부정사가 주어일 때 문장 뒤로 보내고, 주어 자리에 가주어 it을 쓴다.

**지문 해석**

당신은 일주일 중 어떤 요일을 가장 싫어하는가? 대부분의 사람은 월요일이라고 말한다. 재미있고 편안한 주말은 끝이 난다. 그리고 사람들은 직장 혹은 학교로 되돌아가야 한다. 월요일은 대부분의 사람에게 스트레스를 준다. 놀랍게도 월요일의 스트레스는 우리의 건강을 위협한다.

스웨덴의 어떤 새로운 연구는 언제 사람들이 심장마비를 일으키는지를 조사했다. 연구원들은 놀라운 것을 알게 되었다. 사람들은 다른 요일보다 월요일에 심장마비를 일으킬 확률이 11%나 더 높다. (심장마비는 보통 이른 아침에 발생한다.) 사람의 스트레스 수준은 심장마비를 일으키게 할 수 있다. 사람들은 매주 월요일에 많은 스트레스를 받는다. 그래서 그들은 월요일에 심장마비를 많이 일으키게 된다.

불행하게도 월요일에 스트레스를 피하는 것은 불가능하다. 그러나 당신은 운동, 심호흡, 그리고 재미있는 영화를 봄으로써 당신의 스트레스 수준을 낮출 수 있다. 그러면 당신은 심장마비를 피할 수 있고, 건강을 유지할 수 있다.

## 내신 대비 실전 Test

pp.16~17

| 정답 | 1 ③ 2 ① 3 ④ 4 ② 5 Unlike 6 ⑤ 7 He wants his students to come to school early. 8 ② 9 My father wants me to become a doctor. 10 flavonoids 11 ④ 12 ⑤ 13 ② 14 ③ 15 lower |
|---|---|

문제 해설

**1** prefer(선호하다): to like one thing more than another(하나의 것을 다른 것보다 더 좋아하다)
① 가능성: 어떤 것이 일어날 가능성
② 인기 있는: 많은 사람에 의해 사랑받는
④ 연구: 어떤 주제에 대하여 배우기 위한 공부
⑤ 개선하다: 어떤 것을 더 좋게 만들다

**2** ②, ③, ④, ⑤는 유의어 관계인 반면 ①은 반의어 관계이다.

**3** take place: 열리다, 개최되다

**4** provide A for B: B에게 A를 제공하다
우유는 몸에 단백질을 제공해준다.

**5** unlike: ~와 다르게/닮지 않은
펭귄은 조류지만, 그들은 날 수 없다.
= 대부분의 조류와 다르게 펭귄은 날 수 없다.

**6** ⑤번에서 주어가 They로 복수이므로 복수 동사 believe가 와야 한다.
① 나무들은 우리에게 과일을 제공해준다.
② 나는 당신이 그 시험에 통과하기를 원한다.
③ Jake는 다른 학생들과 다르게 피곤해 보인다.
④ 그는 주말에 캠핑 가는 것을 좋아한다.
⑤ 그들은 그것이 가능하다고 믿는다.

**7** want + 목적어 + to부정사: ~가 …하는 것을 원하다
그는 자기 학생들이 학교에 일찍 오는 것을 원한다.

**8** 주어가 복수일 때는 복수 동사, 단수일 때는 단수 동사로 일치시켜 써야 한다.
Stella와 나는 친한 친구이다. 우리는 항상 서로를 돕는다. 그녀는 문제가 있을 때 나에게 이야기한다.

**9** want + 목적어 + to부정사: ~가 …하는 것을 원하다

**[10-12]** p.8 01 지문 해석 참고

**10** These는 바로 앞 문장에 있는 flavonoids를 가리킨다.

**11** 다크 초콜릿이 건강에 몇 가지 이로운 점을 가지고 있다는 연구 결과를 말하는 (C), 구체적으로 건강에 어떤 이점이 있는지를 예를 들어 말해주는 (A), 그래서 초콜릿 먹는 것을 부담 없이 즐기되 너무 많이 먹지 말라는 (B)의 내용으로 이어지는 것이 자연스럽다.

**12** parents, children은 복수 주어이므로 (a)와 (b)에 복수 동사인 tell과 have가 오고, study는 단수 주어이므로 (c)에는 단수 동사 says가 와야 한다.

**[13-15]** p.14 04 지문 해석 참고

**13** 빈칸 앞에는 사람들은 월요일에 많은 스트레스를 받기 때문에 심장마비를 더 많이 일으킨다는 내용이 나오고, 빈칸 뒤에는 월요일에 스트레스를 피하는 것은 불가능하다고 말하고 있으므로 ② '불행하게도'가 가장 알맞다.
① 고맙게도 ③ 다행히 ④ 중요하게 ⑤ 다행히도

**14** '사람들은 다른 요일보다 월요일에 심장마비를 일으킬 확률이 11%나 더 높다'라는 주어진 문장은 연구원들이 알게 된 놀라운 사실이므로 ③에 들어가는 것이 가장 알맞다.

**15** reduce는 '줄이다'라는 뜻으로 lower(낮추다)과 바꿔 쓸 수 있다.

# CHAPTER 02 Titles

## 내신 실전 적용 독해

p.18

**정답** ④

아침 식사를 거를 때 발생하는 여러 가지 문제를 설명하는 내용이므로 ④ '아침 식사를 거르는 것의 영향'이 제목으로 가장 알맞다.

① 당신의 뇌에 에너지를 공급하는 방법들
② 건강하지 않은 생활 방식
③ 바람직한 다이어트: 아침을 먹는 것
⑤ 수업 시간에 집중하는 방법

**지문 해석** 아침 식사를 하는 것은 매우 중요하다. 아침 식사를 거르면, 당신의 뇌는 충분한 에너지를 얻지 못한다. 그러면 당신은 수업 시간에 집중할 수 없게 될 것이다. 그래서 당신은 많이 배우지 못할 것이다. 아침 식사를 거르는 것은 또한 점심시간 전에 당신을 배고프게 만들 것이다. 당신은 쉬는 시간에 간식을 먹을지도 모른다. 그 결과로 당신은 점심시간에 배고프지 않을 것이다. 이것은 당신의 식사 주기를 망칠 것이다. 그리고 그것은 건강하지 않은 생활 방식으로 이어지게 될 것이다.

## 05

p.21

| 정답 | 1 ⑤ | 2 ③ | 3 ⑤ | 4 their website could handle large amounts of data |
|---|---|---|---|---|

**문제 해설**

**1** 두 개의 유명한 웹사이트 Google과 Yahoo!의 이름이 어떻게 지어졌는지에 관한 일화를 소개하는 내용이므로 ⑤ '두 웹사이트는 어떻게 그들의 이름을 얻게 되었는가'가 제목으로 가장 알맞다.
① Google이 그것의 이름을 갖게 된 방식
② Google과 Yahoo!의 첫 이름
③ Google과 Yahoo!의 뜻
④ 사람들은 어떻게 그들의 웹사이트의 이름을 짓는가

**2** 빈칸 앞 문장에 Googol을 Google로 철자를 잘못 쓴 내용이 있으므로 문맥상 ③ '틀린'이 가장 알맞다.
① 긴 ② 짧은 ④ 중요한 ⑤ 큰

**3** ⑤ '사람들은 Yahoo!라는 이름을 어떻게 생각하는가?'는 글에서 언급되지 않았다.
① Yahoo!의 두 명의 설립자들은 누구인가? (11~12행)
② Yahoo!의 원래 이름은 무엇인가? (13~14행)
③ Yahoo!라는 이름은 어디에서 왔는가? (10~11행)

④ 왜 사람들은 매일 Yahoo!를 방문하는가? (1~2행)

**4** Googolplex는 매우 큰 숫자를 뜻하는 것으로 그들의 웹사이트가 많은 양의 정보를 처리할 수 있었기 때문에 그들이 그 이름을 좋아했다고 했다. (5~6행)

Q: 왜 Google의 설립자들은 Googolplex라는 이름을 좋아했는가?

A: 그들의 웹사이트가 많은 양의 정보를 처리할 수 있었기 때문에

**구문 해설**

01행 Millions of people visit Google and Yahoo! **to search** for information daily.

- to search는 to부정사의 부사적 용법으로 목적을 나타내며 '~하기 위해서'라는 뜻이다.

02행 **Have** you ever **wondered how they got** their names?

- 〈Have + 주어 + (ever) + 과거분사〉는 '~해 본 적이 있나요?'라는 뜻의 현재완료 시제로 경험을 물어볼 때 사용된다.
- how they got 이하는 동사 wondered의 목적어로 쓰인 간접의문문으로 〈의문사 + 주어 + 동사〉의 어순이다.

08행 Both Page and Brin liked the incorrect spelling, so they **named their company Google**.

- 〈name + A(목적어) + B(목적격보어)〉는 'A를 B라고 이름 짓다'라는 뜻으로 목적어와 목적격보어에는 명사가 온다.

**지문 해석**

매일 수백만의 사람들이 정보를 찾기 위해서 Google과 Yahoo!를 방문한다. 당신은 그것들이 어떻게 그 이름을 갖게 되었는지 궁금해 본 적이 있는가? 그 이름들 뒤에 숨겨진 이야기들은 흥미롭다.

Larry Page와 Sergey Brin은 Google을 설립했다. 처음에, 그들은 Googolplex라는 이름을 사용하기를 원했다. Googolplex는 매우 큰 숫자이다. 그들은 그들의 웹사이트가 많은 양의 정보를 처리할 수 있었기 때문에 그 이름을 좋아했다. 하지만 Page는 그것을 Googol로 짧게 줄이기를 원했다. 그러나 Page의 친구인 Sean Anderson이 그 이름의 철자를 잘못 써서 Google을 썼다. Page와 Brin 둘 다 틀린 철자를 좋아했고, 그래서 그들은 자신들의 회사를 Google이라고 이름 지었다.

Yahoo!의 역사도 재미있다. '걸리버 여행기'라는 책에서 Yahoo는 거칠고 무례한 생명체들이다. 설립자 Jerry Yang과 David Filo는 그들이 Yahoo와 비슷하다고 생각했다. 그래서 그들은 자신들의 웹사이트 이름을 Yahoo!로 바꿨다. 원래 그들은 '월드 와이드 웹에 대한 Dave와 Jerry의 안내'를 사용할 계획이었다.

## 06

pp.22~23

**서술형 핵심 문법** When I feel sad, I eat some chocolate. [I eat some chocolate when I feel sad.]

| 정답 | **1** ⑤ **2** ① **3** ⑤ **4** 혈당을 낮추기 위해서 몸에서 많은 양의 인슐린을 분비해야 하는 것<br>**5** 올리브유, 식초 |
|---|---|

**문제 해설**

**1** 차와 우유, 흰 빵과 잼 등 함께 먹으면 건강에 유익하지 않은 음식들의 조합을 소개하는 내용이므로 ⑤ '이런 음식들은 함께 먹지 마라'가 제목으로 가장 알맞다.

[문제] 글의 제목으로 가장 알맞은 것은?

① 어떤 음식들이 잘 어울리는가

② 차를 마시는 나쁜 습관

③ 우리 몸 안에서 카페인의 역할

④ 무엇이 당뇨병을 일으킬 수 있는가

**2** '하지만 그것들은 건강에 좋지 않은 조합이다'는 주어진 문장은 많은 사람이 차에 우유를 넣어 마신다는 문장과

우유에 있는 단백질은 차의 항산화제를 쓸모 없게 만든다는 문장 사이인 ①에 오는 것이 적절하다.

**3** 무지방 드레싱을 샐러드에 곁들어 먹으면 채소의 영양분들이 잘 흡수되지 않는다고는 했지만, 다이어트에 효과적인지는 언급되어 있지 않다. (11~12행)

**4** That은 앞 문장의 내용, 즉 '혈당을 낮추기 위해서 몸에서 많은 양의 인슐린을 분비해야 하는 것'을 가리킨다.

**5** 샐러드는 무지방 드레싱 대신에 올리브유와 식초와 함께 먹으면 좋다고 했다. (12~13행)

**구문 해설**

04행 Proteins in the milk **make** the antioxidants in tea **useless**.
- 〈make + 목적어 + 형용사〉는 '~을 …하게 만들다'라는 뜻으로 형용사는 목적어를 설명해주는 목적격보어이다.

05행 And the caffeine in the tea **prevents** your body **from absorbing** the calcium in the milk.
- 〈prevent + 목적어 + from + v-ing〉는 '~이 …하는 것을 막다'라는 뜻이다.

09행 Then, your body **needs to release** lots of insulin **to bring** your blood sugar down.
- 〈need + to부정사〉는 '~할 필요가 있다' 또는 '~해야 한다'라는 뜻이다.
- to bring은 to부정사의 부사적 용법의 목적으로 '~하기 위해서'라는 뜻이다.

11행 But the nutrients in plants **are** not **absorbed** well with fat-free dressing.
- 〈be동사 + 과거분사〉는 '~되다'라는 뜻의 수동태이다.

**지문 해석**

베이컨과 달걀과 같은 몇몇 음식들은 잘 어울린다. 하지만 당신이 어떤 음식을 함께 먹을 때, 그것들은 당신의 몸에 해를 끼칠 수 있다.

차와 우유는 둘 다 건강에 좋다. 많은 사람은 그들의 차에 우유를 부어 마신다. 하지만 그것들은 건강에 좋지 않은 조합이다. 우유에 있는 단백질은 차의 항산화제를 쓸모 없게 만든다. 그리고 차 속의 카페인은 당신의 몸이 우유의 칼슘을 흡수하는 것을 막는다.

흰 빵과 잼은 또 다른 좋지 않은 조합이다. 당신이 그것들을 같이 먹을 때, 당신의 혈당은 빠르게 올라간다. 그러면 당신의 몸은 당신의 혈당을 낮추기 위해서 많은 양의 인슐린을 분비해야 한다. 그것은 당뇨병을 일으킬 수 있다.

요즘에는 사람들이 무지방 드레싱을 곁들인 샐러드를 먹는 것을 좋아한다. 하지만 채소의 영양분들은 무지방 드레싱과 먹으면 잘 흡수되지 않는다. 대신에 올리브유와 식초가 샐러드에 좋다.

# 07

p.25

| 정답 | 1 ⑤ | 2 ④ | 3 ③ | 4 (This) twelve-hour clock |
|---|---|---|---|---|

**문제 해설**

**1** 에티오피아는 적도에 가까이 위치해 일 년 내내 일조량이 거의 같아 새벽부터 해질 때까지, 해질 때부터 새벽까지 12 시각으로 나눈 시계를 사용한다는 내용이므로 ⑤ '에티오피아에서 시간을 구별하는 방식'이 제목으로 가장 알맞다.

① 에티오피아의 일조량
② 에티오피아의 시계는 왜 신뢰받을 수 없는가
③ 에티오피아에서는 언제 해가 뜨고 지는가
④ 에티오피아는 어디에 위치해 있는가

**2** 에티오피아는 적도에 가까이 위치하여 일 년 내내 일조량이 거의 같기 때문에 12 시각으로 나눈 시계를 사용한다고 했다. (2~4행)

**3** 빈칸 앞에 12 시각으로 나눈 시계는 외국인들을 혼란스럽게 한다는 내용이 나오고, 빈칸 뒤에는 그것이 에티오

피아인들에게 일리가 있다는 상반되는 내용이 나오므로 ③ '그러나'가 가장 알맞다.

① 그리고 ② 왜냐하면 ④ 그래서 ⑤ ~할 때

**4** it은 바로 앞 문장에서 언급된 (This) twelve-hour clock을 가리킨다.

구문 해설

01행 Around the world, most people tell time **the same way**.

• the same way는 '같은 방식으로'라는 뜻의 부사구이다.

06행 At 6 o'clock Ethiopian time, Ethiopians **usually** eat lunch.

• usually는 '보통, 대개'라는 뜻의 빈도부사로, be동사 뒤 또는 일반동사 앞에 위치한다.

09행 But it **makes sense to** Ethiopians, and they are proud of their unique ways.

• make sense는 '일리가 있다, 타당하다'라는 뜻이며, 뒤에 '~에게'라는 대상을 나타내기 위해 전치사 to를 사용한다.

지문 해석

세계 각지에서 대부분의 사람은 같은 방식으로 시간을 구분한다. 하지만 아프리카의 한 나라인 에티오피아는 다르다. 에티오피아는 적도에 가깝다. 그래서 일조량이 일 년 내내 거의 같다. 그 결과로 많은 에티오피아 사람들은 12 시각 시계를 사용한다. 1에서 12까지의 하나의 주기는 새벽부터 해질 때까지이다. 나머지 하나의 주기는 해질 때부터 새벽까지이다.

그래서 다른 지역이 오전 7시일 때, 에티오피아는 1시이다. 에티오피아의 시간 6시에 에티오피아 사람들은 보통 점심을 먹는다. 다른 나라에서 오후 6시에 해가 질 때, 에티오피아는 12시이다.

이러한 12 시각 시계는 많은 외국인을 혼란스럽게 만든다. 그러나 그것은 에티오피아 사람들에게 일리가 있으며, 그들은 그들의 독특한 방식을 자랑스럽게 여긴다. 그러니 당신이 에티오피아를 방문한다면, 시간을 구분하는 그들의 방식을 기억하라.

## 08

pp.26~27

서술형 핵심 문법 There are hundreds of cars on the street.

| 정답 | **1** ⑤ | **2** ③ | **3** (1) T (2) F | **4** ecofriendly | **5** Biomethane, waste |
|---|---|---|---|---|---|

문제 해설

**1** 생활 폐기물에서 만들어지는 재생 가능한 바이오 메탄을 사용하여 환경 오염을 줄이는 영국의 버스를 소개하는 내용이므로 ⑤ '환경에 도움을 주는 버스'가 제목으로 가장 알맞다.

[문제] 글의 제목으로 가장 알맞은 것은?

① 바이오 메탄은 무엇이며, 무엇에 쓰이는가

② 가정 폐기물을 줄이는 방법

③ 새로운 형태의 재생 가능한 에너지

④ 환경을 살리는 방법

**2** 친환경적인 버스가 그 지역의 가정 폐기물에서 연료를 얻음으로, 쓰레기를 줄이고 환경 오염도 덜 시킨다는 내용 중에 (c) '그 지역에는 100개가 넘는 버스 노선이 있다'는 문장은 글의 흐름과 무관하다.

**3** (1) 사람들은 바이오 메탄을 그들의 집과 차량의 연료로 사용할 수 있다고 했다. (3~4행)

(2) 똥 버스가 전 세계적으로 주목을 받고 있지만, 아직 전 세계적으로 운행되고 있지는 않다. (13~15행)

**4** '환경에 해를 끼치지 않는'이라는 뜻을 가진 단어는 ecofriendly(친환경적인)다.

**5** 바이오 메탄은 재생 가능한 에너지의 한 형태이고, 그것은 사람과 음식 쓰레기에서 만들어진다. 영국의 한 버스는 그것을 연료로 사용하며, 그것은 '똥 버스'라고 불린다.

구문 해설

01행 **Have** you ever **heard** of biomethane?

- 〈Have + 주어 + (ever) + 과거분사〉는 '~해 본 적이 있나요?'라는 뜻의 현재완료 시제로 경험을 물어볼 때 사용된다.

02행 It is a type of gas **made from** human and household waste.

- made는 앞에 오는 명사 gas를 수식하는 과거분사이다. from 이하 전치사구는 made에 연결되어 '~로부터 만들어진'이라는 뜻이다.

12행 By **turning** poo **into** energy, it is reducing waste.

- 〈turn A into B〉는 'A를 B로 바꾸다'라는 뜻이다.

13행 It also produces **less** pollution **than** gasoline engines **do**.

- 〈less ~ than …〉은 '…보다 덜 ~한'이라는 뜻의 비교급 구문이다.
- do는 앞에 나온 produce를 대신하는 대동사로서 반복을 피하기 위해서 쓰였다.

지문 해석

당신은 바이오 메탄에 대해서 들어본 적이 있는가? 그것은 사람과 가정 폐기물로부터 만들어진 기체의 한 종류이다. 사람들은 그것을 그들의 집과 차량의 연료로 사용할 수 있다. 그러면 그들은 휘발유와 같은 화석 연료를 사용할 필요가 없다. 바이오 메탄은 재생 가능한 에너지의 한 형태이다.

영국에는 '바이오 버스'라고 불리는 버스가 있다. 그것은 평범해 보이지만, 그것의 엔진은 사람의 배설물과 음식 쓰레기로부터 만들어진 바이오 메탄을 연소시킨다. 그래서 사람들은 그것을 '똥 버스'라고 부른다.

똥 버스는 친환경적인 버스이다. 그것은 그 지역의 3만 2천이 넘는 가정에서 나온 쓰레기를 사용한다. (그 지역에는 100개가 넘는 버스 노선이 있다.) 똥을 에너지로 바꿈으로써, 그것은 쓰레기를 줄이고 있다. 그것은 또한 휘발유 엔진보다 오염 물질을 더 적게 배출한다. 그것은 전 세계적으로 주목을 받고 있다. 언젠가 당신도 당신의 나라에서 똥 버스를 타게 될 것이다.

## 내신 대비 **실전 Test**

pp.28~29

정답

**1** wonder **2** ④ **3** ② **4** ④ **5** ③ **6** ④ **7** When I feel bad, I watch funny videos. [I watch funny videos, when I feel bad.] **8** ① **9** There are many tall buildings in New York. **10** found **11** ④ **12** ① **13** ④ **14** ③ **15** tea and milk

문제 해설

**1** wonder(궁금해하다, 궁금하다): 무엇을 알려는 소망을 갖다

나는 그가 파티에 올지 안 올지 궁금하다.

**2** incorrect와 correct는 반의어 관계이므로 빈칸에는 benefit(혜택을 주다)의 반의어 ④ harm(해를 끼치다)이 알맞다.

틀린 : 올바른 = 혜택을 주다 : 해를 끼치다

① 증가하다 ② 태우다 ③ 흡수하다 ⑤ 설립하다

**3** make sense: 일리가 있다, 타당하다

**4** 등위 접속사 and는 구와 구를 대등하게 연결해주므로 ④ to dance가 알맞다.

멕시코 사람들은 노래하고 춤추기를 좋아한다.

**5** 〈from A to B〉는 'A부터 B까지'를 뜻하고, 〈prevent + 목적어 + from + v-ing〉 '~이 …하는 것을 막다'라는 뜻이다.

- A부터 Z까지 모든 것의 목록이 여기에 있다.
- 따뜻한 차는 당신이 감기에 걸리는 것을 막아준다.

6 ④번의 there는 '저기, 거기'라는 의미의 부사이며, 다른 문장에 쓰인 there는 뜻이 없이 문장을 유도하는 역할을 한다.

① 방에는 두 명의 사람들이 있다.
② 질문이 있나요?
③ 벽에는 그림이 없다.
④ 저기를 보세요.
⑤ 아니요, 냉장고에는 아무것도 없어요.

7 ①번의 접속사 when은 '~할 때'라는 뜻으로 뒤에 주어, 동사가 온다. when이 이끄는 절이 문장 앞에 올 경우에는 절 뒤에 콤마(,)를 쓴다.

8 ①번의 등위 접속사 and는 단어와 단어, 구와 구, 절과 절을 대등하게 연결하므로 buying이 아니라 buy의 과거형 bought가 와야 한다.

① 그녀는 손목시계를 잃어버려서 새것을 샀다.
② 우리는 월요일부터 금요일까지 학교에 간다.
③ 해가 질 때, 하늘은 아름답다.
④ 공원에는 나무들과 꽃들이 있다.
⑤ 그는 피곤할 때, 커피를 마신다.

9 '~이 있다'라고 할 때 There is/are를 쓰며, There are 뒤에는 복수명사가 온다.

**[10-12]** p.20 05 지문 해석 참고

10 '회사와 같은 어떤 것을 시작하다'라는 뜻을 가진 단어는 found(설립하다)이다.

11 However로 시작하는 주어진 문장은 그들이 Googolplex라는 이름을 좋아했다는 내용 뒤인 ④에 오는 것이 가장 알맞다.

12 ⓐ는 '걸리버 여행기'에 등장하는 생물인 Yahoos이고, ⓑ~ⓔ는Yahoo!의 설립자들을 가리킨다.

**[13-15]** p.22 06 지문 해석 참고

13 빈칸이 들어 있는 문장이 However로 시작하므로 몇몇 음식들은 잘 어울린다고 한 앞 문장의 내용과 상반되는 ④ '그것들은 당신의 몸에 해를 끼칠 수 있다'가 들어가야 알맞다.

① 그것들은 당신에게 좋다
② 그것들은 잘 어울린다
③ 그것들은 도움이 될 수 있다
⑤ 그것들은 놀랍게 바뀐다

14 어떤 음식은 함께 먹으면 몸에 해를 끼칠 수 있다는 (B), 함께 먹으면 좋지 않은 음식의 첫 번째 예인 차와 우유에 관한 (C), 또 다른 나쁜 조합의 예인 흰 빵과 잼에 대한 (A)로 이어지는 것이 자연스럽다.

15 they는 바로 앞 문장에 나온 tea and milk를 가리킨다.

CHAPTER
# 03 Cause and Effect

## 내신 실전 적용 독해

p.30

**정답** ④

결과를 나타내는 접속사 therefore 앞 문장에서 겨울은 춥고 눈이 와서 동물들이 먹이를 구하기 힘들다는 원인이 나온다. (1행)

**지문 해석** 겨울은 흔히 춥고 눈이 온다. 그러면 동물들은 먹이를 찾는 것이 힘들다. 그러므로 많은 동물이 겨울 동안에 잠을 잔다. 이것은 겨울잠이라고 불린다. 겨울잠을 자는 동안, 동물들은 죽은 것처럼 보인다. 그들은 매우 천천히 숨을 쉬고, 그들의 체온은 떨어진다. 그래서 동물들은 많은 에너지가 필요하지 않다. 그러므로 그들은 겨울 동안 먹이를 먹지 않고서도 생존할 수 있다. 하지만 따뜻한 봄이 오면, 그들은 깨어난다. 그리고 그들은 배가 매우 고프기 때문에, 많은 먹이를 먹는다.

## 09

p.33

| 정답 | 1 ③ | 2 ⑤ | 3 ③ | 4 양파를 자르기 전에 물에 담그거나, 냉동고에 넣는 것 |
|---|---|---|---|---|

**문제 해설**

1 양파를 자를 때 눈물이 나는 이유와 그것을 방지하는 방법을 설명하고 있으므로 ③ '양파가 당신을 울리는 이유'가 제목으로 가장 알맞다.
① 양파의 비밀
② 양파를 자르는 방법
④ 양파는 어떤 화학 물질을 가지고 있는가
⑤ 눈이 따끔거리는 것을 멈추는 방법들

2 밑줄 친 ⓐ tears flow 바로 다음에 '따끔거리는 것을 멈추기 위해서'라고 이유가 나온다.

3 양파를 자를 때 보호 안경을 쓰라는 내용은 언급되지 않았다.

4 바로 앞 문장에 나오는 내용, 즉 '양파를 자르기 전에 물에 담그거나, 냉동고에 넣는 것'을 가리킨다.

**구문 해설**

02행 You probably **started crying**.
- start는 to부정사와 동명사를 모두 목적어로 취할 수 있다.

03행 **Cutting** an onion **releases** chemicals **called** amino acid sulfoxides.
- 동명사 주어(Cutting)는 '~하는 것'이라고 해석되고, 단수 취급하므로 단수 동사(releases)를 사용해야 한다.
- 과거분사 called는 '~라고 불리는'이라는 뜻으로 앞의 명사를 수식하는 형용사 역할을 한다.

08행 Fortunately, there are some ways **to avoid crying** when you cut an onion.
- to부정사의 형용사적 용법은 앞에 나온 명사를 수식하며 '~하는, ~할'로 해석한다.
- avoid는 동명사를 목적어로 취하는 동사로 '~하는 것을 피하다'라는 뜻이다.

**지문 해석** 당신은 양파를 잘라 본 적이 있는가? 당신이 그렇게 한 후에 무슨 일이 일어났는가? 아마도 당신은 울기 시작했을 것이다. 이것에 대한 이유가 있다. 양파를 자르는 것은 아미노산 술폭시드라는 화학 물질을 방출한다. 이 화학 물질들이 공기 중으로 퍼지면, 그것들은 기체를 생성한다. 그 기체가 당신의 눈과 접촉하면, 그것은 산성 물질을 형성한다. 그러면 그 산성 물질이 산화되어 당신의 눈을 따끔거리게 만든다. 그래서 그 따끔거림을 멈추기 위해서 눈물이 흐른다.

다행스럽게도 당신이 양파를 자를 때 우는 것을 피할 몇 가지 방법이 있다. 먼저, 양파를 자르기 전에 그것을 물에 담그거나, 냉동고에 넣어라. 이것은 기체가 퍼져서 당신의 눈에 닿는 것을 막아준다. 두 번째로, 촛불을 켜라. 그것은 기체를 태워 없앨 것이다. 마지막으로, 당신의 입안에 숟가락을 넣어라. 기체는 숟가락에 들러붙게 될 것이고, 그래서 당신의 눈에 닿지 않을 것이다.

# 10

pp.34~35

**서술형 핵심 문법** This puppy looks cute and feels soft.

| 정답 | 1 ⑤ | 2 ④ | 3 ③ | 4 breeds | 5 340 breeds of dogs and 42 breeds of cats |
|---|---|---|---|---|---|

**문제 해설**

1 두 번째와 세 번째 단락에서 개는 고양이와 달리 여러 가지의 일을 해야 했고, 수백 년 전부터 개량을 시작했기 때문에 개의 품종이 더 다양하다는 이유가 나온다.

2 빈칸 앞에는 사람들이 고양이는 쥐를 잡기 위해 길렀다는 한 가지 이유가 나오는 반면, 빈칸 뒤에는 사람들이 개를 기른 이유는 여러 가지가 있었다는 내용으로 빈칸에는 ④ '반면에'가 가장 알맞다.
① 그 결과 ② 게다가 ③ ~에도 불구하고 ⑤ ~뿐만 아니라

3 사람들이 개를 길러온 이유로 사냥, 동물 몰기, 장소 보호하기, 썰매 끌기가 있다고 했다. 쥐를 잡는 것은 고양이를 기른 이유이다.
① 사냥 ② 썰매 끌기 ③ 쥐 잡기 ④ 동물 몰기 ⑤ 장소 보호하기

4 types는 '종류들, 종들'이라는 의미로 글에 나온 breeds(품종들)와 바꿔 쓸 수 있다.

5 오늘날 개의 품종은 340종이 있지만, 고양이의 품종은 42종만 있다고 했다. (11~12행)
Q: 오늘날 얼마나 많은 개와 고양이의 품종이 있는가?
A: 오늘날 340품종의 개와 42품종의 고양이가 있다.

**구문 해설**

01행 But **look** closely **at** them.
• look at은 '~을 보다'라는 의미로 at 뒤에는 대상을 나타내는 목적어가 온다.

06행 For example, they used dogs **for hunting**, **herding** animals, **protecting** places, and **pulling** sleds.
• 전치사 for의 목적어로 hunting, herding, protecting, pulling이 이끄는 동명사구가 쓰였다.

07행 So humans created new breeds of dogs because dogs **had to do** different tasks.
• have to는 '~해야 한다'라는 뜻이며 뒤에는 동사원형이 온다. 과거형은 had to로 '~해야 했다'라는 뜻이다.

09행 This **resulted in** many different types of dogs.
• result in은 '결과적으로 ~을 낳다'라는 뜻으로 뒤에 결과에 해당하는 내용이 나온다.

**지문 해석**

개와 고양이는 두 가지의 인기 있는 반려동물이다. 하지만 그것들을 자세히 보아라. 대부분의 고양이 품종은 비슷하게 보인다. 하지만 개의 품종은 크기, 체형, 얼굴, 그리고 색깔에서 상당히 달라 보인다. 이것에 대한 이유가 있다.

사람들은 개와 고양이를 오래전에 길들였다. 그들은 고양이는 쥐를 잡기 위해서 길렀다. 반면에 사람들은 개를 여러 이유로 길렀다. 예를 들어, 그들은 사냥, 동물 몰기, 장소 보호하기, 그리고 썰매 끌기에 개를

이용했다. 그래서 사람들은 개가 여러 가지의 일을 해야 했기 때문에 개의 새로운 품종을 만들었다. 이것은 결과적으로 많은 다양한 개의 종류를 낳았다.

게다가 사람들은 수백 년 전에 개의 품종을 개량하기 시작했다. 하지만 그들은 고양이의 품종은 대략 75년 전쯤에 개량하기 시작했다. 그 결과 오늘날 340품종의 개가 있다. 하지만 고양이는 겨우 42품종이 있다.

# 11

p.37

| 정답 | 1 ②, ④  2 ⑤  3 (1) T (2) F  4 oxygen, contagious |
|---|---|

**문제 해설**

**1** 글에서 하품하는 이유로 언급된 첫 번째는 숨을 깊게 쉬지 못해 몸에 산소가 부족해서이고, 두 번째는 하품이 전염성이 있어서 다른 사람이 하품하는 것을 보면 따라 하게 된다고 했다.

**2** 우리 몸에 산소가 부족할 때 하품을 함으로써 몸에 산소를 가져온다는 내용을 설명하는 중에 (e) '하품할 때, 입을 가리는 것을 잊지 마라'라는 문장은 글의 흐름과 무관하다.

**3** (1) 모든 사람은 하품하며, 심지어 아기들도 엄마의 뱃속에서 하품한다고 했다. (1~2행)
(2) 하품은 몸에 산소를 가져오고, 몸에서 이산화탄소를 제거한다고 했다. (8~9행)
(1) 아기들은 그들의 엄마의 배 속에 있을 때 하품을 한다.
(2) 당신이 하품할 때, 당신의 몸에서 산소가 제거된다.

**4** 모든 사람은 하품한다. 산소의 부족은 우리의 몸에 더 많은 산소를 가져오기 위해서 우리가 하품하도록 만든다. 하품하는 것은 또한 전염성이 있다. 그래서 다른 사람이 하품할 때, 우리는 하품을 한다.

**구문 해설**

01행 Even babies **in their mothers' bodies** yawn.
• 전치사 in이 이끄는 전치사구가 주어 babies를 수식하고 있다.

05행 So our bodies get **less** oxygen.
• less는 little의 비교급으로 '더 적은, 덜한'이라는 뜻이다.

06행 A lack of oxygen **makes** us **feel** tired.
• 〈make + 목적어 + 동사원형〉은 '~가 …하도록 만들다'라는 뜻으로 사역동사 make의 목적격보어 자리에는 동사원형이 온다.

12행 What happens when you **see** someone **yawn**?
• 〈see + 목적어 + 목적격보어〉는 '~가 …하는 것을 보다'라는 뜻으로 지각동사의 목적격보어 자리에는 동사원형이나 현재분사가 온다.

**지문 해석**

모든 사람은 하품한다. 심지어 아기들도 엄마의 뱃속에서 하품한다. 왜 우리는 하품을 하는가? 과학자들은 확신하지는 못한다. 하지만 그들은 몇 가지 견해를 가지고 있다.

한 이론에 따르면, 호흡이 하품에 영향을 준다는 것이다. 우리가 지루하거나 피곤할 때, 우리는 심호흡을 하지 않는다. 그래서 우리의 몸은 산소를 덜 얻게 된다. 산소의 부족은 우리가 피곤함을 느끼도록 만든다. 몸은 산소를 필요로 해서 우리가 하품하도록 만든다. (당신이 하품할 때, 입을 가리는 것을 잊지 마라.) 이것은 산소를 가져오고, 몸에서 이산화탄소를 제거한다.

또 다른 이론은 하품하는 것은 전염성이 있다는 것이다. 다시 말해서 한 사람이 다른 사람을 하품하게 만들 수 있다. 당신은 누군가가 하품하는 것을 보면 무슨 일이 일어나는가? 아마 당신도 하품하고 싶은 생각이 들 것이다. 지금 당장 그것을 시험해봐라. 누군가를 보면서 하품을 해라. 그 사람 또한 하품했는가?

# 12

pp.38~39

서술형 핵심 문법　I became happier and more cheerful than before.

| 정답 | 1 (1) F (2) T | 2 ④ | 3 ③, ⑤ | 4 That causes us to get smaller. | 5 measure |
|---|---|---|---|---|---|

**문제 해설**

1 (1) 우리의 신축성 있는 연조직은 우리가 잠을 잘 때 원래의 형태로 되돌아간다고 했다. (7~9행)
(2) 우리가 잠을 잘 때는 몸이 수평이 되어 중력이 우리 키에 영향을 미치지 못한다고 했다. (12~13행)

2 As a result(그 결과)로 시작하는 주어진 문장은 낮에 사람들이 걸을 때, 연조직이 압착되어 뼈 사이의 공간이 줄어든다는 내용에 이어지는 것이 자연스러우므로 ④에 오는 것이 알맞다.

3 우리의 낮 동안 키가 작아지는 결과에 대한 원인으로 두 번째 문단에서 ③ '무릎과 척추의 연조직이 압착된다'는 것과, 세 번째 문단에서 ⑤ '중력이 척추의 추간판 사이의 물을 밀어낸다'는 것이 언급되었다.
① 중력은 우리의 키에 영향을 미치지 않는다.
② 우리가 잠을 잘 때, 우리의 몸은 수평이 된다.
④ 무릎의 연조직이 원래의 형태로 돌아간다.

4 '~가 …하는 원인이 되다'는 〈cause + 목적어 + to부정사〉 구문을 쓴다.

5 '특별한 도구를 사용하여 어떤 것의 크기를 알아내다'라는 뜻을 가진 단어는 measure(측정하다)이다.

**구문 해설**

05행 **While** we walk **during** the day, the tissue in both places **gets squeezed**.
- while은 '~하는 동안'이라는 뜻의 접속사로 뒤에 〈주어 + 동사〉가 오지만, during은 '~ 동안, ~ 중에'라는 의미의 전치사로 뒤에 명사가 온다.
- 〈get + 과거분사〉는 '~하게 되다'라는 뜻이다.

06행 This **makes** the spaces between the bones **grow** smaller.
- 〈make + 목적어 + 동사원형〉은 '~가 …하도록 만들다'라는 뜻으로 사역동사 make의 목적격보어 자리에는 동사원형이 온다.

11행 That **causes** us **to get** smaller.
- 〈cause + 목적어 + to부정사〉는 '~가 …하는 원인이 되다'라는 뜻이다.

**지문 해석**

아침에 당신의 키를 재라. 그러고는 밤에 다시 키를 재라. 당신은 아침에 대략 1cm 키가 더 크다. 놀랐는가?
연질의 신축성 있는 조직이 몸의 두 부분을 덮고 있다. 그것들은 무릎과 척추이다. 우리가 낮에 걷는 동안, 두 곳의 조직은 압착하게 된다. 이것은 뼈 사이의 공간을 더 작게 만든다. 그 결과 우리는 낮 동안 키가 더 작아진다. 하지만 우리가 잠을 잘 때, 무릎과 척추의 연조직은 그것의 원래 형태로 되돌아간다.
중력 또한 우리의 키에 영향을 미친다. 우리가 서 있는 동안, 그것은 척추의 추간판 사이의 물을 밀어낸다. 그것은 우리가 더 작아지게 하는 원인이 된다. 그러나 우리가 잠을 잘 때, 우리의 몸은 수평이 된다. 그러므로 중력은 우리의 키에 영향을 미치지 않는다.
이런 두 가지 이유로 우리의 키는 낮과 밤에 달라진다.

## 내신 대비 **실전 Test**

pp.40~41

**정답**

**1** ③ **2** ④ **3** ② **4** ④ **5** ④ **6** ④ **7** ③ **8** Korean food is becoming more popular around the world. **9** This will prevent the disease from spreading. **10** ① **11** tame **12** ⑤ **13** ② **14** ③ **15** smaller

**문제 해설**

**1** original(원래의): created or done for the first time(처음으로 만들어진 또는 된)
① 전염성의: 한 사람으로부터 다른 사람에게 퍼지는
② 지루한: 무언가에 흥미가 없는
④ 흐르다: 한 방향으로 계속해서 움직이다
⑤ 보호하다: 위험으로부터 무언가를 지키다

**2** reach: 이르다, 닿다
기린은 높은 나무에 있는 나뭇잎에 닿을 수 있다.
① 압착하다 ② 퍼지다 ③ 유지하다 ⑤ 없애다

**3** result in: 결과적으로 ~을 낳다

**4** 〈prevent + 목적어 + from + v-ing〉는 '~가 …하는 것을 막다/방지하다'라는 뜻으로 전치사 from 뒤에는 동명사 ④ going이 와야 한다.
허리케인은 우리가 밖에 나가는 것을 막았다.

**5** feel like는 '~하고 싶은 생각이 들다'라는 뜻으로 뒤에 동명사가 오고, 감각동사 feel 뒤에는 형용사가 와서 '~한 느낌이 들다'라는 뜻이다.
• 나는 지금 집에 가고 싶은 생각이 든다.
• 실크 스카프는 부드러운 느낌이 든다.
① 보이다 ② 맛이 나다 ③ 들리다 ⑤ 냄새가 나다

**6** ④의 형용사 big의 비교급은 bigger로 more가 필요하지 않다.
① 그 드레스를 입은 당신은 아름답게 보인다.
② 이것을 보기 위해 더 가까이 와라.
③ 나는 내가 공주인 것 같은 생각이 들어요!
④ 이 셔츠가 더 크다.
⑤ 그 치과의사는 내가 사탕을 먹는 것을 막았다.

**7** 감각동사 look 뒤에는 형용사가 와야 한다.
무슨 일이 있었어요? 오늘 당신은 ________하게 보여요.
① 행복한 ② 사랑스러운 ③ 피곤하게 ④ 바쁜 ⑤ 졸린

**8** 형용사 popular의 비교급은 앞에 more를 써서 만든다.
한국 음식은 전 세계적으로 더 인기를 얻고 있다.

**9** prevent + 목적어 + from + v-ing: ~가 …하는 것을 막다/방지하다

**[10-12]** p.34 10 지문 해석 참고

**10** ⓐ는 앞 문장에 나온 개와 고양이를 가리키지만, 나머지는 humans(사람들)를 가리킨다.

**11** '무언가를 지배하기 더 쉽게 만든다'라는 뜻을 가진 단어는 tame(길들이다)이다.

**12** '이것은 결과적으로 많은 다양한 개의 종류를 낳았다'는 주어진 문장은 사람들은 개가 여러 가지의 일을 해야 했기 때문에 개의 새로운 품종을 만들었다는 내용에 이어지는 것이 자연스러우므로 ⑤가 가장 알맞다.

**[13-15]** p.38 **12** 지문 해석 참고

**13** 빈칸 앞에는 우리가 잠을 잘 때 우리의 몸은 수평이 된다고 했고, 빈칸 뒤에는 중력이 우리의 키에 영향을 미치지 못한다는 결과를 말하고 있으므로 빈칸에는 ② '그러므로'가 가장 알맞다.

① 예를 들어  ③ 게다가  ④ 하지만  ⑤ 다시 말해서

**14** 우리가 낮에 걷는 동안 연조직이 압착되어 우리의 키가 더 작아진다는 (B), 우리가 서 있는 동안, 중력이 척추의 추간판 사이의 물을 밀어내 우리의 키가 더 작아진다는 (C), 이런 두 가지 이유로 낮과 밤에 우리의 키가 달라진다는 결론인 (A)의 내용으로 이어지는 것이 자연스럽다.

**15** 빈칸 앞의 내용으로 보아 (a), (b)에는 '더 작아진다'는 small의 비교급 smaller가 들어가는 것이 알맞다.

# CHAPTER 04 Guessing Unknown Words

## 내신 실전 적용 독해

p.42

**정답** ④

앞 문장에서 즉시 집 밖으로 나와야 한다고 했으므로 문맥상 멈추지 말고 신속하게 움직이라는 내용이 되어야 자연스럽다. 따라서 hesitate는 ④ pause(잠시 멈추다, 머뭇거리다)라는 의미이다.

**지문 해석** 당신은 한밤중에 잠이 깨서 연기 냄새를 맡는다. 당신의 집에 불이 났다! 당신은 무엇을 해야 하는가? 먼저 소방서에 전화해야 하는가? 아니면 집에서 안전한 곳을 찾아야 하는가? 당신은 즉시 집 밖으로 나와야 한다. 주저하지 마라. 또한 아무것도 들고나오지 마라. 만약 연기가 나면, 바닥에 가깝게 몸을 낮춰라. 연기는 올라가므로, 바닥 근처에 신선한 공기가 더 많다. 당신이 바깥으로 나온 후에는, 소방서에 전화해도 된다.

① 일어나다  ② 떠나다  ③ 서두르다  ⑤ 호흡하다

## 13

p.45

| 정답 | 1 ③ | 2 ⑤ | 3 ⑤ | 4 bacteria, farts |
| --- | --- | --- | --- | --- |

**문제 해설**

**1** 저항성 전분이 많은 음식을 섭취했을 때 방귀를 뀌게 되는 원리와 이것이 우리 몸에 어떤 이점이 있는지를 설명하는 내용이므로 글의 요지는 ③ '방귀를 뀌게 만드는 음식들은 당신에게 좋을 것이다'가 가장 알맞다.

① 어떤 음식들은 당신의 방귀 냄새를 나쁘게 만들 수 있다.

② 콩과 사과에는 저항성 전분이 풍부하다.

④ 박테리아는 우리의 몸에서 중요한 역할을 한다.

⑤ 당신은 방귀를 뀔 때, 당황해서는 안된다.

**2** 냄새가 나는 기체를 방귀로 'remove'한다는 것은 문맥상 '제거하다, 없애다'가 되어야 자연스럽다. 따라서 ⓔ 'get rid of(없애다)'와 같은 의미이다.

ⓐ 발생하다  ⓑ 비웃다  ⓒ 방출하다  ⓓ 돕다

**3** 박테리아가 저항성 전분을 분해할 때 냄새가 나는 기체를 방출하는데, 우리 몸이 방귀로 이 기체를 제거한다고 했다. (8~10행)

**4** 당신의 장에서 박테리아가 저항성 전분을 분해할 때, 그것들은 냄새가 나는 기체를 방출한다. 그러면 그것은 당신의 몸에서 제거된다. 이것이 당신의 방귀가 나쁜 냄새가 나는 이유이다.

**구문 해설**

03행 It **smells terrible**, and everyone laughs at you.

- 〈smell + 형용사〉는 '~한 냄새가 나다'라는 뜻이다. 형용사 자리에 부사를 쓰지 않도록 주의해야 한다.

04행 You are embarrassed, but you **should not be**.

- 조동사 should는 '마땅히 ~해야 한다'라는 뜻이며 뒤에 동사원형이 온다. 부정형은 should 뒤에 not을 쓴다.
- be 뒤에는 반복을 피하기 위해 embarrassed가 생략되어 있다.

14행 But the resistant starch can **help** you **avoid** getting sick.

- 〈help + 목적어 + (to)동사원형〉는 '…가 ~하는 것을 돕다'라는 뜻으로 목적격보어 자리에 to부정사나 동사원형이 올 수 있다.

**지문 해석**

당신은 점심으로 콩을 먹는다. 얼마 후에 당신은 교실에 앉아 있다. 당신은 당신의 몸에서 이상한 느낌을 받는다. 갑자기 그것이 일어난다: 당신은 큰 소리로 방귀를 뀐다. 그것은 끔찍한 냄새가 나고, 모두 당신을 비웃는다. 당신은 당황스럽겠지만, 당황해서는 안된다. 사실 방귀를 뀌는 것은 좋은 신호이다.

콩, 바나나, 그리고 사과와 같은 음식에는 많은 저항성 전분이 들어있다. 모든 사람은 그들의 장 안에 박테리아를 가지고 있다. 그 박테리아가 저항성 전분을 분해할 때, 그것들은 냄새가 나는 기체를 방출한다. 그러면 당신의 몸은 이 기체를 방귀로 제거한다. 동시에 박테리아는 분자를 방출한다. 그것은 혈액이 장으로 흐르는 것을 도와주고, 병든 세포를 제거한다.

그러므로 저항성 전분이 풍부한 음식을 먹는 것을 피하지 마라. 물론 당신은 방귀를 뀔 것이다. 하지만 저항성 전분은 당신이 병에 걸리는 것을 피하도록 도와줄 것이다.

# 14

pp.46~47

**서술형 핵심 문법** She is cooking spaghetti for dinner.

| 정답 | **1** (1) T (2) F | **2** ④ | **3** ③ | **4** beat | **5** 결혼식 날 |
|---|---|---|---|---|---|

**문제 해설**

**1** (1) 스코틀랜드에서는 친구들은 종종 신랑과 신부에게 쓰레기를 던진다고 했다. (7행),
(2) 한국에서는 하객들이 식이 끝난 후 신랑의 발을 말린 생선으로 때린다고 했다. (9~11행)

**2** 중국의 Tujia 전통에서 사람들은 신부가 결혼식 날 우는 것을 기대한다고 했지만 ④ '중국의 결혼식에서 신부들이 얼마나 오랫동안 우는가?'는 언급되어 있지 않다.
① 사람들은 어떻게 결혼식을 축하하는가? (2~4행)
② 스코틀랜드 결혼식에서 사람들은 무엇을 던지는가? (7행)
③ 사람들은 왜 한국 신랑의 발을 때리는가? (11행)
⑤ 중국인 신부는 결혼식에서 왜 우는가? (15~16행)

**3** 빈칸 다음에 스코틀랜드, 한국, 그리고 중국의 독특한 결혼 풍습들이 예로 소개되고 있으므로 빈칸에는 ③ '독특한 결혼 풍습들'이 가장 알맞다.
① 몇 가지 비슷한 의식들
② 축하하는 전형적인 방법들
④ 신랑 신부를 위한 시험들
⑤ 많은 결혼 의식들

4 한국의 하객들은 식이 끝난 후에 신랑의 맨발을 때린다(beat)는 내용이 먼저 나오고, 신랑의 발을 묶고 말린 생선으로 slap 한다고 했으므로 slap은 beat와 같은 의미임을 알 수 있다.

5 앞 문장에서 신부들이 결혼식에서 울기를 기대받는다는 내용이 나오고, 신부들은 the big day를 위해 많은 시간 동안 연습한다고 했으므로 the big day는 결혼식 날임을 알 수 있다.

구문 해설

02행 People celebrate them **by singing**, **dancing**, and **eating** delicious food.

- 〈by + v-ing〉는 '~함으로써'라는 뜻으로 수단이나 방법을 나타낸다.

12행 Perhaps **the strangest** one of all is a Tujia tradition from China.

- 형용사나 부사의 최상급은 most 또는 -(e)st를 붙여서 만들고, 앞에 the를 쓴다.

12행 Brides **are expected** to cry at their weddings.

- 〈be동사 + 과거분사〉는 수동태로 are expected to cry는 '울기를 기대받다'라는 뜻이다.

15행 They think **the more beautifully** they cry, **the luckier** they will be.

- 〈the + 비교급, the + 비교급〉은 '더 ~할수록, 더 …하다'라는 뜻이다.

지문 해석

결혼식은 사람들의 삶에서 중요한 행사이다. 사람들은 노래 부르고, 춤추고, 맛있는 음식을 먹음으로써 그것들을 축하한다. 하지만 몇몇 나라에는 독특한 결혼 풍습들이 있다.

스코틀랜드에서는, 친구들은 종종 신랑과 신부에게 쓰레기를 던진다. 그들은 신랑 신부가 그들의 결혼생활에서 겪을 어려운 시간에 대비하도록 도와주고 있다. 한국에서는, 결혼식 하객들은 식이 끝난 후에 신랑의 맨발을 때린다. 그들은 신랑의 발을 함께 묶고 말린 생선으로 때린다. 그들은 결혼생활을 위한 신랑의 힘을 시험해 보는 것이다.

아마도 모든 것 중에서 가장 이상한 것은 중국의 Tujia 전통이다. 신부들은 그들의 결혼식에서 울기를 기대받는다. 그 결과 그들은 결혼식 날 전에 많은 시간 동안 연습한다. 결혼을 한 후에 신부들은 하객들 앞에서 운다. 그들은 신부가 더 아름답게 울수록, 더 행운이 있을 거라고 생각한다.

# 15

p.49

| 정답 | 1 ④ | 2 ② | 3 ③ | 4 Frisbee의 회전 운동이 Frisbee에 가속도를 주기 때문에 |
|---|---|---|---|---|

문제 해설

1 Frisbee가 어떻게 만들어지게 되었는지와 그것의 비행 원리를 설명한 내용이므로 ④ 'Frisbee의 기원과 그것이 나는 방법'이 제목으로 가장 알맞다.

[문제] 글의 제목으로 가장 알맞은 것은?

① Frisbee를 가지고 노는 방법

② Frisbee가 인기 있는 이유

③ Frisbee는 얼마나 빠른가

⑤ Frisbee 발명가의 삶

2 이어지는 문장에서 '그것은 금속으로 만든 것보다 더 잘 날았다'라고 했으므로 문맥상 두 사람이 금속이 아닌 플라스틱으로 Frisbee를 새롭게 만들어냈다는 내용이 되어야 자연스럽다. 따라서 invented는 ② created(만들어 냈다)라는 의미이다.

① 날았다 ③ 팔았다 ④ 불렀다 ⑤ 회전했다

3 William Frisbie가 파이를 팔던 철판 접시를 학생들이 던지며 놀았는데 후에 Walter Morrison과 Warren Franscioni가 Frisbee라고 부른 플라스틱 원반을 발명했다고 했다. (7~8행)

4 Frisbee의 회전 운동이 Frisbee에 가속도를 주어 Frisbee가 오랫동안 공중에서 날 수 있다고 했다. (12~14행)

구문 해설

08행 It flew **better than** metal **ones**.
- better는 부사 well의 비교급으로 better than은 '~보다 더 잘'이라는 뜻이다.
- ones는 앞에 나오는 plates를 대신해서 쓰였다.

08행 They **called it the Frisbee**.
- 〈call + A(목적어) + B(목적격보어)〉는 'A를 B라고 부르다'라는 뜻이다.

13행 This **lets** it **fly** in the air for a long time.
- 〈let + 목적어 + 동사원형〉은 '~을 …하게 하다'라는 뜻이다. 사역동사 let은 목적격보어에 동사원형이 온다.

지문 해석

공원을 방문해 보아라, 그러면 당신은 아마도 비행접시를 목격하게 될 것이다. 그것은 미확인 비행 물체인가? 아니다, 그것은 확인 비행 물체인 Frisbee이다. Frisbee는 운반하거나 가지고 놀기 쉽기 때문에 인기가 있다. 하지만 그것의 시작은 소박했다.

1871년, William Frisbie는 얇은 철판 접시에 파이를 팔았다. 학생들은 빈 접시를 던지면서 "Frisbie!"라고 소리치곤 했다. 후에 Walter Morrison과 Warren Franscioni는 플라스틱 원반을 발명했다. 그것은 금속으로 만든 것보다 더 잘 날았다. 그들은 그것을 'Frisbee'라고 불렀다.

Frisbee는 그것의 디자인 덕분에 잘 난다. 곡선으로 이루어진 윗부분을 가진 Frisbee는 비행기의 날개와 같은 모양이다. 그것이 날 때, 공기는 그것의 아래에서보다 위에서 더 빨리 이동한다. 이것이 들어 올리는 현상을 만들어서, 그것은 회전하면서 난다. Frisbee의 회전 운동은 그것에 가속도를 준다. 이것은 그것이 공중에서 오랫동안 날 수 있게 해준다.

# 16

pp.50~51

서술형 핵심 문법 I believe that you are telling the truth.

| 정답 | 1 ④ 2 ③ 3 ② 4 Jupiter is mostly made of gas.<br>5 it has no solid ground to weaken storms |
|---|---|

문제 해설

1 1800년대에 목성의 대적점은 지구보다 4배 이상 더 컸고, 오늘날은 지구보다 1.3배 더 크다고 했다. (10~12행)

2 첫 문단에서 목성은 대적점을 가진 큰 행성이라고 했고, 마지막 문단에서 오늘날 대적점의 크기가 지구보다 1.3배 더 크다는 내용으로 gigantic은 ③ '큰'이라는 의미임을 유추할 수 있다.
① 다채로운 ② 아름다운 ④ 작은 ⑤ 환상적인

3 '하지만 그것은 예전에는 더 컸다'는 주어진 문장은 1800년대에는 대적점이 지구보다 4배 이상 더 컸다는 내용 앞인 ②에 오는 것이 가장 알맞다.

4 '~로 이루어지다'는 be made of를 사용한다. mostly는 '주로, 대부분'이라는 의미의 부사로 be동사 뒤에 온다.

5 목성은 대부분 기체로 이루어져 있어서 폭풍을 약하게 만들 단단한 땅이 없다고 글에 언급되어 있다. (8~9행)
Q: 목성은 왜 오랫동안 거대한 폭풍을 가지고 있는가?
A: 그것은 폭풍을 약하게 만들 단단한 땅을 가지고 있지 않기 때문에

구문 해설

05행 In fact, it has winds **blowing** more than 640 kilometers per hour.
- 현재분사는 형용사처럼 명사를 수식할 수 있다. 수식어구가 긴 경우에는 명사 뒤에 위치한다.

06행 The storm **has been** on Jupiter **for** at least 150 years and maybe **for** more than 400 years.

• 현재완료 계속은 과거에 시작된 일이 현재까지 계속되고 있음을 나타낼 때 사용한다. '지금까지 ~해왔다'라는 뜻이며 주로 for, since와 함께 쓴다.

08행 So it has no solid ground **to weaken** storms.

• to weaken은 앞에 나온 명사 ground를 수식하는 to부정사의 형용사적 용법으로 '~할, ~하는'으로 해석한다.

10행 Today, the Great Red Spot is 1.3 **times bigger than** the Earth.

• 〈~ times + 비교급 + than〉은 비교하는 대상보다 '~배 더 …한'이라는 뜻으로 times 앞에 배수를 나타내는 숫자가 온다.

지문 해석 어떤 행성들은 알아보기 쉽다. 지구는 파랗고, 화성은 빨갛고, 그리고 토성은 아름다운 고리들을 가지고 있다. 그리고 목성은 대적점이 있는 큰 행성이다.

목성에 있는 대적점은 무엇일까? 그것은 거대한 폭풍이다. 사실 그것은 시속 640km 이상으로 부는 바람을 가지고 있다. 그 폭풍은 최소 150년, 아마도 400년 이상 동안 목성에 존재해 왔다. 어떻게 그것이 가능한가? 목성은 대부분 기체로 이루어져 있다. 그래서 폭풍을 약하게 만들 단단한 땅이 없다.

오늘날, 대적점은 지구보다 1.3배 더 크다. 하지만 그것은 예전에는 더 컸다. 1800년대에 그것은 지구보다 4배 이상 더 컸다. 그 이후로 그것은 점점 작아지고 있다. 과학자들은 그것이 언젠가 사라질 수 있다고 생각한다. 그러면 사진 속의 목성의 모습은 변하게 될 것이다.

## 내신 대비 실전 Test

pp.52~53

**정답**

**1** ④ **2** ① **3** ② **4** ③ **5** ④ **6** ⑤ **7** ④
**8** You can avoid getting a cold if you get a flu shot. **9** The ball is spinning in the air.
**10** 신랑 신부가 결혼생활에서 겪을 어려운 시간에 대비하도록 돕기 위해서 **11** ③
**12** ④ **13** ⑤ **14** ② **15** break down

**문제 해설**

**1** '부끄러움이나 수줍음을 느끼는'이라는 뜻을 가진 단어는 ④ embarrassed(당황스러운)이다.
① 끔찍한 ② 단단한 ③ 벌거벗은 ⑤ 초라한

**2** '행성'을 의미하는 단어인 ① planet은 ② 화성, ③ 목성, ④ 지구, ⑤ 토성을 모두 포함할 수 있다.

**3** be made of: ~로 이루어지다
물은 산소와 수소로 이루어져 있다.
① ~을 제거하다 ③ ~을 비웃다 ④ ~을 가지고 놀다 ⑤ 분해하다

**4** as는 '~할 때, ~함에 따라'의 의미로 동시에 일어나는 상황이나 시간을 나타낼 때 쓰인다.
• 사람들은 나이가 들어감에 따라 지혜로워진다.
• 당신이 운동할 때 건강해질 것이다.

**5** think 뒤에 접속사 that이 와서 목적절을 이끈다.
나는 그 영화가 훌륭하다고 생각한다.

**6** ⑤에서 현재진행형을 만들 때 주어가 They이면 be동사는 are를 쓴다.
① 당신이 그것을 피할 수 없다면, 그것을 즐겨라.
② 엄마는 지금 음악을 듣고 계신다.
③ 해가 질 때, 하늘은 아름답다.
④ 나는 내가 수학을 잘한다고 생각한다.
⑤ 그들은 서로 얘기를 나누고 있다.

**7** 지금 진행 중인 동작을 나타내는 현재진행형으로 〈am/are/is + v-ing〉 형태를 쓰는데, 주어가 단수일 때 be동사는 is, 복수일 때는 are를 쓴다.

• Dave는 지금 점심으로 샌드위치를 먹고 있다.

• Jenny와 나는 지금 수학을 공부하고 있다.

**8** avoid + v-ing: ~을 피하다

당신이 예방주사를 맞는다면, 감기에 걸리는 것을 피할 수 있다.

**9** am/are/is + v-ing: ~하고 있다, ~하는 중이다

**[10-12]** p.46 14 지문 해석 참고

**10** 스코틀랜드에서 친구들이 신랑 신부에게 쓰레기를 던지는 이유는 신랑 신부가 결혼생활에서 겪을 어려운 시간에 대비하도록 돕기 위한 것이라고 했다.

**11** '그 결과 그들은 결혼식 날 전에 많은 시간 동안 연습한다'는 주어진 문장은 신부들은 결혼식에서 울기를 기대받는다는 문장 뒤인 ③에 오는 것이 자연스럽다.

**12** 마지막 문단에서 신부는 결혼식 날 신랑이 아니라 하객들 앞에서 운다고 했다.

**[13-15]** p.44 13 지문 해석 참고

**13** It은 바로 앞에 나온 ⑤ molecule(분자)을 가리킨다.

① 당신의 몸 ③ 저항성 전분 ③ 냄새가 나는 기체 ④ 방귀

**14** 방귀를 뀌는 것은 좋은 신호임을 말하는 (C), 방귀를 뀌는 과정과 몸에 미치는 긍정적인 효과를 설명하는 (A), 그러므로 방귀를 뀌게 만드는 저항성 전분이 풍부한 음식을 먹는 것을 피하지 말라는 (B)의 내용으로 이어지는 것이 자연스럽다.

**15** '무언가를 더 작은 조각으로 나누다'라는 뜻을 가진 단어는 break down(분해하다)이다.

# CHAPTER 05 | Identifying Cohesive Devices: Pronoun

## 내신 실전 적용 독해

p.54

**정답** ②

대명사 it은 그의 엄마를 화나게 만들어 엄마가 그에게서 가져가 버린 것으로 첫 번째 문장에 나온 단수명사 ② '그의 휴대폰'을 가리킨다.

① 하루 ③ 흥미 ④ 힘든 시간 ⑤ 그의 생활 방식

**지문 해석** Matt는 그의 휴대폰을 가지고 노는 데 하루에 5시간 이상의 시간을 보내곤 했다. 그는 다른 활동에는 흥미를 잃었다. 그의 엄마는 화가 나서, 그녀는 그로부터 그것을 가져가 버렸다. 처음에 Matt는 힘든 시간을 보냈다. 그는 지루했고, 무엇을 해야 할지 몰랐다. 하지만 그는 천천히 그의 생활 방식을 바꾸었다. 그는 더 많은 책을 읽었다. 그는 야외 활동을 했다. 그는 또한 그의 친구들, 가족과 함께 더 많은 시간을 보냈다. 휴대폰 없이 사는 것은 결국 그렇게 나쁘지는 않았다.

# 17

p.57

| 정답 | 1 ① | 2 ⑤ | 3 갑판 아래는 배의 흔들림이 덜했기 때문에 | 4 sick |
|---|---|---|---|---|

**문제 해설**

1 대화문에 쓰인 "under the weather"가 무슨 뜻이며, 왜 그런 의미를 갖게 되었는지 설명하는 내용이므로 ① '아프다는 것에 관한 표현'이 제목으로 가장 알맞다.
② 장거리를 여행하는 방법
③ 날씨와 항해의 연관성
④ 당신이 아플 때
⑤ 과거에 사람들이 여행한 방법들

2 ⓐ~ⓓ는 "under the weather"라는 표현을 가리키며, ⓔ는 앞 문장에 나온 배들이 앞뒤로 흔들리는 것을 가리킨다.

3 날씨가 좋지 않을 때 사람들은 갑판에 머물 수 없었고, 배의 흔들림이 덜한 갑판 아래로 내려갔다고 했다. (12~14행)

4 많은 사람이 "under the weather"라는 표현을 그들이 아플 때 사용한다고 했으므로, sick과 바꿔 쓸 수 있다. (4~5행)

**구문 해설**

01행 **It's time for** school.
- ⟨It's time for ~⟩는 '~할 시간이다'라는 뜻으로 뒤에 명사나 동명사가 온다.

13행 Instead, they went below deck **as** the rocking there was **less** noticeable.
- as는 '~때문에'라는 의미의 이유를 나타내는 접속사로 뒤에 ⟨주어 + 동사⟩가 온다.
- less는 little의 비교급으로 '(정도가) 덜한'이라는 뜻이다.

14행 Passengers **had to** go under the deck **because of** the weather.
- have to는 '~해야 한다'라는 뜻의 조동사로 뒤에 동사원형이 온다. have to의 과거형은 had to로 '~해야 했다'라고 해석한다.
- because of는 '~ 때문에'라는 뜻의 전치사구로 뒤에 명사가 온다. 반면 접속사 because 뒤에는 주어와 동사가 있는 절이 온다.

15행 So the expression "under the weather" **was born**.
- be born은 수동태로 '태어나다'라는 뜻이다.

**지문 해석**

엄마: 일어나! 학교에 갈 시간이야.
Sam: 엄마, 저 아파요.

Sam의 말은 무슨 뜻일까? 날씨가 그의 위에 있다는 것일까? 그는 자신이 아프다고 말하고 있다. 많은 사람은 그들이 아플 때 이 표현을 사용한다. 그런데 그것은 어디에서 생겨난 것일까?

역사가들은 그것이 바다에서 생겨났다고 믿는다. 과거에는 비행기가 없었다. 그래서 사람들은 배로 장거리를 여행했다. 배들은 보통 맑은 날씨에 항해했다. 하지만 때때로 날씨가 안 좋게 바뀌었다. 바람이 불고, 비가 내렸다. 배들은 앞뒤로 흔들렸다. 그것은 승객들이 뱃멀미하는 것을 야기했다.

궂은 날씨에 사람들은 배의 맨 위의 갑판에 머물 수 없었다. 대신에 그들은 갑판 아래로 갔는데, 거기에는 배의 흔들림이 덜했기 때문이었다. 승객들은 날씨 때문에 갑판 아래로 내려가야 했다. 그래서 "under the weather"라는 표현이 생겨났다.

# 18

pp.58~59

**서술형 핵심 문법** Wash your hands after you come back home.

| 정답 | 1 (1) F (2) T | 2 ③ | 3 ④ | 4 the closest island | 5 survive |
|---|---|---|---|---|---|

**문제 해설**

**1** (1) 무인도에서 살아남기 위한 조언으로 뿌리나 열매와 같은 먹을 수 있는 음식을 찾고, 물고기도 잡을 수 있다고 했다. (13행)
(2) 물 없이는 3~4일밖에 살 수 없다고 했다. (7~8행)
(1) 무인도에는 보통 식품 공급원이 없다.
(2) 당신은 4일 이상 살아남기 위해서 식수가 필요하다.

**2** 음식을 하고, 도움을 요청하는 신호를 보내기 위해 불을 지피라고 했지만, 동물들의 접근을 막기 위해 불을 지피라는 것은 언급되지 않았다.

**3** 빈칸 앞에 무인도에서 살아남기 위한 여러 가지 조언이 나와 있고, 빈칸 뒤에도 긍정적인 태도를 유지하고 희망을 가지라는 조언이 나오므로 설명을 덧붙일 때 쓰는 연결어 ④ '무엇보다도'가 가장 알맞다.
① 그 결과 ② 하지만 ③ 그럼에도 불구하고 ⑤ 대신에

**4** 대명사 it은 앞 문장에 나온 단수명사 the closet island(가장 가까운 섬)를 가리킨다.

**5** '힘들거나 위험한 상황에서 살아남다'라는 뜻을 가진 단어는 survive(생존하다)이다.

**구문 해설**

03행 You probably feel **frightened**.
- ⟨feel + 형용사⟩는 '~한 느낌이 들다'라는 뜻으로, '무서워하는'이라는 뜻의 형용사 frightened가 주어의 상태를 나타내는 주격보어로 쓰였다.

04행 But calm down and think about **what** you need **to survive**.
- what은 '~하는 것'이라는 뜻으로 전치사 about의 목적어로 쓰인 명사절을 이끄는 관계대명사이다.
- to survive는 to부정사의 부사적 용법으로 목적을 나타내며 '~하기 위해서'라는 의미이다.

09행 Build a shelter to **protect yourself from** bad weather and animals.
- yourself는 '너 자신'이라는 뜻의 재귀대명사로, 목적어가 주어 자신을 가리킬 때 재귀대명사를 쓴다.
- ⟨protect + 목적어 + from ~⟩은 '~로부터 …을 보호하다'라는 뜻이다.

**지문 해석**

당신은 열대의 섬으로 휴가를 가고 있다. 하지만 당신의 비행기가 추락한다. 당신은 생존해서 가장 가까운 섬으로 헤엄쳐 간다. 하지만 그곳은 무인도이다. 당신은 아마 두려움을 느낄 것이다. 하지만 진정하고 생존하기 위해서 당신이 필요로 하는 것에 대해 생각해라. 여기 생존을 위한 몇 가지 조언이 있다.
- 시냇물과 같은 식수의 원천을 찾아라. 당신은 물 없이는 3~4일밖에 살 수 없다.
- 궂은 날씨와 동물로부터 자신을 보호할 은신처를 지어라.
- 음식을 하고, 도움을 요청하는 신호를 보내기 위한 불을 지펴라.
- 해변에 H-E-L-P라고 써라. 누군가가 당신의 긴급구조요청 메시지를 보고 당신을 구해줄 수 있다.
- 뿌리나 열매와 같은 먹을 수 있는 음식을 찾아라. 당신은 또한 바다에서 낚시할 수도 있다.

무엇보다도 긍정적인 태도를 유지하고 긴장을 풀어라. 지나가는 비행기나 배의 누군가가 당신을 구해 줄 것이다.

# 19

p.61

| 정답 | 1 ② | 2 ⑤ | 3 ③ | 4 he wanted people to enjoy nature and have adventures |
|---|---|---|---|---|

**문제 해설**

1 대명사 this는 보통 앞에 나온 구나 절 단위의 내용을 가리키는데, 여기서는 문맥상 첫 번째 문장에 나온 ② '보물상자를 발견하는 것'을 가리킨다.

2 경찰이 Fenn에게 보물상자를 회수할 것을 부탁했지만, 그가 거절했다고 했다. (9~11행)

3 '하지만 찾는 일은 쉽지 않다'라는 주어진 문장은 그 상자를 찾던 중에 세 사람이 죽었다는 내용 앞인 ③에 오는 것이 가장 알맞다.

4 Fenn은 사람들이 자연을 즐기고, 모험하기를 원했기 때문에 보물을 가져가는 것을 거절했다고 했다. (10~11행)
Q: 왜 Fenn은 보물상자를 회수하는 것을 거절했는가?
A: 그는 사람들이 자연을 즐기고, 모험하기를 원했기 때문에

**구문 해설**

01행 Imagine **finding** a box **full of** treasure.
- 동명사 finding이 이끄는 구는 동사 imagine의 목적어로 쓰였다.
- full of는 '~로 가득 찬'이라는 뜻으로 앞에 나온 명사 box를 수식한다.

08행 Three people **have died while** searching for it.
- 〈have + 과거분사〉 형태의 현재완료는 과거의 일이 현재까지 영향을 미칠 때 사용된다.
- while은 '~하는 동안에'라는 뜻의 접속사로 보통 뒤에 〈주어 + 동사〉가 오지만, 〈대명사 주어 + be동사〉는 종종 생략되기도 한다. 여기서는 they were가 생략되었다.

10행 He said no because he **wanted** people **to enjoy** nature and **have** adventures.
- 〈want + 목적어 + to부정사〉는 '~가 …하기를 원하다'라는 뜻인데 여기서는 두 개의 to부정사 to enjoy와 (to) have가 목적격보어로 쓰였다.

12행 **Some** say the whole thing is a trick. **Others** say Fenn already took the box back.
- 〈Some ~ Others …〉는 다수의 무리 중 '어떤 사람들은 ~, 또 다른 사람들은 …'이라고 말할 때 쓴다.

**지문 해석**

보물로 가득 찬 상자를 발견하는 것을 상상해 보아라. 신나지 않겠는가? 이런 일이 실제로 일어날 수 있다. 하지만 먼저, 당신은 미국의 로키산맥으로 여행을 떠나야 한다.

2010년, Forrest Fenn은 2백만 달러의 보물로 상자를 채웠다. 그러고는 그는 그것을 로키산맥에 묻었다. 그는 또한 그 보물을 찾기 위한 단서가 있는 시를 썼다. 매년 사람들은 그것을 찾아 나선다. 그들은 부유해지는 것을 꿈꾼다. 하지만 찾는 일은 쉽지 않다. 그것을 찾던 중에 세 사람이 죽었다. 그래서 경찰은 Fenn에게 그의 보물을 가져가 달라고 부탁했다. 그는 사람들이 자연을 즐기고, 모험하기를 원했기 때문에 거절했다.

어떤 사람들은 모든 것이 속임수라고 말한다. 또 다른 사람들은 Fenn이 이미 그 상자를 가져갔다고 말한다. 이런 소문에도 불구하고, 사람들은 여전히 그 보물을 찾고 있다. 당신도 이 보물찾기에 참여하기를 원하는가?

# 20

pp.62~63

**서술형 핵심 문법** We will go on a picnic tomorrow.

| 정답 | 1 ⑤ | 2 ③ | 3 ⑤ | 4 그리스에서 하이힐을 신는 것 | 5 similar, strange |
|---|---|---|---|---|---|

**문제 해설**

1 싱가포르, 덴마크, 베네치아 등 세계 여러 곳에 있는 특이한 법을 소개하는 내용이므로 이 글의 주제는 ⑤ '세계의 특이한 법'이 가장 알맞다.
① 국가에서의 법의 역할
② 세계적으로 법이 비슷한 이유
③ 국가들이 법을 제정하는 방법
④ 사람들의 권리를 보호하기 위한 법

2 앞 문단에서 세계 여러 곳의 특이한 법을 소개하였고, 빈칸 앞에 not이 있는 것으로 보아 ③ '곤란에 처하다'가 들어가야 내용 연결이 자연스럽다.
① 유적을 훼손하다
② 많은 돈을 벌금으로 부과받다
④ 갈등을 피하다
⑤ 당신의 권리를 보호하다

3 그리스에서는 고대 유적을 훼손시킬 수 있기 때문에 하이힐을 신는 것이 위법이라는 내용 중에 (e) '하이힐은 처음에 남자들이 신었다'라는 문장은 글의 흐름과 무관하다.

4 대명사 It은 내용 흐름과 무관한 (e)를 뺀 앞에 있는 문장 (d)에 있는 그리스에서 하이힐을 신는 것을 가리킨다.

5 대부분의 국가는 비슷한 법을 가지고 있다. 하지만 어떤 곳은 이상한 법을 가지고 있다. 당신은 이곳들을 방문하기 전에 이러한 법들을 알아야 한다.

**구문 해설**

02행 They **want** people **to live** together **without** conflict.
- ⟨want + 목적어 + to부정사⟩는 '~가 …하기를 원하다'라는 뜻으로 to부정사는 목적격보어이다.
- 전치사 without은 뒤에 명사가 와서 '~ 없이'라는 뜻이다.

05행 This law **was passed to keep** public places **clean**.
- ⟨be동사 + 과거분사⟩는 수동태로 was passed는 '통과되었다'라는 뜻이다.
- to keep은 to부정사의 부사적 용법의 목적으로 '~하기 위해서'라는 뜻이다.
- ⟨keep + 목적어 + 목적격보어⟩는 '~을 …하게 유지하다'라는 뜻이다.

08행 **If** parents want to use different names, they **need to** get approval from the government.
- 조건의 접속사 if는 '만약 ~한다면'이라는 뜻이다.
- ⟨need + to부정사⟩는 '~해야 한다'라는 의미이다.

10행 People **who** feed the pigeons in Venice, Italy, will get fined $700.
- 관계대명사 who가 이끄는 관계대명사절은 앞에 나온 사람 선행사 people을 수식한다.

**지문 해석**

전 세계의 국가들은 사람들의 권리를 보호하기 위해 법을 제정한다. 그들은 사람들이 갈등 없이 함께 살기를 원한다. 그래서 대부분의 국가는 비슷한 법을 가지고 있다. 하지만 어떤 곳들은 이상한 법을 가지고 있다.

싱가포르에서는 껌을 수입할 수 없다. 이 법은 공공장소를 깨끗하게 유지하기 위해서 통과되었다. 덴마크는 아이들의 이름을 짓는 것에 관한 공식적인 지침을 가지고 있다. 목록에는 7천 개의 승인된 이름들이 있다. 만약 부모들이 다른 이름을 사용하기를 원하면, 그들은 정부로부터 승인을 받아야 한다. 이탈리아 베네치아에서 비둘기에게 먹이를 주는 사람들은 700달러의 벌금을 부과받게 될 것이다. 그 시는 그것들이 사람들의 건강에 좋지 않다고 생각한다. 그래서 그들은 더 많은 비둘기를 원치 않는다. 마지막으로, 그리스에서는 하이힐을 신지 마라. (하이힐은 처음에 남자들이 신었다.) 그것은 그것들이 고대 유적들을 훼손시킬 수 있기 때문에 위법이다.

만약 당신이 이곳들을 방문한다면, 이러한 이상한 법을 기억하라. 그러면 당신은 곤란에 처하지 않을 것이다.

# 내신 대비 실전 Test

pp.64~65

| 정답 | |
|---|---|
| | 1 treasure 2 ⑤ 3 ② 4 ① 5 ④ 6 ③ 7 is going to |
| 정답 | 8 It can cause many problems to happen. 9 Tom asked me to borrow my book. |
| | 10 ② 11 ④ 12 배들이 앞뒤로 흔들리는 것 13 ⑤ 14 ① 15 conflict |

**문제 해설**

**1** treasure(보물): 금과 같이 가치 있는 것들의 모음
만약 당신이 숨겨진 보물을 찾는다면, 당신은 부유해질 것이다.

**2** ①, ②, ③, ④는 반의어 관계인 반면 ⑤는 유의어 관계이다.

**3** calm down: 진정하다

**4** ask + 목적어 + to부정사: ~에게 …할 것을 부탁하다/요청하다
엄마는 나에게 오늘 집에 일찍 올 것을 부탁했다.

**5** 부정명령문은 Don't를 동사원형 앞에 쓰고, 명령문은 동사원형으로 시작하는데 형용사 앞에는 be동사의 동사원형인 Be를 쓴다.
• 교실에서는 껌을 씹지 마라.
• 공공장소에서는 조용히 해라.

**6** ③에서 조동사 will 뒤에는 동사원형이 와야 한다.
① 물이 없는 사막을 상상해라.
② 나에게 화내지 마라.
③ 그녀는 당신의 거짓말을 믿을 것이다.
④ 엄마는 나에게 숙제를 할 것을 요청했다.
⑤ 스트레스는 당신을 아프게 하는 원인이 될 수 있다.

**7** will은 be going to로 대신할 수 있다.
하늘을 보아라. 태양이 곧 뜰 것이다.

**8** cause + 목적어 + to부정사: ~가 …하는 것을 야기하다/~가 …하는 원인이 되다
그것은 많은 문제가 발생하는 것을 야기할 수 있다.

**9** ask + 목적어 + to부정사: ~에게 …할 것을 부탁하다/요청하다

**[10-12]** p.56 17 지문 해석 참고

**10** cause + 목적어 + to부정사: ~가 …하는 것을 야기하다/~가 …하는 원인이 되다

**11** '하지만 때때로 날씨가 안 좋게 바뀌었다'는 주어진 문장은 바람이 불고, 비가 내렸다는 나쁜 날씨의 예를 보여주는 문장 앞인 ④에 들어가는 것이 가장 알맞다.

**12** 바로 앞 문장에 나온 내용, 즉 '배들이 앞뒤로 흔들리는 것'을 가리킨다.

**[13-15]** p.62 20 지문 해석 참고

**13** ⓔ에서 부정명령문은 not이 아니라 don't를 동사원형 앞에 쓴다.

**14** 어떤 곳들은 이상한 법을 가지고 있다는 (B), 이상한 법이 있는 곳들을 예를 들어 설명해주는 (C), 이곳들을 방문할 때 이상한 법들을 기억하면 곤란에 처하지 않을 것이라는 (A)의 내용으로 이어지는 것이 자연스럽다.

**15** '사람들 사이의 의견 불일치 또는 싸움'이라는 뜻을 가진 단어는 conflict(갈등, 분쟁)이다.

CHAPTER

# 06 Compare & Contrast

**내신 실전 적용 독해** p.66

**정답** ④

빵은 맛있고 훌륭한 에너지원이며, 전 세계적으로 인기가 있다는 것이 공통점으로 언급되었다.

**지문 해석** 빵은 맛있고, 훌륭한 에너지원이다. 그래서 그것은 전 세계적으로 인기가 있다. 하지만 그것은 여러 가지 다른 모양과 맛을 가지고 있다. 프랑스에서는 바게트가 인기 있다. 그것은 길고, 가는 흰 빵 덩어리이다. 그것의 겉은 딱딱하고, 속은 쫄깃하다. 인도에서 난은 인기 있는 납작하고, 둥근 빵이다. 사람들은 보통 난을 버터 또는 카레와 함께 먹는다. 그리고 베이글은 가운데에 구멍이 뚫려 있는 쫄깃한 둥근 빵이다. 폴란드 사람들이 그것들을 즐겨 먹는다. 그들은 그들의 베이글 위에 크림치즈를 펴 바른다.

## 21

p.69

**정답** **1** (1) F (2) T **2** ⑤ **3** ③ **4** (영국) 사람들의 오른손이 그들을 지나가는 사람들에게 더 가까웠던 것

**문제 해설**

**1** (1) 영국과 과거 영국의 식민지였던 국가에서는 사람들이 좌측에서 운전한다고 했다. (8~9행)
(2) 미국에서는 마차 운전자들이 4륜 마차의 왼쪽 말 위에 앉았다고 했다. (10~11행)

**2** 마차 운전자들은 다른 마차가 지나가는 것을 보기 위해 길의 오른쪽에 머물렀다고 했다. (12~13행)

**3** 영국에서는 말을 타고 좌측통행을 했고, 미국에서는 4륜 마차를 타고 우측통행을 했던 차이점이 있지만, 두 나라 모두 ③ '교통수단으로 말을 이용했다'라는 공통점이 있다.

| 영국 | (A) | 미국 |
| --- | --- | --- |
| • 사람들은 말을 탔다.<br>• 사람들은 좌측에서 운전했다. | | • 4륜 마차가 인기가 있었다.<br>• 사람들은 우측에서 운전했다. |

① 사람들은 원래 좌측에서 운전했다.
② 사람들은 원래 우측에서 운전했다.
④ 사람들은 말보다 4륜 마차를 선호했다.
⑤ 사람들은 그들의 오른손으로 말에 채찍질했다.

**4** 앞 문장의 내용, 즉 '(영국) 사람들의 오른손이 그들을 지나가는 사람들에게 더 가까웠다는 것'을 가리킨다.

**구문 해설**

01행 **Driving** on the wrong side of the road **is** dangerous.
• 동명사 주어는 '~하는 것'이라고 해석하며, 단수 취급하므로 뒤에 단수 동사가 온다.

08행 That made **it** easier **to wave or to draw a sword**.
• 목적어로 사용된 to부정사구가 긴 경우, 문장 뒤로 보내고 그 자리에 가목적어 it을 쓴다.

12행 They stayed on the right side of the road **to see** other wagons **passing** by.
• to see는 to부정사의 부사적 용법으로 목적을 나타내며 '~하기 위해서'라는 뜻이다.

• 〈see + 목적어 + 현재분사〉는 '~가 …하는 것을 보다'라는 뜻으로 목적격보어로 현재분사가 쓰일 때는 동작이 진행 중임을 나타낸다.

**지문 해석** 잘못된 차선에서 운전하는 것은 위험하다. 어떤 나라에서는 사람들은 좌측에서 운전하지만, 또 어떤 나라에서는 사람들이 우측에서 운전한다. 왜 그들은 다른가?

영국에서 사람들은 종종 말을 타곤 했다. 그들은 다른 사람들의 왼쪽에 탔다. 그래서 그들의 오른손이 그들이 지나가는 사람들에게 더 가까웠다. 그것은 손을 흔들거나 칼을 뽑는 것을 더 쉽게 만들었다. 오늘날, 영국과 과거 영국의 식민지였던 국가에서는 사람들이 좌측에서 운전한다.

그러나 미국에서는 4륜 마차가 인기가 있었다. 마차 운전자들은 왼쪽에 있는 말 위에 앉았다. 그들은 왼손으로 4륜 마차를 운전했고, 오른손으로 말에 채찍질했다. 그들은 다른 4륜 마차들이 지나가는 것을 보기 위해서 도로의 우측에 머물렀다. 오늘날, 미국을 포함하여 세계의 다른 나라들은 우측에서 운전한다.

## 22

pp.70~71

**서술형 핵심 문법** Everyone can answer the question.

| 정답 | 1 ⑤ | 2 ③ | 3 ⑤ | 4 positive | 5 Upcycling, creativity, environment |
|---|---|---|---|---|---|

**문제 해설**

**1** 업사이클링은 물건을 분해하지 않고 물건을 다른 용도로 쓰는 것으로 에너지나 물을 필요로 하지 않는 환경에 도움을 준다는 내용이므로 ⑤ '환경을 위한 업사이클링'이 제목으로 가장 알맞다.

[문제] 글의 제목으로 가장 알맞은 것은?
① 재활용이 중요한 이유
② 언제 업사이클링이 시작되었는가
③ 환경에 도움을 주는 방법
④ 무엇이 업사이클 될 수 있는가

**2** 빈칸 앞에 업사이클링은 물건들을 분해하지 않는다는 내용이 나오고, 빈칸 뒤에는 물건들을 사용하기 위한 다른 방법들을 찾는다는 상반되는 내용이 나오므로 ③ '대신에'가 가장 알맞다.

① 그래서 ② 다시 말하면 ④ 게다가 ⑤ 예를 들어

**3** 첫 단락에서 재활용과 업사이클링의 공통점으로 환경에 긍정적인 영향을 주는 것을 언급했다. 두 번째 단락부터 둘의 차이점을 대조적으로 보여주고 있는데 ①, ③, ④는 재활용에 관한 내용이며, ②는 업사이클링에 관한 내용이다.

**4** '어떤 상황이 더 좋아질 것이라고 믿는'이라는 뜻을 가진 단어는 positive(긍정적인)이다.

**5** 업사이클링은 오래된 물건들을 분해하지 않는다. 사람들은 그것들은 다른 방법으로 사용한다. 그것은 단지 창의성을 필요로 하며, 환경에 도움이 되는 좋은 방법이다.

**구문 해설**

01행 But **few** know about upcycling.

• few는 수량형용사로 '거의 없는'이라는 부정의 의미지만, a few는 '몇 개의'라는 긍정의 의미를 지닌다. 둘 다 셀 수 있는 명사에 쓰인다.

05행 **It** requires energy and water **to break down the materials**.

• 주어로 쓰이는 to부정사구가 긴 경우, 문장 뒤로 보내고 그 자리에 가주어 it을 쓴다.

06행 And the quality of the new products is often **worse than** the original **ones**.

• bad의 비교급인 worse는 than과 함께 쓰여 '~보다 더 나쁜'이라는 뜻이다.
• ones는 앞에 나온 명사 products를 대신하여 쓰였다.

11행 And their quality is often better or **the same as** the originals.

• the same as는 '~와 같은'이라는 뜻으로 as 뒤에는 비교하는 대상이 온다.

지문 해석 모든 사람은 재활용이 환경에 도움을 줄 수 있다는 것을 안다. 하지만 업사이클링에 대해 알고 있는 사람은 거의 없다. 두 가지 모두 환경에 긍정적인 영향을 주지만, 그것들은 몇 가지 차이점을 가지고 있다.

사람들이 재료를 재활용할 때, 그것들은 분해된다. 그 다음에 그것들은 새로운 제품으로 다시 만들어진다. 재료를 분해하는 것은 에너지와 물이 필요하다. 그리고 새롭게 만들어진 제품의 질은 종종 원래의 것보다 더 나쁘다.

업사이클링은 물건들을 분해하지 않는다. 대신에 사람들은 그것들을 사용하기 위한 다른 방법들을 찾는다. 예를 들어, 누군가는 문을 식탁으로 바꿀지도 모른다. 또 다른 사람은 빈 플라스틱병으로 꽃병을 만들지도 모른다. 업사이클링 제품을 만드는 것은 단지 창의성이 필요하다. 그리고 그것들의 질은 종종 원래의 것보다 더 좋거나 같다.

업사이클링은 새로운 것이 아니다. 사람들은 돈을 아끼기 위해서 오래된 물건으로 새로운 제품을 만들곤 했다. 그러나 오늘날 우리는 업사이클링을 함으로써 환경에 도움을 줄 수 있다.

# 23

p.73

| 정답 | 1 ④ | 2 ② | 3 ⑤ | 4 blue |
|---|---|---|---|---|

문제 해설

**1** 회사들이 수익을 늘리기 위해서 소비자들이 선호하는 색상을 알아내서 광고에 활용한다는 내용이므로 ④ '색깔은 마케팅에 중요하다'가 요지로 가장 알맞다.

① 흰색은 여성이 제일 좋아하는 색깔이다.
② 회사는 많은 돈을 벌기를 원한다.
③ 남성과 여성은 둘 다 파란색을 좋아한다.
⑤ 많은 쇼핑객은 갑작스러운 결정을 내린다.

**2** 대부분의 쇼핑객이 제품의 포장 색깔에 근거하여 갑작스러운 구매 결정을 한다는 (B), 이에 대한 구체적인 수치를 제시하는 (A), 그래서(So) 회사들이 쇼핑객들이 좋아하는 색깔을 알아내서 광고에 활용하려 한다는 (C)의 내용으로 이어지는 것이 자연스럽다.

**3** 연구 결과에 따르면, 남성은 짙은 색을 선호하고, 여자는 연한 색을 선호한다고 했다. (10~12행)

**4** 바로 앞 문장에 나온 남성과 여성이 둘 다 가장 좋아하는 blue(파란색)를 가리킨다.

구문 해설

08행 So they tried to figure out **which colors shoppers like**.

• 의문사 which가 이끄는 절이 figure out의 목적어로 쓰인 간접의문문으로 〈의문사 + 주어 + 동사〉의 어순이다.

12행 **That is why** packaging for women's products often includes white.

• That is why는 '그것이 바로 ~한 이유이다'라는 뜻으로, why 뒤에는 〈주어 + 동사〉가 온다.

13행 However, **both** men **and** women like blue **more than any other color**.

• 〈both A and B〉는 'A와 B 둘 다'라는 뜻이다.
• 〈비교급 + than any other + 단수명사〉는 비교급을 이용한 최상급 표현으로 '어떤 다른 ~보다 더 …한'이라는 뜻이다.

지문 해석 당신은 상점에 쇼핑하러 간다. 하지만 살 것들이 많이 있다. 당신은 어떤 것을 살지 모른다. 당신은 어떻게 결정하는가?

(B) 연구자들은 대부분의 쇼핑객이 갑작스러운 결정을 내린다는 것을 알게 되었다. 그들은 또한 종종 제품의 포장 색깔에 근거하여 물건을 선택한다. (A) 사실 모든 구매의 약 90%는 색깔에 근거한다. 회사들은 가능한 한 많은 돈을 벌기를 원한다. (C) 그래서 그들은 쇼핑객들이 어떤 색깔을 좋아하는지 알아내기 위해 노력했다. 그런 방식으로 회사들은 그것들을 그들의 광고에 사용할 수 있었다.

그들의 연구에 따르면, 남성들은 짙은 색깔을 선호한다. 그래서 남성을 위한 포장재에는 종종 검은색이 포함된다. 하지만 여성들은 더 연한 색깔을 선호한다. 그것이 바로 여성 제품의 포장재에는 종종 흰색이 포함되는 이유이다. 그러나 남성과 여성 둘 다 어떤 다른 색깔보다도 파란색을 더 좋아한다. 그래서 그 색깔이 포장재에 흔하다.

# 24

pp.74~75

서술형 핵심 문법 I usually go to school by bus.

정답 **1** ⑤ **2** ③ **3** ④ **4** alike **5** (1) Look exactly alike (2) Share the same DNA

문제 해설

**1** 이란성 쌍둥이는 두 개의 별개의 난자가 아기로 발달하면서 태어난다고 했다. (9~10행)

**2** '그 이유로 그들은 거의 항상 두 명의 남자아이이거나 두 명의 여자아이이다'라는 주어진 문장은 그 이유에 해당하는 '일란성 쌍둥이들은 같은 DNA를 공유한다'는 문장 뒤인 ③에 오는 것이 가장 알맞다.

**3** ⓓ는 일란성 쌍둥이를 가리키고, 나머지는 모두 이란성 쌍둥이를 가리킨다.

**4** identical은 '똑같은, 동일한'이라는 의미로 alike(비슷한, 같은)와 의미가 같다.

**5** (1) 일란성 쌍둥이는 똑같아 보인다고 했다. (4행)
(2) 일란성 쌍둥이는 같은 DNA를 공유한다고 했다. (6행)

| 일란성 쌍둥이 | 이란성 쌍둥이 |
|---|---|
| • 한 개의 난자에서 발달함 | • 두 개의 서로 다른 난자에서 발달됨 |
| • (1) 똑같아 보임 | • 다르게 보임 |
| • 비슷하게 행동함 | • 다르게 행동함 |
| • (2) 같은 DNA를 공유함 | • 같은 유전자의 반을 공유함 |

구문 해설

01행 **When** we see two identical boys or girls, we know **they are twins**.
• when은 시간을 나타내는 부사절을 이끄는 접속사로써 '~할 때'라는 뜻이다.
• know의 목적어로 쓰인 명사절을 이끄는 접속사 that이 생략되었다.

02행 **Let's look** at the two most common types of twins.
• 〈Let's + 동사원형〉은 '~하자'라는 뜻의 청유문이다.

04행 Identical twins **look exactly alike**.
• alike는 '비슷한, 같은'이란 뜻의 형용사로서, 지각동사 look 뒤에 와서 '비슷해 보이다, 같아 보이다'라고 해석한다.
• exactly는 '정확히, 꼭'이라는 의미의 부사로 형용사 alike를 수식하고 있다.

12행 **Unlike** identical twins, fraternal twins are usually one boy and one girl.
• unlike는 '~와 다르게'라는 뜻의 전치사로 뒤에 명사가 온다.

지문 해석

우리가 두 명의 똑같은 남자아이들 또는 여자아이들을 볼 때, 우리는 그들이 쌍둥이라는 것을 안다. 하지만 쌍둥이들은 생김새와 성격에서 다를 수 있다. 두 가지의 가장 흔한 쌍둥이 유형을 보자.

일란성 쌍둥이들은 똑같아 보인다. 그들은 엄마가 임신했을 때, 엄마의 난자 하나가 두 개로 나뉘면서 태어난다. 일란성 쌍둥이들은 같은 DNA를 공유한다. 그 이유로 그들은 거의 항상 두 명의 남자아이이거나 두 명의 여자아이이다. 그들은 또한 종종 비슷하게 행동한다. 그들은 똑같은 성격과 호불호를 가지고 있을 것이다.

이란성 쌍둥이들은 정확히 닮아 보이지는 않는다. 그들은 두 개의 별개의 난자가 아기로 발달하면서 태어난다. 이란성 쌍둥이들은 같은 DNA를 공유하지 않는다. 그들은 대략 같은 유전자의 반 정도만을 공유한다. 이란성 쌍둥이들은 일란성 쌍둥이들과는 다르게 대개 한 명은 남자아이이고 한 명은 여자아이이다. 그들은 보통의 남매처럼 행동한다.

## 내신 대비 **실전 Test**

pp.76~77

정답

**1** ③ **2** ② **3** ⑤ **4** ④ **5** can **6** ② **7** They used to go fishing every weekend. **8** ① **9** I want to become an English teacher. **10** ④ **11** ② **12** recycling, upcycling **13** ② **14** ③ **15** item

문제 해설

**1** common(흔한, 공통의): existing in many places(많은 곳에 존재하는)
① 위험한: 누군가에게 해를 끼칠 가능성이 있는
② 공유하다: 무언가를 다른 사람들과 함께 사용하다
④ 창의성: 새로운 무언가를 만들어내는 능력
⑤ 갑작스러운: 빠르게 일어나거나 행해지는

**2** goods와 products는 유의어 관계이므로 빈칸에는 similar(비슷한)의 유의어 ② alike(비슷한, 같은)가 알맞다.
① 이전의 ③ 보통의 ④ 별개의 ⑤ 틀린

**3** draw a sword: 칼을 뽑다

**4** 빈도부사는 be동사 뒤, 일반동사 앞에 위치한다. ④ not은 동사 앞에서 단독으로 쓰일 수 없으므로 알맞지 않다.
나는 ________ 나의 남동생과 물건을 공유한다.
① 대개 ② 종종 ③ 항상 ⑤ 가끔

**5** 조동사 can은 be able to로 대신할 수 있다.
그녀는 영어와 중국어를 말할 수 있다.

**6** to부정사를 목적어로 취하는 동사에는 hope, need, expect, decide, plan 등이 있다. ② avoid는 동명사를 목적어로 취한다.
나는 가까운 미래에 그녀를 만나기를 ________.
① 원한다 ③ 희망한다 ④ 계획한다 ⑤ 기대한다

**7** used to + 동사원형: ~하곤 했다

**8** ①의 빈도부사는 be동사 뒤에 와야 한다.
① 그는 가끔 학교에 늦는다.
② 나는 콘서트에 가기로 결정했다.
③ 그녀는 파티에 올 수 있다.
④ 나의 부모님은 나를 절대 때리지 않으신다.
⑤ 그 가수는 한때 유명했다.

**9** want + to 부정사: ~하기를 원하다

**[10-12]** p.70 22 지문 해석 참고

**10** 빈칸 다음에 오는 문단에서 재활용과 업사이클링의 차이점을 설명하고 있으므로 ④ '그것들은 몇 가지 차이점을 가지고 있다'가 들어가야 알맞다.
① 사람들은 그것들에 대해서 모른다
② 그것들은 꽤 비슷하다
③ 그것들은 많은 유사점을 가지고 있다
⑤ 그것들은 환경에 해를 끼칠 수 있다

**11** For example로 시작하는 주어진 문장은 사람들이 물건들을 분해하지 않고 다르게 사용할 방법을 찾는다는 것의 예시로 ②에 오는 것이 가장 알맞다.

**12** Both는 앞에서 언급된 두 가지 recycling(재활용)과 upcycling(업사이클링)을 가리킨다.

**[13-15]** p.72 23 지문 해석 참고

**13** They는 바로 앞 문장에서 언급된 복수명사를 가리키는데, 문맥상 물건을 고르는 주체인 ② shoppers(쇼핑객들)임을 알 수 있다.
① 연구자들 ③ 결정들 ④ 회사들 ⑤ 제품들

**14** want + to 부정사: ~하기를 원하다

**15** '구매할 물건들의 목록에 있는 하나의 물건'이라는 뜻을 가진 단어는 item(물품, 품목)이다.

# WORKBOOK ANSWER KEYS

## CHAPTER 01 pp.04~05

**A**
1 이점, 혜택
2 인식하다, 알아보다
3 결정
4 줄이다
5 피하다, 방지하다
6 threaten
7 dislike
8 instead
9 create
10 excuse

**B**
1 festival
2 famous
3 yell
4 character
5 prevent
6 scary

**C**
1 In fact
2 surprising
3 Thanks to
4 high in
5 are likely to

**D**
1 have → to have, 나는 당신에게 행운이 있기를 원한다.
2 with → for, 인터넷은 사람들에게 많은 정보를 제공한다.
3 his → him, 그와는 다르게 나는 버스를 타고 학교에 간다.
4 want → wants, Jason은 내가 그의 생일 파티에 오기를 원한다.

**E**
1 helps you stay healthy
2 The music festival takes place
3 Thanks to him, my English skills improved

**F**
1 I want you to get better soon.
2 The flower has no smell, unlike other flowers.
3 It is likely to rain tomorrow.

## CHAPTER 02 pp.06~07

**A**
1 무례한, 거친
2 가정
3 궁금해하다, 궁금하다
4 쓰레기, 폐기물
5 붓다, 따르다
6 shorten
7 useless
8 vehicle
9 release
10 unique

**B**
1 handle
2 absorb
3 creature
4 dawn
5 harm
6 wild

**C**
1 Millions of
2 go well together
3 are proud of
4 plan to
5 throughout

**D**
1 feel → I feel, 나는 행복할 때, 음악에 맞춰 춤을 춘다.
2 into → to, 그 가게는 월요일부터 금요일까지 연다.
3 is → are, 동물원에는 많은 야생 동물들이 있다.
4 nicely → nice, 이 크리스마스 머그잔은 독특하고 멋지다.

**E**
1 We sat on the beach and watched the sunset
2 There are some ways to reduce
3 He worked hard from dawn to dusk

**F**
1 search, for
2 received, attention
3 make, sense

## CHAPTER 03 pp.08~09

**A**
1 수평의
2 (짐승을) 몰다
3 따끔거리다
4 이론, 생각
5 조직
6 stretchy
7 height
8 chemical
9 yawn
10 spread

**B**
1 happen
2 keep
3 affect
4 bored
5 task
6 remove

**C**
1 stuck to
2 A lack of
3 according to
4 go back to
5 result in

**D**
1 to get → from getting, 손을 씻는 것은 네가 감기에 걸리는 것을 막아줄 수 있다.

2 softly → soft, 그녀의 목소리는 부드럽고, 사랑스럽게 들렸다.
3 to go → going, 가끔 나는 어린 시절로 돌아가고 싶은 생각이 든다.
4 more long → longer, 여름에는 낮이 더 길어진다.

E
1 more expensive
2 better
3 earlier
4 more deeply

F
1 It looks delicious but tastes bad.
2 A lack of sleep can make you tired.
3 This will prevent a similar event from happening.

## CHAPTER 04 pp.10~11

A
1 당황스러운
2 행성
3 고체의, 단단한
4 기념하다, 축하하다
5 던지다
6 humble
7 disappear
8 ceremony
9 smelly
10 practice

B
1 expect
2 garbage
3 empty
4 weaken
5 spin
6 terrible

C
1 As a result
2 rich in
3 laughed at
4 get rid of
5 is made of

D
1 as → that, 나는 그가 나를 비웃고 있다고 생각한다.
2 to drink → drinking, 당신은 너무 많은 커피를 마시는 것을 피해야 한다.
3 that → as, 그녀는 영화를 보면서 잠이 들었다.
4 catches → is catching, 그는 지금은 맨손으로 물고기를 잡고 있다.

E
1 As the sky became dark
2 A man is throwing garbage
3 that the plant gets rid of bad smells

F
1 I believe (that) his dream will come true.
2 They are preparing for the music festival.
3 You should avoid practicing the piano at night.

## CHAPTER 05 pp.12~13

A
1 제정하다
2 두려움을 느끼는
3 승객
4 공인된
5 시
6 shelter
7 approval
8 ancient
9 adventure
10 mean

B
1 import
2 bury
3 trick
4 edible
5 distance
6 illegal

C
1 calm down
2 get in trouble
3 comes from
4 go on vacation
5 full of

D
1 speak, 공공장소에서는 큰 소리로 말하지 마라.
2 to crash, 그 끔찍한 폭풍은 우리 비행기가 추락하게 했다.
3 to imagine, 우리 선생님은 우리에게 인터넷 없는 삶을 상상해 보라고 요청했다.
4 will not be, 당신의 어머니는 당신에게 화내지 않을 것이다.

E
1 caused people to enjoy nature
2 Don't worry too much
3 I will feed your cat

F
1 The doctor asked him to take a walk every day.
2 Despite the rain, they will go on a treasure hunt.
3 Calm down and listen to his advice.

## CHAPTER 06 pp.14~15

A
1 영향, 효과
2 임신한
6 dangerous
7 common

3 보통의
4 (손을) 흔들다
5 품질
8 company
9 separate
10 sudden

B
1 identical
2 save
3 purchase
4 former
5 require
6 choose

C
1 drew a sword
2 figure out
3 divided into
4 pass by
5 based on

D
1 use → used, 나는 어렸을 때, 자전거를 타곤 했다.
2 protects → protect, 우리는 재활용을 함으로써 환경을 보호할 수 있다.
3 always is → is always, 하와이 날씨는 항상 따뜻하다.
4 buying → to buy, 나는 미술 수업을 위한 재료를 사기 원한다.

E
1 I am able to learn
2 He never shares his toys
3 the quality of goods used to be worse

F
1 You can save energy with this product.
2 I hope to develop my English skills.
3 He usually rides a horse on the weekend.

# Reading Skill로 끝내는 중학 내신 독해 1

Level

## 정답 및 해설

Laws

Architecture

Food

Space

Culture

Science

Story

Entertainment

Art

# Reading Skill로 끝내는 중학 내신 독해 Level 1

## Workbook

Happy House

# Reading Skill로 끝내는 중학 내신 독해 Level 1

# Workbook

Happy House

# Contents
## 목차

CHAPTER

# 01 Main Idea

## Word Practice

**A 다음 영어는 우리말로, 우리말은 영어로 쓰시오.**

1 benefit ____________

2 recognize ____________

3 decision ____________

4 reduce ____________

5 avoid ____________

6 위협하다 ____________

7 싫어하다 ____________

8 대신에 ____________

9 만들어 내다 ____________

10 변명, 핑계 ____________

**B 다음 영영풀이에 알맞은 단어를 보기에서 골라 쓰시오.**

| 보기 | prevent | yell | character | famous | festival | scary |
|---|---|---|---|---|---|---|

1 ____________: an event where people celebrate something

2 ____________: known by many people

3 ____________: to shout loudly because you are angry or excited

4 ____________: a person or an animal in a book or a movie

5 ____________: to keep something from happening

6 ____________: making you feel frightened

**C 다음 문장의 빈칸에 알맞은 말을 보기에서 골라 쓰시오.**

| 보기 | high in | are likely to | in fact | surprising | thanks to |
|---|---|---|---|---|---|

1 He isn't a liar. ____________, he was telling the truth.

2 I have something ____________ to tell you.

3 ____________ his help, I found my backpack.

4 You should try to eat food ____________ protein.

5 People ____________ choose cheaper products.

## Grammar & Writing Practice

**D** **다음 문장에서 틀린 부분을 바르게 고쳐 쓰고, 해석하시오.**

1 I want you have good luck.

→ ______________________________

2 The Internet provides a lot of information with people.

→ ______________________________

3 I go to school by bus, unlike his.

→ ______________________________

4 Jason want me to come to his birthday party.

→ ______________________________

**E** **우리말과 같은 뜻이 되도록 주어진 말을 바르게 배열하시오.**

1 규칙적인 운동은 네가 건강을 유지하도록 도와준다.

Regular exercise ______________________________.

(stay / healthy / you / helps)

2 그 음악 축제는 자라섬에서 열린다.

______________________________ on Jara Island.

(the / festival / takes place / music)

3 그 덕분에 나의 영어 실력은 많이 향상되었다.

______________________________ a lot.

(thanks / my / improved / English skills / to / him)

**F** **우리말과 같은 뜻이 되도록 괄호 안의 말을 이용하여 문장을 완성하시오.**

1 나는 네가 곧 회복되기를 원한다. (get better, soon)

______________________________

2 그 꽃은 다른 꽃들과 다르게 향기가 없다. (has, smell)

______________________________

3 내일은 비가 내릴 가능성이 있다. (be likely to)

______________________________

CHAPTER

# 02 Titles

## Word Practice

### A 다음 영어는 우리말로, 우리말은 영어로 쓰시오.

| | | | |
|---|---|---|---|
| 1 rude | ________ | 6 짧게 하다 | ________ |
| 2 household | ________ | 7 쓸모 없는 | ________ |
| 3 wonder | ________ | 8 차량, 탈 것 | ________ |
| 4 waste | ________ | 9 방출하다 | ________ |
| 5 pour | ________ | 10 독특한 | ________ |

### B 다음 영영풀이에 알맞은 단어를 보기에서 골라 쓰시오.

| 보기 | harm | creature | dawn | wild | absorb | handle |
|---|---|---|---|---|---|---|

1 ________________: to deal with; to be in charge of

2 ________________: to take in a gas or a liquid

3 ________________: a living thing that can move around

4 ________________: the time of day when it begins to get light

5 ________________: to injure or damage someone or something

6 ________________: living or growing in natural conditions

### C 다음 문장의 빈칸에 알맞은 말을 보기에서 골라 쓰시오.

| 보기 | are proud of | plan to | millions of | throughout | go well together |
|---|---|---|---|---|---|

1 ________________ people visit this area from around the world.

2 This tie and shirt ________________.

3 You are really amazing. We ________________ you!

4 We ________________ go on vacation to Europe.

5 The weather in the country is hot ________________ the year.

## Grammar & Writing Practice

**D 다음 문장에서 틀린 부분을 바르게 고쳐 쓰고, 해석하시오.**

1 When feel happy, I dance to music.

→ ______________________________

2 The store is open from Monday into Friday.

→ ______________________________

3 There is many wild animals at the zoo.

→ ______________________________

4 This Christmas mug is unique and nicely.

→ ______________________________

**E 우리말과 같은 뜻이 되도록 주어진 말을 바르게 배열하시오.**

1 우리는 어제 해변에 앉아 일몰을 보았다.

______________________________ yesterday.

(on the beach / the sunset / and / sat / watched / we)

2 공기 오염을 줄일 수 있는 몇 가지 방법들이 있다.

______________________________ air pollution.

(to reduce / ways / are / some / there)

3 그는 젊었을 때, 새벽부터 해질 때까지 열심히 일했다.

______________________________ when he was young.

(dusk / he / to / from / worked / hard / dawn)

**F 우리말과 같은 뜻이 되도록 빈칸에 알맞은 말을 쓰시오.**

1 학생들은 인터넷에서 쉽게 정보를 찾을 수 있다.

Students can easily ________ ________ information on the Internet.

2 아몬드는 많은 영양분을 갖고 있기 때문에 주목을 받아오고 있다.

Almonds have ________ ________ because they have many nutrients.

3 그의 변명은 전혀 타당하지 않다.

His excuse does not ________ ________ at all.

CHAPTER
# 03 Cause and Effect

## Word Practice

### A 다음 영어는 우리말로, 우리말은 영어로 쓰시오.

1 horizontal ____________
2 herd ____________
3 sting ____________
4 theory ____________
5 tissue ____________
6 신축성이 있는 ____________
7 키, 신장 ____________
8 화학 물질 ____________
9 하품하다 ____________
10 퍼지다 ____________

### B 다음 영영풀이에 알맞은 단어를 보기에서 골라 쓰시오.

| 보기 | remove | task | keep | bored | affect | happen |
|---|---|---|---|---|---|---|

1 ____________: to take place, usually without being planned
2 ____________: to own and take care of animals
3 ____________: to cause a change in something or somebody
4 ____________: feeling tired after losing interest in something
5 ____________: something that somebody has to do
6 ____________: to take something away from somewhere

### C 다음 문장의 빈칸에 알맞은 말을 보기에서 골라 쓰시오.

| 보기 | go back to | stuck to | result in | a lack of | according to |
|---|---|---|---|---|---|

1 Look! Some metal spoons ____________ the magician's body.
2 ____________ vitamins can cause serious problems.
3 This summer will be very hot ____________ the weather forecast.
4 Vacation is over. Now it's time to ____________ school.
5 Not studying for a test can ____________ a bad grade.

## Grammar & Writing Practice

**D 다음 문장에서 틀린 부분을 바르게 고쳐 쓰고, 해석하시오.**

1 Washing your hands can prevent you to get a cold.

→ ______________________________

2 Her voice sounded softly and lovely.

→ ______________________________

3 Sometimes I feel like to go back to my childhood.

→ ______________________________

4 The days become more long in summer

→ ______________________________

**E 다음 괄호 안의 단어를 이용하여 비교급 문장을 완성하시오.**

1 The pink shoes are ______________ than the blue ones. (expensive)

2 His original idea was ______________. (good)

3 My brother wakes up ______________ than me. (early)

4 Sit up and breathe ______________. (deeply)

**F 우리말과 같은 뜻이 되도록 괄호 안의 말을 이용하여 문장을 완성하시오.**

1 그것은 맛있게 보이지만, 맛이 없다. (delicious, bad)

______________________________

2 수면 부족은 당신을 피곤하게 만들 수 있다. (sleep)

______________________________

3 이것은 비슷한 사건이 일어나는 것을 막을 것이다. (similar event, happen)

______________________________

CHAPTER

# 04 Guessing Unknown Words

## Word Practice

**A 다음 영어는 우리말로, 우리말은 영어로 쓰시오.**

| | | | |
|---|---|---|---|
| 1 embarrassed | ______________ | 6 초라한 | ______________ |
| 2 planet | ______________ | 7 사라지다 | ______________ |
| 3 solid | ______________ | 8 의식, 식 | ______________ |
| 4 celebrate | ______________ | 9 냄새 나는 | ______________ |
| 5 throw | ______________ | 10 연습하다 | ______________ |

**B 다음 영영풀이에 알맞은 단어를 보기에서 골라 쓰시오.**

| 보기 | empty | spin | expect | terrible | garbage | weaken |
|---|---|---|---|---|---|---|

1 ______________: to think that something will happen

2 ______________: waste that is to be thrown away

3 ______________: containing nothing inside

4 ______________: to make something less strong or powerful

5 ______________: to turn around and around fast

6 ______________: making you feel very upset or afraid

**C 다음 문장의 빈칸에 알맞은 말을 보기에서 골라 쓰시오.**

| 보기 | rich in | get rid of | as a result | laughed at | is made of |
|---|---|---|---|---|---|

1 He was sick. ______________, he did not go to school.

2 Apples are good for you because they are ______________ vitamin C.

3 Many people ______________ his theory at first.

4 This medicine will ______________ your headache.

5 The crown ______________ gold and silver.

## Grammar & Writing Practice

**D 다음 문장에서 틀린 부분을 바르게 고쳐 쓰고, 해석하시오.**

1 I think as he is laughing at me.

→ ______________________________

2 You should avoid to drink too much coffee.

→ ______________________________

3 She fell asleep that she watched the movie.

→ ______________________________

4 He catches fish with his bare hands right now.

→ ______________________________

**E 우리말과 같은 뜻이 되도록 주어진 말을 바르게 배열하시오.**

1 하늘이 어두워지면서 비가 오기 시작했다.

______________________________, it started to rain.
(as / the / dark / sky / became)

2 한 남자가 쓰레기를 길에 버리고 있다.

______________________________ on the street.
(is / garbage / a / throwing / man)

3 그는 그 식물이 나쁜 냄새를 없애 준다고 말한다.

He says ______________________________.
(smells / that / gets rid of / bad / the plant)

**F 우리말과 같은 뜻이 되도록 괄호 안의 말을 이용하여 문장을 완성하시오.**

1 나는 그의 꿈이 이루어질 것이라고 믿는다. (come true)

______________________________

2 그들은 그 음악 축제를 준비하고 있다. (prepare for)

______________________________

3 너는 밤에 피아노 연습하는 것을 피해야 한다. (should, practice)

______________________________

CHAPTER

# 05 Identifying Cohesive Devices: Pronoun

## Word Practice

**A 다음 영어는 우리말로, 우리말은 영어로 쓰시오.**

1 establish ____________________

2 frightened ____________________

3 passenger ____________________

4 official ____________________

5 poem ____________________

6 은신처 ____________________

7 승인 ____________________

8 고대의 ____________________

9 모험 ____________________

10 의미하다 ____________________

**B 다음 영영풀이에 알맞은 단어를 보기에서 골라 쓰시오.**

| 보기 | edible | bury | distance | import | illegal | trick |
|---|---|---|---|---|---|---|

1 ____________________: to bring a product from another country to your own

2 ____________________: to put something into the ground

3 ____________________: the act of making a person believe that something false is true

4 ____________________: safe or good enough to eat

5 ____________________: the amount of space between two places

6 ____________________: not allowed by the law

**C 다음 문장의 빈칸에 알맞은 말을 보기에서 골라 쓰시오.**

| 보기 | full of | calm down | go on vacation | comes from | get in trouble |
|---|---|---|---|---|---|

1 Please ____________________ and take a deep breath.

2 Don't do it. I don't want you to ____________________.

3 This fruit ____________________ a tropical island.

4 I will ____________________ to Hawaii next week.

5 The bus was ____________________ passengers after the soccer game.

## Grammar & Writing Practice

**D 다음 괄호 안에서 알맞은 것을 고르고, 해석하시오.**

1 Don't (speak / be speak) loudly in public places.

→ ______________________________

2 The terrible storm caused our plane (crashing / to crash).

→ ______________________________

3 Our teacher asked us (imagine / to imagine) life without the Internet.

→ ______________________________

4 Your mother (will be not / will not be) angry with you.

→ ______________________________

**E 우리말과 같은 뜻이 되도록 주어진 말을 바르게 배열하시오.**

1 그 모험은 사람들이 자연을 즐기도록 만들었다.

The adventure ______________________________.

(caused / to / nature / people / enjoy)

2 너무 걱정하지 마라. 우리는 구조될 것이다.

______________________________. We will be rescued.

(too much / worry / don't)

3 당신이 휴가를 간 동안에, 내가 당신의 고양이에게 먹이를 줄 것이다.

While you go on vacation, ______________________________.

(will / your / feed / I / cat)

**F 우리말과 같은 뜻이 되도록 괄호 안의 말을 이용하여 문장을 완성하시오.**

1 그 의사는 그에게 매일 산책을 하라고 요청했다. (take a walk)

______________________________

2 비에도 불구하고, 그들은 보물찾기하러 갈 것이다. (go on a treasure hunt)

______________________________

3 진정하고, 그의 충고를 들어라. (listen to, advice)

______________________________

CHAPTER

# 06 Compare & Contrast

## Word Practice

**A 다음 영어는 우리말로, 우리말은 영어로 쓰시오.**

1 impact ________________

2 pregnant ________________

3 regular ________________

4 wave ________________

5 quality ________________

6 위험한 ________________

7 흔한, 공통의 ________________

8 회사 ________________

9 서로 다른 ________________

10 갑작스러운 ________________

**B 다음 영영풀이에 알맞은 단어를 보기에서 골라 쓰시오.**

| 보기 | require | identical | former | purchase | save | choose |
|---|---|---|---|---|---|---|

1 ________________: exactly the same or very similar

2 ________________: to keep something for use in the future

3 ________________: the act of buying something

4 ________________: before the present time or in the past

5 ________________: to need something

6 ________________: to decide which people or things you want

**C 다음 문장의 빈칸에 알맞은 말을 보기에서 골라 쓰시오.**

| 보기 | pass by | divided into | based on | figure out | drew a sword |
|---|---|---|---|---|---|

1 He ________________ and attacked the enemy.

2 I can't ________________ how to solve this problem.

3 We ________________ two teams and played soccer.

4 I ________________ the park on my way to school.

5 The movie is ________________ a famous novel.

## Grammar & Writing Practice

**D 다음 문장에서 틀린 부분을 바르게 고쳐 쓰고, 해석하시오.**

1 I use to ride a bike when I was young.

→ ______________________________

2 We can protects the environment by recycling.

→ ______________________________

3 The weather always is warm in Hawaii.

→ ______________________________

4 I want buying some materials for art class.

→ ______________________________

**E 우리말과 같은 뜻이 되도록 주어진 말을 바르게 배열하시오.**

1 나는 새로운 것을 빠르게 배울 수 있다.

______________________________ new things quickly.

(able / learn / I / am / to)

2 그는 결코 그의 장난감을 그의 남동생과 공유하지 않는다.

______________________________ with his brother.

(toys / never / he / shares / his)

3 과거에는 상품의 질이 더 나빴었다.

In the past, ______________________________.

(of goods / used / worse / the quality / be / to)

**F 우리말과 같은 뜻이 되도록 괄호 안의 말을 이용하여 문장을 완성하시오.**

1 당신은 이 물건을 가지고 에너지를 절약할 수 있다. (energy)

______________________________

2 나는 나의 영어 실력을 향상시키기를 희망한다. (skills)

______________________________

3 그는 주말에 대개 말을 탄다. (on the weekend)

______________________________

# Reading Skill로 끝내는 중학 내신 독해 1 Level

## Workbook